TOBACCO:
A HISTORY

TOBACCO:
A HISTORY

V. G. Kiernan

Hutchinson Radius

Hutchinson Radius
An imprint of Random Century Ltd
20 Vauxhall Bridge Road
London SW1V 2SA

Random Century Australia (Pty) Ltd
89-91 Albion Street, Surry Hills, NSW 2010,
Australia

Random Century New Zealand Limited
PO Box 40-086, Glenfield, Auckland 10, New Zealand

Random Century South Africa (Pty) Ltd
PO Box 337, Bergvlei, 2012, South Africa

First published by Hutchinson Radius 1991

© 1991 by Victor G. Kiernan

British Library Cataloguing in Publication Data
Kiernan, V. G.
Tobacco: A history.
I. Title
394.1

ISBN 0 09 174216 1

Filmset in Ehrhardt by SX Composing Ltd, Rayleigh, Essex
Printed and bound in England by Butler and Tanner Ltd,
London and Frome

Contents

1.	Origins	1
2.	The World Learning	6
3.	Europe: Pipe, Snuff-box, Cigar	27
4.	A Girdle Round About the Earth	53
5.	The Conversion of Women	79
6.	Religion Reconciled	100
7.	At Rest, At Work, On the March	117
8.	Pipe and Drum	134
9.	A Ministering Angel	158
10.	Men of Action	173
11.	Thought and Fancy	183
12.	To Smoke or Not to Smoke	206
13.	Man's Best and Worst Friend	223
	Books and Other Sources Quoted	234

To Brian Smith
with gratitude for much friendly
interest and active help

Origins

At that blest hour when nicotine and coffee,
The day's first cup and cigarette, unite
And soar into the brain, with sleep still fluffy,
Like bee and queen-bee on their nuptial flight . . .

The Two Commissars, Bombay, 1944

Everyone who is or has been a smoker must have a private history of his own. I grew up in a non-smoking household; at the start of my second year as a student I reached the point of regaling myself with one cigarette a day. I partook of it after tea, in front of a smoky little fire, with Boswell's *Tour to the Hebrides*, then first read, for company. Those were the most exquisite smoking moments, and Boswell one of the best-loved books, of my life; linked with them in memory is the gradual deepening of clear October skies outside to a peculiar electric blue. Before long the daily ration inevitably increased. It has left me with recollections of turning to a cigarette for a morsel of warmth in winter among snowy hills, oftenest in Lakeland, or for an illusion of coolness on tropical nights. In a very small tent after a climb of Ben Nevis on a wet day I was restored by a 'Manikin', a small cheap cigar. Fragrance from a cigarette on a summer day in Norway, on the rim of a vast deep valley into which I was to descend, still floats in some recess of my mind.

There were times when I wanted badly to smoke, and had no tobacco, and others when I had no means of lighting it. A sunny spell of camping and walking in the Shetlands left images, among those of Pictish brochs and Norse settlements, of wrestlings with a cigarette-lighter that refused to work. Another frustration I owed to a bout of sandfly fever on my first visit to Lahore, in a still un-divided India. Getting back to a friend's house at the end of a long walk through the streets in a temperature of 104°, I learned that my own temperature had risen to the same figure. It was a first ex-perience of what became in time unpleasantly familiar: the dis-gusting flavour, like mouldy straw burning, of tobacco poisoned by fever, its consolations cut off just when most acutely pined for.

A happier Indian memory is the hookah, or 'hubble-bubble', the water-pipe that was the great restorative of early generations of Britons there. As a student I had tried to get used to a pipe, but somehow it was always going out, and its fumes never seemed as seductive as those from other men's pipes have often done. The hookah was perfectly Elysian. I had a simple one with me during a summer month at Almora, in the Himalayan foothills, where I had some writing to do and not much time to do it. I sat most of the day at a table on the balcony of a small wooden cottage, with a spacious view over the vale, scribbling and imbibing – for an hour at a time, with no discordant sensations to follow – its ineffably cool gurglings.

Cigarettes predominated, however, and brought penalties wor-sening with time. One was a faint but persistent fuzziness in the head; another, a fear of becoming enslaved and dependent, pos-sibly some day languishing in jail bereft of their support. In the early 1950s lung cancer was only beginning to be muttered about; rising costs were a more indubitable evil. Rolling small cigarettes with a toy-like gadget gave a partial defence, but gloomy calcula-tions beset my mind – of how many pounds a year one 'real' ciga-rette a day meant. Attempts to keep to a fixed daily limit were more painful than successful. Efforts to give up smoking alto-gether came to nothing.

Finally deliverance came through an accidental sequence of causes starting with a snow-fall on 25 January 1952, and a visit to the Botanical Garden at Edinburgh to view the white trees and lawns. On the way home I had to call at the University Library, then crammed into the Old College, and hunt for some tome in a cellar thick with the dust of ages. By the fireside that evening I smoked what I little guessed was to be my last cigarette on this planet. Next day I had a painfully sore throat; being engaged to take the chair nine days later at a meeting in what used to be the Oddfellows' Hall, I heroically resolved to smoke no more until this was over. The meeting was addressed by Sir John Pratt, the diplomat, authority on China, and brother of the better known Boris Karloff, the actor. He had been relieved of a post of adviser at the Foreign Office, because of his criticism of Britain's participation in the Korean war, and now at an advanced age was touring the country and denouncing British policy with a vigorous flow of what he himself called 'vituperation'.

Next day I was giving him lunch before he went on to Aberdeen, and told him my little story. He listened sympathetically, gave me a harrowing account of someone he had known who had smoked himself to death, and exhorted me never to start again. With feelings as though of having heard an inspired prophet, I went and sat on Carlton Hill, and took my vows. For a couple of days I had to evade all the work I could; after that, the ordeal so long feared proved surprisingly mild. Chewing gum was helpful, if undignified. For a month my weight went up abruptly, but then returned to normal. For weeks and months I went on taxing the patience of acquaintances by telling them how many days it was since I gave up smoking. Not long ago I came on a memorandum tucked into a book on the 999th day.

Meanwhile one of my rewards was the disappearance of a chronic snuffling cold in the head and rusty throat. Among others I would like to be able to specify an improved temper, a sunnier disposition, and a greatly strengthened intellect; but whether these things could be said truthfully I have not been able to decide. Nevertheless, yearly when able on 25 January I have made a pilgrim tour of the Botanical Garden, and remembered my day of liberation. It was by way of a substitute for what had dropped out of my life that I made a hobby of noting down all the tobacco stories and allusions I came on in the course of my meandering reading; their number has swollen year by year.

It is on material from the resulting collection that this little book has been founded: anecdotes of all sorts about tobacco and its progress round the world, testimonies of how men and women and nations have thought of it. They are arranged here by periods and regions, and, still more, by themes. Fact and fiction may seem oddly mixed, but the two have always been interwoven, and their boundaries are indistinct.

It was only while putting together tobacco episodes from everywhere that I came to realise what a unique force this herb has been, all through modern times, how immense a sway it has exercised over human lives in almost every sphere. Without attempting a systematic history – an encyclopedic task – I have tried to present my offerings in such a way as to make readers aware of this incalculable power of a plant unknown outside the Americas until five centuries ago, and then quite suddenly known and craved for everywhere. It has been an element in modern history strangely overlooked by historians, a great many of whom have written lengthy volumes without once feeling called upon to mention it.

Each quotation is followed by the author's name (if not given nearby in the text) and a page or chapter number, in brackets: a short title of the work is given if more than one work by the same author is cited; fuller details of the source will be found in an alphabetical list of writers at the end of the book. Among works of reference drawn on, particular acknowledgement is due to the *Penguin Dictionary of Historical Slang;* among museums and displays, to the splendid Tony Irvine collection, illustrating every aspect of tobacco history, whose home when I visited it was the 'House of Pipes' in the Sussex village of Bramber. Various sidelights on the intimate relationship between tobacco and modern warfare come from the stores of diaries, letters, etc, in the National Army Museum and the Imperial War Museum in London.

Many individuals have given me help or suggestions: in the forefront my wife, on medical matters and the cinema; my brother, whose collection of West African pipes includes one that was being smoked by a market woman in Nigeria while he bargained for it with her; and my friend Brian Smith, the Shetland archivist, whose flow of information has enriched my knowledge of tobacco history and habits, especially in his own islands. My thanks are due also to Mr Hermann Bessler for permission to reproduce a passage from some unpublished memoirs of his late wife, the Georgia Hale of *The Gold Rush*.

2

The World Learning

[My greenhouse] wants only the fumes of your pipe to make it perfectly delightful. Tobacco was not known in the golden age. So much the worse for the golden age. This age of iron, or lead, would be insupportable without it; and therefore we may reasonably suppose that the happiness of those better days would have been much improved by the use of it.

William Cowper, letter to Rev. W. Bull,
3 June 1783

To any devoted smoker the world before tobacco must look a barren place, whatever his respect for Aristotle or Dante. Tobacco titillates three senses, smell and sight and touch, but above all the nose. According to current experiments in artificial nose-building, the organ has a million nerve-ends, each sensitive to one of a score of smells. These wind their way into our inmost consciousness. Man's nose is his seat of nostalgia, linking him with a remote four-footed past. It has always craved for pleasing odours, primarily associated with satisfying foods. It must seem curious that we have, in English at least, so few words to classify the sensations it yields; from 'perfume' to 'stink' is a broad gap with few verbal stepping-stones.

Had tobacco been known anciently in the Old World, doubtless it would have been added to the creature comforts of all the Hindu heavens and many others, by popular fancy if not by ecclesiastical warrant. Mankind endowed its deities with incense-seeking nostrils because its own inhalings gratified it so keenly; here too it has made them in its own image. It was no more absurd of Amerindians to offer tobacco to the spirits than of Greeks or Hebrews to offer heaven the savour of roast meat; the steam of the altar was the distilled essence of the sacrifice. It found a more refined successor in the incense that has pervaded temples from Europe to China, and that to the simple worshipper's mind has been as pleasurable to those on high as to those here below. Some vestige of a fire-worship once everywhere practised may linger in the gently glowing tip of either burning taper or lighted cigarette, a reassurance akin to that provided by camp fires lit to repel wild beasts and demons.

Romans at their banquets could no more do without garlands round their heads, and unguents poured over their hair, than without wine. They were doing their best for the nasal need that would eventually be met, more effectively if less artistically, by tobacco. 'No one can read Horace', it has been well said, 'without feeling that he had the true spirit of the tobacco cult' ('Alpha', p 43). Hotspur's fop in _Henry IV Part I_ carried a scent-box to protect his nose from the effluvia of a battlefield, and long before that day aromatic herbs had been credited with medicinal virtues. They may be thought of as forerunners of snuff; and some herbs in use in various parts of the Old World pointed the way towards smoking-tobacco. Ancient pipes have often been unearthed, and it appears that men have tried experiments with willow bark, roots, mushrooms, sawdust, hemp, rose leaves and other flowers. Ongés tribesmen in the Andaman Islands, far off the highway of history, learned to smoke certain dried leaves in rude pipes made from crab claws (Singh, N. Iqbal, p 69).

Nearly all such makeshifts were swept aside at once by the emergence of that potent genie lurking for so long, incognito, in the American forests. 'Nicotiana' was given its botanical classification by Linnaeus in 1753, with two species, _Nic. tabacum_ and _Nic. rustica_; there were others, but none has survived in use, and _Nic. rustica_ only here and there, in Russia under the name of _makhorka_. Tobacco spread round the world by trade, and then by being adopted as a crop by local cultivators. It possessed, as the historian Braudel has said, the supreme asset of flexibility in adapting itself to the most diverse climates and soils (Braudel, pp 189-90). Or, as J.K. Galbraith writes in his autobiographical account of Scottish farming in southern Ontario, the notion that tobacco is 'a heat-loving plant which matures only under a subtropical sun . . . is a myth perpetated by the tobacco ads' (p 2).

Its uniqueness as a new benison for humanity is shown in its suddenly entering the Old World and spreading over so much of it like wildfire – claiming so high a place in every sphere of social and private life, appealing to every race, every class, every time of life from adolescence to the grave, and to both sexes. Europe jumped at tobacco as eagerly as North America at alcohol. Clearly in each case there had been a void, an inarticulate need awaiting fulfilment. Tobacco-smoking in the 'West' now appears destined to a brief life-span of a few centuries, by contrast with the age-old reign of alcohol to which no end is yet in sight. But the tobacco years have been world history's grandest – and most terrible – hitherto, in terms of effort, conflict, achievement, transformation in every field. To all this, tobacco's contribution is impossible to measure, but it has been immense.

A northern Amerindian legend told of a meeting between a withered old man and a stalwart youth; the senior proposed that they should spend the night talking about themselves.

> He then drew from his sack a curiously wrought antique pipe, and having filled it with tobacco, rendered mild by a mixture of certain leaves, handed it to his guest . . .
> 'I blow my breath', said the old man, 'and the stream stands still . . . '
> 'I breathe', said the young man, 'and flowers spring up over the plain.'

At sunrise the youth, who was Spring, recognised his companion as Winter, and as he did so the old man melted away into nothing, leaving behind him a single white flower (Twain, *Mississippi*, chap 59).

Wherever in the Americas tobacco may have had its birthplace, its use was widespread by the time the Europeans arrived and stumbled on the New World's best-loved product. Montezuma is said to have smoked a ceremonial pipe after dinner. Many clay pipes were dug up in later days near Mexico City, some decorated with human shapes; similar ones, and others with animal figures, turned up in very old Indian funeral mounds, most of them carved from hard stone like porphyry (Fairholt, pp 18ff). In Peru, by contrast, tobacco was only taken for medicinal purposes, generally in the form of snuff (Mason, p 143). This, like the pipe, was native to America, and we hear of well-made snuff-mills, or grinders, in early Brazil. Raleigh's account of his voyage up the Orinoco speaks of tribes, handsome and healthy, who were greatly addicted to tobacco (Mackenzie, pp 84-5).

Tobacco played so prominent a part in American rituals that one may wonder whether its use originated from religion; though it might be asked why this plant, rather than any other, should have been thought acceptable to heaven, if it had not already made itself agreeable to human nostrils. Conceivably the first virtue that recommended it to men was the mild intoxication it could induce. Shamans or medicine men, at any rate, did look to it to assist their visions or trances, and this mystic association might well win for tobacco a place in religion (Huxley, F., pp 289-90). An early explorer of the north-west Pacific coast reported that the Chinook Indians had no great fondness for drink, and despised drunkards, but 'They are very fond of smoking tobacco and they inhale the smoke, which intoxicates them and makes them ill, but they keep on doing it' (Franchère, p 107).

Ritual practices may have struck Europeans most. Spaniards in the Maya region of Central America were astonished by a ceremony resembling baptism, directed by four old men representing *Chacs* or rain-gods, with incense, tobacco, and holy water as offerings (Coe, p 167). It does not appear that tobacco was made other use of there. 'Red Indians' of the north made gifts of tobacco to the spirits of the dead and those of the cliffs, waterfalls, rapids they had to encounter on their journeys. Raleigh's expeditionists in Virginia in 1588 saw tobacco offered to deities, but also smoked by mortal men in clay pipes: heaven and earth might thus be said to have shared in a communal festival. So long as tribal belief and custom survived intact, tobacco kept its station. 'An Indian believed that to smoke was to pray', one writer says of the Plains Indians in the later 19th century.

> A portable altar, the pipe was a combination of important symbols. The pipestone bowl represented the Mother Earth. The wooden stem represented all growing things. Red porcupine quillwork was a symbol of magic power. By mingling his breath with sacred tobacco and divine fire, the smoker (i.e., the worshiper) put himself in tune with the universe. (Miller, pp 170-71).

A translation has been made of the text of a ceremony of condolence performed by an Iroquois tribe when an honoured member died, in conjunction with delegates from another of the allied 'Six Nations'. It begins with the mourners welcoming their visitors as they come along the forest trail. 'You keep seeing the footmarks of our forefathers', they say, 'and all but perceptible is the smoke where they used to smoke the pipe together.' Then they join in smoking, to appease any hostile spirits that may be lurking near (Bierhorst, p 127). A long-drawn-out Navajo prayer service or purification is accompanied by offerings, among them four reeds, each painted with insignia of the god it is dedicated to. After an invocation the reeds are filled with locally grown tobacco, and the reciter celebrates a mystic union –

> Now the yellow leaf am I,
> Now the broad leaf am I –.

Figuratively the reeds are set alight by the sun's rays, and the patient under exorcism repeats after the chanter a long petition –

> I have made your sacrifice.
> I have prepared a smoke for you ... (Bierhorst, pp 293-4).

If faith or auto-suggestion can cure, this picturesque rite may be expected to do as much good as any other.

Tobacco came into affairs of war and peace, inter-tribal and even, when white men became involved, international. Exploring in the 1850s, Francis Parkman found a strong Sioux expedition against the Crows preparing, each band under its own headman, though this chief organiser seemed to want to divert it against the Snake tribe; his aim was revenge for the death of a son 'whose scalp we saw at the fort with tobacco attached to signify a wish of peace' on the part of the killers (Parkman, p 445). When Crow Indians planned reprisals for slain relatives, a bereaved warrior might carry round the war-pipe and ask for support in a raid. 'If his friends smoked the pipe with him, they committed themselves to assist him and temporarily acknowledged his leadership' (Miller, p 165). A war-pipe might be a tomahawk with a bowl above the blade. A 'calumet' or pipe of peace was a tribal heirloom, ornamented with feathers and other decorations by the women. It was this pipe that fired the imagination of white men, and that they joined at times in smoking.

Crows in Parkman's time were 'nomad hunters, living on the buffalo and planting only a little tobacco for use in their religious ritual' (Parkman, p 609). It may be conjectured that such practices would tend to encourage a general spread of agriculture and settled life. Some tribes were adopting this, and from them tobacco was spreading to the hunting peoples. 'The Calif Indians picked it wild, and the Tlingit of the Northwest coast grew it, their only crop' (Coon, pp 213-14). As in the Old World, multifarious herbs were resorted to in areas where tobacco was not yet available; for instance by the Micmacs of Nova Scotia, one of whose substitutes was bearberry leaf, smoked in pipes made of stone, bone, bark, or – as can be seen in the provincial museum at Halifax – lobster claws. Only one such herb survived in competition with tobacco, *kinneekinick*, the dried and chopped inner bark of the red willow, smoked by itself or mixed with tobacco.

Tobacco was widely traded as well as grown. One Iroquois tribe earned the name of 'Tobacco Indians' by its love of smoking and its habit of selling part of its crop. Some Indians of the north and far west and Eskimos of the far north were first brought tobacco by white men, who had learned to smoke from other Indians, as they pushed their way over the continent. Tobacco grown in the colonies often displaced native crops. Everywhere it seems to have met with a warm welcome; it could help to allay the tensions, anxieties, insecurities that must haunt any life as precarious as the Indians' often was.

Established in the New World from early in the 16th century, the Spaniards and Portuguese claimed possession of the entire continent. They did their best to keep out intruders more commercially-minded than themselves, while failing to recognise, more than very sluggishly, opportunity staring them in the face. As J.H. Parry says, 'Tobacco has made more fortunes than all the silver of the Indies, but not mainly for Spaniards' (p 241). Their procurements from the Indies did before long include some tobacco, a limited part of which was re-exported to other European countries at a good profit. It was one of the crops raised by the Jesuits on their mission settlements, and carried down-river to the ports. By the mid-16th century Spain was smoking cigars, ahead of anyone else; by 1558 it was growing tobacco, and next year Jean Nicot, the French ambassador, sent to his court the cigars which were to confer his name (though without immortalising it) on nicotine, much as the forgotten Amerigo Vespucci gave his Italian name to America. By the early 17th century, when the pipe was spreading like wildfire in Britain, snuff was winning popularity in Paris. It must be supposed that the pipe was better suited to the stolid Teutonic temperament, snuff to the excitable Gallic.

It seems curious that England, buying from Spain the Seville oranges that Shakespeare punned on, and the sherry wine of Xérez that ascended so bewitchingly into Falstaff's brain, did not get more tobacco by the same route. It had, it seems, to be brought into the country by Englishmen before it could be accepted, even though learned of by them from 'savages'. Several individuals have been given the credit for first introducing England to what Elizabethans often called the 'drinking' of tobacco-smoke, as people do today in India. Sir John Hawkins, Drake, Raleigh have been candidates; but Raleigh is agreed to have been the first to bring smoking into fashion. He is said to have been smoking as he watched the execution of the Earl of Essex in 1601, and, 17 years later, just before his own. Englishmen might today be going into shops to buy a pound of *Uppowoc*, if the name picked up by his settlers in Virginia had not been supplanted by another American word which in English became 'tobacco', in French 'tabac', in Hindustani 'tumbaku'. From Brazil the Portuguese brought and long used a third name, *petun* or *petum*.

Tobacco, like sugar, was habit-forming, and so had a boundless market – a revolutionary fact of economic history. Production might seem equally limitless, given that half an ounce of seed can give birth to some 20,000 plants (Calder, pp 177, 252). Gigantic volumes of smoke can be imagined billowing out from their tiny prison, as if from an atomic explosion. Colonial territories in America were natural places for tobacco to be grown, and make fortunes for their owners. It exhausted the soil too quickly, however, to suit the smaller West Indian islands where cultivation was tried. Henry Winthrop, son of the founder of Massachusetts, settled in 1627 in Barbados, but the leaf he sent home was '"verye ill conditioned, fowle, full of stalkes and evill coloured"' (Dunn, p 50).

English enterprise fared better on the North American mainland. In the early days of Virginia tobacco was the only significant market crop. Two-thirds of the growers were smallholders; but with soil soon exhausted the advantage lay with men who could acquire extensive plantations. Wealthy planters could afford trips to England to make direct selling arrangements. Richard Lee, with thousands of acres to found a family on, spent much time in England during the Commonwealth. He had a warehouse and counting-house in London, and an estate in Essex, with a coach to carry him daily to the City, and two sons at Oxford (Sachse, pp 118-9). One of the chief facts about tobacco is the enormous amount of money that has been made out of it, and is still being made.

Big-scale cultivation brought a spread of black slavery, which enabled Virginia and Maryland to expand their exports sixfold between 1663 and 1699. More and more thousands of Africans were taking the *via dolorosa* to American shores. In 1664 a vessel chartered by a Dutch and Jewish group sailed from Amsterdam carrying 350 slaves, illicitly obtained from Portuguese Angola, to Curaçao for sale to the Spaniards; it returned laden with bullion and Venezuelan tobacco. Amsterdam was a staple or clearing-house for tobacco from America, some of it coming by way of England to be cured there (Israel, pp 242, 264-5). Before long other countries were trying to develop their own processing industries, but down to 1700 Dutch supremacy remained intact; Amsterdam had 23 factories, half of them Jewish. Tobacco had become big business.

Smoking had gripped the Dutch about the same time as the English, and when they were the leading businessmen of Europe. Under Spanish rule from early in the 16th century, they developed close commercial relations with Spain, until a long war, with England at times an ally, won them their independence. Holland was tobacco's chief gateway into northern Europe, as Spain was into the southern countries, and Portugal into much of Asia, round whose coasts it was acquiring ports and trading stations. By the late 1630s tobacco from the New World was being mixed with a coarse tobacco grown in Holland, which made it too cheap for English shippers to compete with in the Baltic.

A broad dividing-line was drawing itself between stronger flavours, known as 'oronoko', and a range of milder ones. In the English settlements the former were most at home in Maryland, the latter in Virginia. In northern Europe 'oronoko' was most in demand, in France the other kind. Holland imported from South as well as North America. A leading part in the curing business was taken by Jews, of families originally Spanish or Portuguese before the expulsion from the Peninsula at the end of the 15th century; they still had useful family connections with Brazil. An increasing proportion of imported tobacco hailed from Venezuela, with 'Cracostabak' or Caracas tobacco the commonest brand. When Madrid for a while suppressed tobacco-growing there, the efforts of Dutch interlopers to gain a foothold on the coast were largely paralysed (Israel, pp 66, 106).

Tobacco-growing and smoking quickly spread from the

Netherlands into Germany, whose people before long rivalled the Dutch in enthusiasm. Bans imposed in several of the principalities were quite ineffective. They had more effect, though only temporarily, in Muscovy, where smokers were threatened with public flogging, nose-slitting, even for a second offence death. A rational argument for the prohibition, which must have weighed with other governments too, was that old wooden towns could easily suffer from careless pipe-lighting, or from smokers falling asleep with pipes in their mouths. But in 1646 the seductive prospect of revenue caused tobacco to be legitimised as a State monopoly. Peter the Great (1689-1725) travelled as a youth in Holland and England, and came back a moderniser and a voluminous smoker. His more conservative subjects regarded him as a false pretender on the throne, and as possessed by the Devil – which would convincingly explain why he

> hobnobbed with foreigners, burdened his subjects with recruitments [conscription] and taxes, cut off beards, donned strange coats, smoked tobacco, and – a reference to his calendar reform – stole eight years from God. (Avrich, p 141)

In England, on the contrary, the adoption of tobacco owed nothing to royal patronage. A queen could not be seen with a pipe in her mouth, and James I was a fanatical opponent. James was everything bad, the poet Swinburne is said to have declared one day at the Arts Club, 'but I love him, I worship him, because he slit the throat of that blackguard Raleigh, who invented this filthy smoking' (Benham, p 513). If he had the Devil to dinner, James himself thundered, he would give him a pipe. His *Counterblaste to Tobacco* solemnly warned smokers that they were making a spectacle of themselves to all civilised nations: it was 'a custom loathsome to the eye, hateful to the nose, harmful to the brain, dangerous to the lungs' (Brand, pp 363-4). His diatribe fell on mostly deaf ears; the voice of the people declared, like that of Parliament in another way, against any divine right of kings to decide. In 1619 the London clay pipe makers were formed into a chartered body, with a coat of arms showing a 'Moor', or dusky native, holding a pipe and a roll of tobacco.

Dogmatic though he was, James was also hard up, and the temptation of increased revenue led him to reduce the import duty, especially on tobacco from Virginia. Prices fluctuated widely in those early days. An ounce might cost two or even three days' earnings of an artisan or labourer, yet consumption spread quickly among all classes. John Aubrey, the gossip-collector, remembered hearing his grandfather – a first-generation smoker – say that in his day 'one pipe was handed from man to man round the table' (p 45). There might be some impulse of sociability in this, as well as economy; bottles circulated likewise. The well off had silver pipes, ordinary folk might be content with a walnut shell and a straw stem. Poverty helped to keep pipe-sharing common much later, in Ireland for example.

Smuggling did something to lower the cost. About 1636 a large fortified tobacco store was built on the coast of Glamorgan, as a point of entry for large quantities of West Indian produce (*Guardian*, 14 October 1982). Tobacco could be cheapened much further, as it was in Holland, by being grown at home, and cultivation did in fact spread quite widely; Gloucestershire and adjacent counties took the lead. Bacon's philosophic eye could hardly miss so novel a phenomenon. Growing was profitable, he learned, but the crop was judged 'too dull and earthy', and he suggested treatment by heating (Lee, vol 1, p 512). A pamphlet of 1615 was entitled *An Advice How to Plant Tobacco in England;* it drew an alarming picture of the dirtiness of Spanish curing, and its pernicious effects (Wright, p 457). But revenue was more easily collected on imports, and home growing came under repeated bans. One was imposed in 1655, under the Commonwealth, and called forth an ironical protest: a welcome from the hangman, on the ground that apart from tobacco-growing there was no other work to be had in some districts, so everyone took to sheep-stealing, and thus gave him plenty of employment (Pepys, 19 September 1667, ed n).

Parliamentary taxation, with an army to pay, was stiff, and the excise system planned by Pym fell heavily on articles like beer and tobacco. Here must be a main cause of the Commonwealth's deepening unpopularity, and the jubilant recall of Charles II in 1660. But Charles too had his pockets to think of, and in 1667 Pepys heard that troops sent into the countryside, supposedly to suppress an insurrection, were really going into Gloucestershire to destroy a tobacco crop: this had been repeatedly done before, with the result that the Winchcombe area was 'a miserable poor place' (19 January 1667). What did more to put an end to cultivation in the later decades of the century was the rapid increase and falling price of imports from North America. By the 1670s a pound could be bought for a shilling or less. By the end of the century the English were seen by foreign visitors as a race of smokers.

Scots were not far behind. It was simple for James I to inflict anti-tobacco edicts on his native land, even though absent in London, but far harder to get them enforced, as their frequent re-petition was really an admission. One of 1616 denounced tobacco as 'ane weade so infective as all young and ydill personis ar in maner bewitchet theirwith' (Donaldson, p 235). It may partly be because of old French links, persisting in spite of the Reformation, that snuff became more a favourite than in England. A student at St Andrews, William Cleland, wrote 'A Mock Poem upon the Ex-pedition of the Highland Host' sent into Galloway in 1678 to crush the Covenanters or religious objectors. Each trooper, he said, carried a bag of onions, a snuff-grinder, and a pipe stuck in his bonnet (Prebble, p 60).

When Sir George Carew, busy helping to conquer Ireland, sent a gift of Irish hawks and hounds to Sir Robert Cecil, chief minister of James I and son of Elizabeth's, Cecil sent him in return Vene-tian glasses and tobacco (Rowse, p 212). Smoking was growing fashionable, and an easy means of attracting notice. A man about town, Thomas Dekker advised in 1609, before the food was brought in at a tavern should 'draw out his Tobacco-box, the ladell for the cold snuffe into nosthrill, the tongs and prining-Iron: All which artillery may be of gold or silver (if he can reach to the price of it)' – and display his smoking tricks, 'the *Whiffe*, the *Ring*, For these are complements that gaine Gentlemen no mean re-spect' (*Hornbook*, p 43).

John Selden, the lawyer, observed that just as some dislike sermons, but might learn to enjoy them, it was the same with 'that which is the great pleasure of some men, tobacco; at first they could not abide it, and now they cannot be without it' (p 128, on 'Pleasure'). For adolescents wanting to feel grown up and in the swim, learning to smoke was becoming a necessary accomplishment. Ben Jonson gives us a rich young man from the country, Kastril, who tells 'a Tobacco Man' how he has been learning to take tobacco like 'the angry boys', and now wants to master duelling (*Alchemist*, Act 3 Scene 2). In the last scene to Kastril drags in his sister, to be married to Lovewit, and tells him

> an thou canst take tobacco and drink, old boy,
> I'll give her five hundred pound more to her marriage' –

and Lovewit responds with alacrity: 'Fill a pipe full, Jeremy.'

It is easy to see how smoking could come to be associated with ruffianism. In another Jonson play a woman says of someone that

> He tauk so desperate, and so debausht,
> So baudy like a courtier and a lord,
> God bless him, one that tak'th tobacco. (*New Inn*, Act 2)

And Richard Brathwait, a critic of social manners, wrote in the 1620s of how bullies sometimes forced their way into theatres,

> furnished with Tinder, Match, and a portion of decayed *Barmoodas*, they smoake it most terribly . . . and in the end grow distastefully rude to all the Companie. (Gurr, p 48)

Walter Scott's young hero Nigel was being shown, about that time, round 'Alsatia', the old sanctuary area of Whitefriars in London, which had become a refuge of outlaws, when he encountered a pair of them, '"smoking like moving volcanoes"', as his guide remarked, 'shaggy, uncombed ruffians, whose enormous moustaches were turned back over their ears' (*Nigel*, chap 17). In a Star Chamber case of riotous behaviour in 1631 a woman was charged with forging a will in favour of her son, and he with entering a property by force, 'an aggravating circumstance being that he had "whiffed tobacco" in the face of the rightful owner' (Tanner, p 278).

But tobacco was quickly finding customers among more ordinary folk. Of the luxuries brought into Europe for mass consumption by the colonial discoveries, it was the first to reach the common man; it must have done much to secure his approval for the conquests, and all that went with them, including the slave trade. In 1614, when tobacco was being sold in taverns and inns, and by apothecaries and tobacconists, Barnabe Rich made an attempt to calculate annual sales. They were swollen in London, the chief place of import, by stocks being always available: about half a million pounds were coming in annually by the late 1620s, and smaller amounts at the west coast ports (Clark, P., p 135). Small quantities could be 'drunk' from a communal pipe at the alehouse, that English institution so ably chronicled by Peter Clark. This was in fact the principal retailing point, and we hear that anyone taking his seat there was likely to be at once invited to try a pipe (pp 135, 228).

Robert Burton, author of *The Anatomy of Melancholy,* thought that England carried off the palm for the number of its smokers, as Holland did for its seamen, France its dancers, Germany its drunkards, Italy its jealous husbands (vol 3, p 303). Englishmen seemed to foreign visitors to be smoking everywhere, and nowhere more than at the theatre. A smell of pipe smoke hung about the indoor playhouses, and the 'lords' rooms' or special boxes at the unroofed ones; it was deemed 'a gentleman-like smell', Sir John Davies commented sarcastically in an epigram (Gurr, p 39). Paul Hentzer, a German in London near 1600, found most of the spectators, not only the fashionables, puffing at long clay pipes, with copious 'defluxion', or spitting, as the result (Ridley, p 333).

Plays themselves often abounded in allusions to tobacco. Among their writers Marlowe was remembered as a smoker, and credited with a saying that 'they who loved not tobacco and boys were fools'. In a play by Dekker a different opinion is expressed by a servant who tells his master that a man like him, foolish enough to lose money gambling, 'is like twenty pounds' worth of tobacco, which mounts into the air' and only proves that 'he is an ass that melts so much money in smoke' (*Fortunatus*, Act 2 Scene 2). However, Shakespeare has puzzled his commentators by never mentioning tobacco. Some modern producers have made up for his forgetfulness; in the Royal Shakespeare Company's impressive 1989 production of *Othello* in modern dress, filmed in 1990, Iago (Ian McKellen) lit a cigarette to assist his scheming thoughts, and the Doge in his council chamber drew on a cigar. Few will doubt that if Falstaff had been born a little later he would have been a tireless pipe smoker.

With the reception of tobacco there sprang up heated argument, which never entirely died down, between those who welcomed it as health-giving and those who, like James I, condemned it as deleterious. Ultimately the hostile party have been proved right, though not for the kind of reasons advanced in the 17th century.

In *The Faerie Queene* when Belphoebe, out hunting, found the wounded knight Timias, one of the herbs she gathered in the woods to heal him was 'divine Tobacco' (Spenser, Book 3 Canto 3). In less pretentious verse a song-writer denied any harmfulness in it –

> Tobacco I love and tobacco I'll take,
> And hope good tobacco I ne'er shall forsake.
> 'Tis drinking and wenching destroys still the creature;
> But this noble fume does dry up ill nature.
>
> (Massingham, p 313).

In sober prose a pamphleteer set out to detail the 'strange and wonderfull operations' of tobacco, as vouched for by physicians; venereal disease was only one of the many ailments it could set right (Chute, Pref. and pp 44-5).

William Barclay, a Scottish enthusiast, talked of its merits as a tranquilliser – something Europe was much in need of, then as now; it brought, he wrote, 'the forgetting of all sorrows and miseries' (Clark, P., p 135). In 1659 Dr Everard commended its value to all hard workers, scholars as well as soldiers, ploughmen, and so on: they 'find great refreshment by it', and many declare they would as soon be deprived of food as of tobacco (Graves, p 34). Snuff was soon being recommended for all head colds, and as better than any of the other substances used as 'sternutatories', or sneeze-bringers (Fairholt, pp 239-40).

Lord Herbert of Cherbury (1583-1648), a nobleman whose memoirs never underrate his own good points, called his attendants to witness that his underwear always stayed fresh and sweet,

> which sweetness also was found to be in my breath above others, before I used to take tobacco, which, towards my latter time, I was forced to take against certain rheumes and catarrhs that trouble me, which yet did not taint my breath for any long time. (p 113)

Herbert's sensitivity on this matter suggests that one charm of tobacco must have been its ability to smother more disagreeable odours. No doubt many in that age took bad smells for granted, but we can see, if only from Shakespeare, that there were noses fastidious enough to detest them. Stenches enveloping the great houses with their multitude of servitors must have been, as Rowse says, 'appalling', and later on it was said that Louis XIV's palace of Versailles could be smelt from three miles away (p 159).

In the Elizabethan theatre pipe smoke could be a screen against the reek of garlic emanating from poorer spectators. To some noses, on the other hand, the remedy might seem a still worse affliction. Anyone who ventures into print, Dekker wrote feelingly, must expect persecution, and be ready to brave 'the stinking tobacco-breath of a satin-gull, the aconited stink of a narrow-eyed critic, the faces of a fantastic stage-monkey' (*Wonderful Year*, pp 161-2).

Another line of attack drew upon stock accounts, and pictures, of American aborigines which linked tobacco with indecency, shameless orgies, cannibalism (Schama, pp 203-4); an early development of 'anti-native' prejudice. West Indian rum, by contrast, could boast itself an offspring of the European genius. Tobacco, it was maintained, would impair memory, or cause impotence. Sundry herbs and spices were often mixed with it, which may in some cases have produced bad results, and faces of smokers in old Dutch paintings of low life sometimes wear a stupefied look. Heavy smoking, combined with heavy drinking of beer, might well have been expected to reduce the whole Dutch nation to stupefaction, yet its effect was apparently, during the era of Dutch greatness, the reverse.

A long poem by Joshua Sylvester was pithily entitled 'Tobacco Battered, and the Pipes Shattered' (Lee, vol 1, p 29). Braudel quotes the French moralist Sébastien Mercier's denunciation of tobacco, coffee and tea as a venomous trinity, and snuff as a noxious powder which deprived Frenchmen of what little memory they could lay claim to (Braudel, p 188). Toxic theses were not left untested. After dinner at Gresham College on 3 May 1665, Pepys watched an experiment of 'a cat killed with the Duke of Florence's poyson, and saw it proved that the oyle of tobacco drawn by one of the Society do the same effect'.

Burton, who of all men might have been counted on to give tobacco good marks as a remedy for melancholy, was antagonised by the excesses he believed too many smokers to be guilty of, including excess of spending at a time when it was still a luxury. He could only admit it as a humble purgative, and laughed at all talk of its 'divine, rare, superexcellent' qualities –

> A good vomit, I confess, a virtuous herbe, if it be well qualified, opportunely taken, and medicinally used, but, as it is commonly abused by most men, which take it as Tinkers do Ale, 'tis a plague, a mischief, a vicious purger of goods, lands, health, hellish, devilish, and damned *Tobacco*, the ruin and overthrow of body and soul. (Vol 2, p 264).

Christian IV of Denmark, brother-in-law of James I, must have listened to similar teachings. Asked whether he made use of the 'crazy-weed', he replied that he was too heedful of warnings that it drove people mad, by clogging brain as well as lungs with smoke, until the arteries burst (Gade, p 159).

About 1600 Asia woke up, and began to smoke. Tobacco was spreading across cultural as well as social boundaries; the sophisti-

cated mandarin of the Hanlin Academy took to it with as much relish as the Eskimo in his igloo. Governments far and wide over
Asia, as over Europe, sought to suppress it, and equally without
avail. Despotic regimes have been able to force their subjects to
take up arms for them, sometimes to change their religion; but
attempts at such a deprivation as this have always failed. Mankind
has found too few comforts to let itself be robbed of them.

By 1600 the Ottoman dominions, stretching from Morocco to
Iraq, were catching the infection, and English merchants were
quick to realise that they, and Persia too, represented an avid market. Religion was invoked by the hostile authorities, but there were
secular considerations too. The Sublime Porte, as the Turkish
government was quaintly known in Europe, may have seen economic objections to a drain of wealth to pay for tobacco imports.
As in Muscovy, fire risks could be an argument. Stamboul was
peculiarly subject to them, as the tall watchtower still standing on
its highest ridge-top reminds the tourist, so much so that it was
considered a duty of the Sultan to show himself on the scene in
person when a fire broke out, day or night. And, as everywhere,
smoking could be denounced as a peril to health and morals.

Murad IV (1623-40) went for the smokers tooth and nail, and
tried moreover to close the coffee-houses which often harboured
them, and could be suspected by a nervous police of being a resort
of malcontents and plotters. A veritable persecution was launched,
and there were many who proved as ready to die for their nicotine
as others have been for their country or faith. Katib Chelebi (d.
1657), the judicious Turkish writer, commented in an essay on
tobacco that as Murad's severity increased, 'so did people's desire
to smoke ... "Men desire what is forbidden", and many thousands of men were sent to the abode of nothingness.' When
Murad was on campaign against Baghdad, 15 or 20 officers were
found guilty of smoking at one halting-place; they were put to
death by torture in his presence. Some soldiers, Chelebi says, kept
short pipes in their sleeves or pockets, and, with what seems
almost incredible hardihood, 'found an opportunity to smoke even
during the executions'. He recommended that those who wanted

to should be allowed to smoke at home; the government could collect revenue from their weakness (pp 51-2, 58).

The great carriers of new things round the coasts of Asia and Africa were the Portuguese, with footholds scattered along the trade routes; within the Islamic world ideas and novelties found other points of diffusion in the centres of pilgrimage. There is a record of a jewelled pipe being presented to the Mughul emperor Akbar, and of his trying it until dissuaded by his physician (Watt, p 796); tobacco was outlawed in 1617 by his son Jehangir. This may have been no more than a formality; in any case smoking spread rapidly, and so did the growing of tobacco, the one important new crop to take root in India during the 17th century. Irfan Habib remarks that this shows a readiness among the peasantry to embrace a new and lucrative branch of farming (pp 45-6, 81).

Any official dislike there may have been was mollified in the usual way by a vista of tax gains, and early in the second half of the century the traveller Manucci reported that tobacco was yielding a considerable revenue at Delhi. Portuguese contact with Bengal commenced in the 1530s, and by 1550 smoking formed 'an indispensable part of the social life there' (Rahim, p 287). By the end of the 17th century it was a 'mass habit' in India at large (Habib, p 94), and Englishmen saw common people smoking pipes on the west coast, cheroots on the Coromandel coast in the south-east. One of them saw even children three or four years old puffing away (Raychaudhuri, p 275). Indians had long been chewers of areca-nut – from a species of palm – wrapped up in its leaf along with other ingredients, to which tobacco was now often added. Some took to chewing tobacco by itself, an Indian authority says (Sharar, p 220).

Frequently tobacco for smoking was combined with other leaves, spices, or sandalwood. It was taken by preference in the water-pipe, whose various designs were quick to make their appearance in the eastern lands. By passing through water the smoke was cooled, and perhaps rendered less noxious; the mouthpiece too was kept cool. The hookah, as it was called in India, could blossom into an article of display, and the Mughul empire, concentrating enormous wealth in the hands of its élite classes – largely, as in British India, foreigners – brought it to full bloom. Some choice specimens are on view in the Victoria and Albert Museum in London, made of inlaid metal or coloured glass; a small one with its mat for the smoker and long tube was brought to England by Clive. For social or literary gatherings a hookah made an ideal centre, the mouthpiece at the end of its long 'snake' being passed round the circle, not touching the lips but held cupped in the hand. Small portable varieties allowed the smoker a cool whiff while walking the hot street. The art of smoking was taking on an inventiveness of true genius, as it never did in over-busy Europe.

In the Far East tobacco reached the Philippines as soon as they were occupied by the Spaniards – from Mexico – before 1600. Japan was reached towards 1590, and gave a ready welcome to both tobacco and Christianity; but tobacco was forbidden between 1607 and 1609, Christianity in 1614, by the new, isolationist rule of the Shogunate. Christianity was destroyed, tobacco persisted. In China smoking spread quickly from the south-east, and by 1640 was a familiar enjoyment of the north. It had little religious pre-judice to contend with, but was deemed undesirable by the government, which probably had the same objection as others to money being exported to pay for it. An edict of 1643 threatened banishment or beheading; the embargo went on being reissued, if only from force of habit, until late in the 18th century. By then tobacco was being grown widely in China, as in Japan, so there was little need of imports. Dermigny remarks on the impressive unanimity of rulers in Asia and Europe in condemning 'the fra-grant intruder from America', and, still more remarkable, their equal failure (pp 1253-4). If all men really are brothers, they have never shown it more than in their surrender to nicotine.

Tobacco spread across north Africa from Egypt and other Turkish dominions, and thence southward into and across the Sahara. Carried by the Portuguese, it reached west Africa quite early in the 17th century and began to be grown there. In 1694 the Royal Africa Company's representative Captain Thomas Phillips had an interview with the king, whose face his counsellors were not allowed to see. He was lolling on a clay throne or platform with dirty old curtains round it.

> He had two or three little black children with him, and was smoaking tobacco in a long wooden pipe, the bole of which, I dare say, would hold an ounce, and rested upon his throne, with a bottle of brandy and a little dirty silver cup by his side . . . (Calder, p 351)

A company agent among the Fula of Gambia in 1738 found that crimes of all sorts, however trifling, were punished by sale into slavery; one man was offered for sale to him because he had stolen a tobacco pipe (Calder, p 454).

3

Europe: Pipe, Snuff-box, Cigar

Tobacco has gone out. To be sure, it is a shocking thing, blowing smoke out of our mouths into other people's mouths, eyes, and noses, and having the same thing done to us. Yet I cannot account, why a thing which requires so little exertion, and yet preserves the mind from total vacuity, should have gone out.

Dr Johnson, St Andrews, 19 August 1773 (Boswell, *Hebrides*)

With William III and his Dutchmen, and then George I and his Germans, the 18th century seemed to be opening propitiously for the pipe, after its neglect under Charles II. William held smoking parties after his hunts, said to have been the model for the royal 'Tobacco Parliament' in Prussia (Libert, p 37). Yet in 'good society' the pipe was soon being given up, in favour of snuff. Perhaps some anti-foreign prejudice played a part in this; more important must have been a turning away from a habit that went on being cherished by the common herd. Ostracism of the pipe can be counted as part of that drawing away of the élite from a popular culture, formerly shared by all, that Peter Burke has found characteristic of early modern Europe. Enjoyment of the pipe by Demos was enough to stamp it now as a vulgarity for a gentleman to eschew, and as too much a leveller of ranks. How much can be ascribed to a dawning sense of cleanliness, however, is hard to say. Smoking could not but add to a natural human proclivity to spitting: Johnson confessed that he had no passion for clean linen, but in Paris he was disgusted to see ladies spitting on the floor. Indoor spitting had been given up, on this side of the Atlantic, by the time smoking regained high-class acceptance.

Thomas Warton's 'Panegyric on Oxford Ale' portrays a hard-up student, in a quiet public house, savouring his evening tankard

> With toast embrown'd, and fragrant nutmeg fraught,
> While the rich draught with oft-repeated whiffs
> Tobacco mild improves. Divine repast!

– and contrasts this modest contentment with the pipeless pleasures of the fashionable coffee-house or tavern where the Proctor seeks his prey. A rhymer of 1731 allowed equal virtue to tobacco's two shapes, or souls –

> Thus dost thou every taste and genius hit,
> In *smoak*, thou'rt wisdom; and in *snuff*, thou'rt wit.
> (Brand, p 365)

Other poets too could be more discerning than men of the world. Jane Austen's Mary Crawford quotes and parodies the verses of Hawkins Browne, in 1736, extolling tobacco in the styles of six contemporary poets, among them Pope –

> Blest leaf! whose aromatic gales dispense
> To Templars [lawyers] modesty, to Parsons sense.
> (*Mansfield Park*, chap.17)

Unpretentious men of respectable status had no need to hide their pipes. The long clay ones later known as 'churchwardens' were earlier dubbed 'aldermen', a title which associates them with a high social rank. William Cowper writing to his friend the Rev. John Newton, that pious ex-slave trader, teases him about his pipe, but adds,

> for your comfort and the honour of that same pipe, that it hardly falls within the line of my censure. You never fumigate the ladies, or force them out of company; nor do you use it as an incentive to hard drinking ... Smoke away, therefore. (18 September 1781)

An inventory of a Sheffield grocer's stock included eight barrels of tobacco, in company with 45 gallons of brandy (Brewer, p 184). Tobacco shops often had outside as a sign a 'Carotte', or picture of a carrot-shaped roll or leaf; an alternative was the head of a dusky Indian, crowned with leaves. Smoking was more and more a part of the lives of ordinary folk, and glowed most warmly in their social gatherings. Self-respecting workmen, however, were alive to the fact that it might be a distraction when there was serious business on hand. Rules framed for meetings of Manchester small-ware weavers in the 1750s stipulated that they must be for orderly discussion of their affairs: they were not coming together 'to regale themselves with Ale and Tobacco, and talk indifferently on all Subjects'. Some Cordwainers' rules about the same time imposed fines for 'calling for drink or tobacco without leave of the stewards' (Thompson, E.P., *Working Class*, pp 418, 421). But an account of a rustic festivity near Aberystwyth in the mid-18th century tells of huge eating, followed by adjournment to the barn to dance until the sweat ran, '"with a great jug of ale at their knees and a piece of tobacco for each one'" (Williams, p 166).

Boswell and Johnson found the inhabitants of Skye consuming 'a vast deal of snuff and tobacco', despite a prevalent shortage of money (Boswell, *Hebrides*, 24 September 1773). Miniature pipes once in use in Scotland were known as 'elfin-pipes' and in Ireland 'fairy-pipes'; romantic legends grew up round them, but their origin must have lain in the poverty which prevented people from smoking more than a wisp of tobacco at a time. During the American War scarcities of tobacco were felt far more widely, and there was some revival of cultivation round Kelso and Jedburgh; England's laws against home growing were not extended to Scotland until 1779. Dealers who had good stocks at the outset made the usual wartime gains, like Scott's tobacconist Mr Quid, who trebled his prices to all except a distant relative, Mrs Bertram, 'whose tortoise-shell snuff-box was weekly filled with the best rappee at the old prices'. On her death we see him amid an impatient throng waiting to hear her will read out, in eager hope of legacies (*Guy Mannering*, chap 18).

From 1718, after the long wars with Louis XIV, Glasgow was

becoming the main port of entry for tobacco, which in the middle years of the century represented nearly half of all Scotland's imports from abroad (Devine, p v). A ring of 'tobacco barons' controlled the business, families moving as time went on into new mansions in George Square, and then into streets with names like Virginia and Havannah. Their trade with the colonies was largely a form of barter. As Adam Smith noted in *The Wealth of Nations*, the planters had little money available for buying what they needed from Britain, so they paid in effect in tobacco, and Britain in goods, often advanced on long credits (vol 1, pp 180, 619-20). They were allowed to export only to Britain, and restrictions on freedom of marketing were to be the main arguments for American independence. In the 1770s, when Smith was writing *The Wealth of Nations,* about 96,000 hogsheads of tobacco were being imported year by year, of which Britain consumed only about 14,000, the rest being re-exported (vol 1, p 417), giving British merchants the easy profits that all businessmen yearn for.

Compulsory passage through Britain added something to the cost of tobacco on the Continent, but it was cheaper than any supplies from Spanish America, burdened as they were by the weight of a State monopoly organisation. Tobacco was likewise one of the most lucrative monopolies of the Portuguese crown, both at home and in the empire; its subjects could not forgo their cherished indulgence, however high the price or bad the quality. Like other monopolies, this one was farmed out to capitalists who paid a fixed annual sum for their privilege (Boxer, *Portuguese Empire*, p 221). A great customer for North American tobacco was France. From 1674 to the Revolution another State monopoly was in force there, with the usual renting out of the operations to big financiers, the 'Farmers-General of the Customs', who bought in bulk, and whom the British intermediaries could not wish to antagonise. Altogether tobacco was an important contributor both to the building up of State power and to the accumulation of capital in private hands.

Holland was a more zealous smoker than ever, and led the field in pipe making, with large-scale manufacturers coming to the front, their staple product being the white clay pipe made at Gouda. This industry, launched in 1647, expanded until it enjoyed 'an extraordinary vogue, especially in France, Germany, and Scandinavia' (Israel, p 267). It flourished into the third quarter of the 18th century, but its products were eventually shut out from Denmark, Prussia and elsewhere, by governments which wanted to see pipes made in their own dominions. By the 1770s Gouda was ruined, but Dutch addiction to tobacco continued to earn the country a not altogether savoury reputation. Foreigners were repelled by the sight of barge-women pouring out smoke; snuff and chewing-tobacco also made themselves at home, and spittoons multiplied with them. Beer and tobacco may be considered the reaction or refuge of the Dutch from their morbidly excessive scrupulosity about cleanliness.

Aristocratic English distaste for smoking had little parallel in Holland, a republic where the powerful burgher class was always at odds with a small class of nobility headed by the House of Orange. When Boswell went to Holland in 1773 as a law student his journal's first allusion to tobacco, soon after his arrival, was unfavourable. Addressing himself, as he often did, in an admonitory tone, he wrote: 'Don't smoke any more because it makes you sick and a foreigner need not do it' (*Boswell in Holland*, p 4). But within a few months his feeling had changed. One of his morning exercises was the composition of ten lines of verse, on any topic that came into his head; those he penned at Utrecht on 21 January 1774 open with a flourish, a combination of ideas, that no other versifier would ever have hit on –

> With the same ease that blackguards feed on tripe
> Have I, James Boswell, learned to smoke a pipe:
> For I am now a very Dutchman grown,
> As all at Utrecht cannot fail to own.
> My father smoked some thirty years ago,
> And I most wisely in his footsteps go. (p 122)

Germany too had its republican sector, in the self-governing Free Cities, and its ordinary folk everywhere were no more perturbed than in England by snobbish etiquette. Coleridge's letters from Germany in 1798-9 bear witness to this. At the big port of Hamburg he found himself among 'Men with pipes of all shapes and fancies ... cane, clay, porcelain, wood, tin, silver, and ivory ... *many* with silver chains and with silver *bole*-covers' (*Collected Letters*, p 431). Peering through windows as he explored the town he saw ladies and gentlemen drinking coffee and playing cards, and – to his astonishment – '*all* the Gentlemen *Smoking* at the same Time'. Male teeth, he noticed, were commonly black and yellow with a Life's *Smoking*' (pp 431,439-40). Knowing the antipathy to tobacco of his friend Wordsworth, who was about to come to Germany, he warned him that he must be prepared to put up with German smoke. 'Here, when my friends come to see me, the candle nearly goes out, the air is so thick' (p 46). But Coleridge's real staggerer came at an open-air dance during a rural excursion. His eye was caught by a slender girl who looked about seventeen, and her partner who

> *waltsed* – with a pipe in his mouth! smoking all the while! and during the whole of this voluptuous Dance the whole of his Face was a fair Personification of true *German Phlegm* (p 507)

Snuff-taking may not look much of an upward step in social refinement. In late 18th-century Venice 'Everyone, man, woman and child, took snuff', and the 'inevitable and unpleasant catarrh' it produced was universal (McClellan, p 38). More elegant habitués prided themselves on being able to stuff their noses without sneezing. A drawing room full of ladies and gentlemen sneezing at one another would have been as repulsive as any pipe smoke; a Napoleon lecturing his Council of State and sneezing at every word would be undignified. But in England, unlike Venice, a taboo on ladies taking snuff in public came to prevail. Early in the 18th century, Thackeray recalled disgustedly in his essay on Steele, it was not so.

> Things were done in that society, and names were named, which would

make you shudder now. What would be the sensation of a polite youth of the present day, if at a ball he saw the young object of his affections taking a box out of her pocket and a pinch of snuff: or if at dinner, by the charmer's side, she deliberately put her knife into her mouth? (*Humourists*)

Snuff created a flourishing market for snuff-boxes, and a whole department of artistic craftsmanship. Japanese lacquer might be used, from the mid-18th century, as a covering; boxes shaped like shoes were admired; at Geneva some snuff-boxes had watches built into them. There were good wooden types, emulating the designs of superior ones, and a cheaper sort for the mass market. Ornamental snuff-boxes were convenient gifts for bestowal by way of compliment, or mementoes that could be exchanged among friends. An embarrassing surplus of them might pile up with a man like Mozart, who could not civilly be rewarded for his private performances with the hard cash he would have greatly preferred. This plethora of boxes littering Europe must have been a tempting target for highwaymen, pickpockets and muggers, and a scene in *The Beggar's Opera* ends with Peachum taking leave of Lockit – 'I must now step home, for I expect the Gentleman about the Snuff-box, that Filch nimm'd two Nights ago in the Park' (Gay, Act 2 Scene 2).

From about 1775 gold boxes became 'the prerogative of ceremony and royalty', as marks of favour which might contain gifts of money or jewels, or the keys of a loyal city (Phillips, P., p 61). The *corbeille* or basket of wedding presents received by Marie Antoinette included 51 watches and 52 snuff-boxes, all gold (Landes, p 441). Byron was behaving in semi-regal style when, planning a second grand tour in 1813, he paid 300 guineas for seven gold snuff-boxes for presentation to grandees who might prove serviceable (Moore, D.L., p 199). And Scott's Colonel Mannering, rewarding his servants for good conduct when the house was attacked by a smuggling gang, tactfully included the uncouth but worthy Dominie Sampson by

begging to exchange snuff-boxes with him. The honest gentleman was much flattered with the proposal, and extolled the beauty of his new snuff-box excessively. 'It looked', he said, 'as if it were real gold from Ophir.'

It *was* real gold, but Sampson had no notion of its cash value and no interest in it (chap 30).

In addition, a historian brings Charles II before us, 'odious, vicious, repulsive-looking with his snuff-plugged nose', and his Scottish agent Lauderdale 'with his red head, fiery face, spectacled nose, gross cheeks, thick sensual lips, and blubbering tongue . . . his hand always rifling the King's snuff-box' (Hewison, pp 116-17). Yet in 18th-century hands snuffing must have lent itself, better than any other mode of tobacco-taking, to niceties of deportment, an eloquence of the well-bred body; and this must have been one of its recommendations to 'the world', as a posturing élite called itself. Like every pastime of such a society – hunting, for instance, or duelling – it acquired a jargon and code of behaviour of its own. A writer prescribed a set of 14 movements required to make the taking of a pinch of snuff truly genteel (Libert, p 10), just as for more practical reasons a long series of commands had to be given before soldiers could fire their muskets in due form.

Scottish fondness for snuff continued among all classes, however. 'The popular southern ideas of a Scotchman and his snuff-box are inseparable,' wrote Dean Ramsay. Common folk up in the north economised their snuff by pushing it up their noses with a quill or small ladle, instead of wastefully sniffing it off their fingers. One tit-bit, known as a 'plugging', was a piece of pigtail-tobacco pushed right into the nostril and kept there. 'I suppose the plug acted', Ramsay comments, 'as a continued stimulant' (p 117). And Lord Gardenstone, the well-known Scottish judge, who died in 1793, formed two great attachments, to snuff and pigs. He had a pig sleeping in his bedroom, with his clothes for its pallet.

> His snuff he kept not in a box, but in a leathern waist-pocket made for the purpose. He took it in enormous quantities, and used to say that if he had a dozen noses he would feed them all. (Ramsay, p 144)

Particularly associated with Scotland was the 'sneeshin'-mill' or mull, a receptacle equipped with a rasp for grating tobacco into rappee, or snuff. It might have a spoon with it, and a hare's foot to wipe the lips after use. Cutting and grinding tobacco at home could be a safeguard against the adulteration that snuff very frequently underwent, as well as helping to kill time; a mull might be of wood, bone, horn, stone, with silver or gold mountings if the owner could afford them.

Countless individuals, some illustrious, others obscure, thus have a place in the annals of snuff. Herzen, the radical exile from Russia who lived for long in England, speaks of an old footman named Bakay in his family's service, who was usually drunk, but had one friend, a Newfoundland dog named Macbeth. He got impatient when Macbeth failed to understand his talk, and then

> he would take snuff angrily and throw what was left on his fingers at Macbeth's nose. The dog would sneeze, make incredibly awkward attempts to get the snuff out of his eyes with his paw, rise in high dudgeon from the bench, and begin scratching at the door. (p 32)

And Turgenev says of the critic and philosopher Belinsky, whom he greatly admired, that 'He laughed happily, like a child. He liked to pace the room, tapping with the fingers of his small, beautiful hands his snuffbox with Russian snuff' (p 108).

Mozart wrote a long account to his father in 1777, from Augsburg, of how he felt insulted by a Baron Bagge and another officer, who kept joking about the papal decoration he wore. They exchanged cutting remarks, sharpening them by offering each other pinches of snuff, until Mozart wound up with the haughty words:

> . . . it would be easier for me to obtain all the orders which it is possible for you to win than for you to become what I am, even if you were to die twice and be born again. Take a pinch of snuff on that.

Upon which the composer took his hat and sword and walked out (p 324).

Smoking revived in Britain among the fashionable, but now with the cigar as its bearer instead of the pipe. This new vogue was arriving from Spain; it might have done so much earlier if Spanish-American tobacco of decent quality had been more plentiful. It is usually held that the cigar spread by way of the warring French and British armies there during the Napoleonic occupation from 1808 to 1814. Parry pushes the starting point further back and further away, to the Seven Years War of 1756 to 1763 when Cuba was occupied by the British and its cigars made a lasting impression on them (p 304). In Britain a high duty on cigars checked their adoption until 1829, when it was scaled down.

Jules Sandeau, the French dramatist, was one European who commented on the subsequent rapid spread of the cigar. Marx, himself a devotee, ironically treated it as one of the tools of Bonapartist demagogy in the creation of the Second Empire. 'As a fatalist,' he wrote of Napoleon III,

> he lives in the conviction that there are certain higher powers which man, and the soldier in particular, cannot withstand. Among these powers he counts, first and foremost, cigars and champagne, cold poultry and garlic sausage. (*Brumaire*)

In lower walks of life smoking had always gone cheerfully on. A letter written by Lord Palmerston in 1805 talked patronisingly about a ball at Romsey, held in some mean rooms of an inn –

> ... the blaze of beauty displayed by the apothecary's daughter and attorney's wife ... the still more dazzling lustre of six tallow candles stuck in tin chandeliers ... the harmonious scrapings of the rheumatic fiddler (who by the by is barber and hairdresser) and the ambrosial exhalation of gin punch and tobacco. (p 37)

But among 'the quality' the old veto persisted for a surprisingly long time, at least as a ban on smoking in most parts of a house, and above all in feminine company. Perhaps it was feared that by savouring forbidden fumes women might catch the infection themselves – as in the end they did. As often, however, with such class-imposed taboos, the womenfolk of families desirous of rising socially were the keenest on adopting them, in order to qualify for acceptance. A story about Manchester life told by Engels to the socialist E.B. Bax illustrates this:

> Engels was on one occasion requested by the master of the house where he was dining, who, notwithstanding the shocked proprieties of his daughters, was addicted to his pipe after dinner, to join him for the purpose of a tranquil smoke in the kitchen! – and this was a well-to-do Manchester manufacturer who lived in a good house! (Bax, p 307)

And as late as 1880 a guest at Battle Abbey found that his host the Duke of Cleveland, very much a man of the old school,

> relegated the smokers to some remote place in the lower regions of the great romantic pile, the approach to which was through devious and confusing passages and turnings. One night, after a more protracted tobacco parliament than usual, one of the smokers, rather a figure of fun in a scanty and very ancient dressing-gown, took the wrong turning and opened the wrong door, and to his dismay found himself in a room where one of our married couples were peacefully slumbering. (Rumbold, pp 199-200)

Old Mr Harding of Barchester, with weary hours to get through in London, was directed to a 'coffee divan': this proved to be a cigar shop, with a smoking-room upstairs, where for a shilling he was given a cigar and a coffee ticket. The coffee was not bad; there were sofas, books, magazines, chess boards; he put his tired feet up, read, and soon fell asleep (Trollope, *Warden*, chap 16). When smoking began to be allowed, around the mid-19th century, in one room of a house, this sanctum too was called a 'divan' (Smith, Albert, *Constantinople*, p 163) – evidence of how the Ottoman East was associated with the beguiling vice. The march of progress ensured that the Bute apartments and state rooms in Cardiff Castle would include both winter and summer smoking rooms.

In a Pinero farce of 1885 the hospitable Mr Posket, as he enters his drawing room after dinner, cigar in hand, is telling his guest and fellow magistrate: 'We smoke all over the house, Bellamy, all over the house. Smoke anywhere, Bellamy – smoke anywhere.' His guest unluckily suffers from bronchitis, and can only suck jujubes (*Magistrate,* Act 1). In public there was the same drift. In 1868 English railways, following Dutch example, had to begin introducing the smoking compartments so often occupied by Holmes and Watson. And 'smoking concerts' were soon being held. On 5 June 1916, the Scottish *Border Telegraph* carried a notice of the ninth annual pantomime, *Dick Whittington*, at King's Theatre, Edinburgh, with the added inducement: 'Smoking At All Performances.'

Despite the appeal of the cigar, the pipe, if of presentable appearance, was recovering its old respectability. Plain clay pipes continued for many smokers to be the standard type; their social status depended on their length. A pipe with a short grimy stem was associated at best with the manual worker, and frequently with the street rowdy (in many middle-class minds there was not much difference between the two). When Disraeli's agitated heroine Sybil was hurrying through London in a cab, and a wheel came off, she was at once surrounded by louts – 'brutality stamped on every feature, and with pipes in their mouths' – and juvenile thieves, one of whom made a snatch at her purse.

> 'No wiolence,' said one of the ruffians, taking his pipe out of his mouth and sending a volume of smoke into Sybil's face, 'we'll take the young lady to Mother Poppy's, and then we'll make a night of it.'

(Happily a policeman appeared in the nick of time, and they took to their heels; Book 5 chap 6).

A longer, more fragile stem betokened (like the mandarin's long fingernails) a man with leisure to loll in his armchair. Pipes of altogether superior stamp were coming in, however, to compete with the cigar. They were capable of an artistic gloss or ornamentation such as our civilised forefathers bestowed on their pistols, or on cannon very unlike the naked monsters of our rude day. Pipe bowls took on, as if by natural growth, the forms of human or animal heads, or negroes, ladies, bearded worthies. In Europe pride of place was won by the meerschaum, just as the nobler kinds of water-pipe held sway in Asia; the name, 'sea-foam', stands for a species of stone from Asia Minor that absorbs hot tobacco juice and gradually takes on a rich dark hue, highly prized by connoisseurs. Meerschaums made their appearance in the later 18th century, and Coleridge discovered in Germany that a good one bought for 4 or 5 guineas would sell for 20 after being used for a year to two (_Collected Letters_, pp 462-3). But new owners were often curiously indifferent as to who had done the smoking and sucking before them.

Ultimate victory was reserved for a later comer, the briar pipe – unconnected with the briar rose; it was made from the tough roots of the southern European _bruyère_. Manufacturing processes were laborious, and called for high skill; the style that established itself was one of elegant simplicity, free of any adornment, which could be regarded as an index of English taste (Libert, p 96). Popular taste, meanwhile, clung to the clay pipe, whose decorated versions would be kept for special occasions. Salisbury was a place where pipes were early made; their makers were incorporated as a craft in 1619. Today its museum contains a large collection, coming down to the 'commemorative' variety in demand in later years. These have spacious bowls with room for miniatures of such events as the London Exhibition of 1862, or 'Donovan's Derby' run in 1889. Winchester Museum has another good collection of clay pipes from the 17th to the 19th-century, many with their makers' marks; one short clay has an image in relief on its bowl of the _Victory_. Dorchester again is well supplied, particularly with pipe-bowls fashioned into human heads. Peterborough Museum has in its section of ceramics a mid-19th century 'snake cigar holder', an unpleasantly writhing thing a foot long; and a late 18th-century pipe from Staffordshire, its stem a labyrinth with the bowl perched on one end of its intricate coils; such experiments must have owed something to the hookah. One may see there too a trio of very ornate and delicate glass pipes, of 'Nailsea' type, from about 1850.

Between the 1830s and the late 1870s consumption of tobacco in Britain rose from 14 oz per head to 1½ lbs (Briggs, p 242). Many Englishmen, 'especially of the common sort', had become enslaved to it, a critic wrote sadly in 1854 (Brand, p 362). Country brewers had learned well before 1800 to supply their tied houses with tobacco and spirits as well as beer (Clark, P., p 266); the museum at Peebles has a penny-in-the-slot tobacco machine of a sort common in 19th-century public houses. Music halls advertised gilded premises where workers could indulge in fantasies of luxurious living. One had a poster inviting patrons into ELEGANTLY APPOINTED SMOKING SALOONS and the MOST MAGNIFICENT SMOKING LOUNGE IN EUROPE (Sobel and Francis, p 51). In the next century working-class incomes improved sufficiently for consumption to double between 1914 and 1939 (Royle, p 280).

Mayhew, the investigator of mid-19th-century London poverty, learned that cigars were no longer being sold much in the streets. They had been sold formerly as smuggled goods, though they might be nothing of the kind: '"Everybody likes a smuggled thing",' a vendor remarked to him (pp 177-8); no doubt there was a touch of excitement in the idea as well as the thought of cheapness. In fact it may have been along the west coast of Scotland that the sturdy old smuggling or 'fair trade' spirit held out longest; Scotland was still a poorer country. In 1771 a hundred men and two hundred horses loaded with contraband had passed defiantly within a mile of Wigtown in Galloway, in spite of soldiers having been sent there to reinforce the customs officers. They lost four horses which fell down dead from heat but also, an exciseman thought, from the too pungent smell of so much tobacco (Irvine, G., p 35).

A friend of Carlyle's, a Dr Stirling, remembered showing Carlyle's brother John a shop where good smuggled tobacco could be got at half price. He laid in a supply, and Thomas, with him on a visit, must have done the same; as a biographer says, 'he always abhorred the meanness of taxing the needs of the common people' (Wilson and MacArthur, p 19). Carlyle's political judgements were highly erratic, but his steady sympathy with smugglers is greatly to his credit. For about 1860, smoking in his garden with a visitor, a blind preacher from America, he denounced the injustice of the tax on tobacco –

> The Government finds it needful to have such a revenue that it must needs lay a tax of some hundreds per cent upon the poor man's pipe, while the rich man's glass of wine pays scarcely one-tenth of this impost. (Wilson, D.A., p 384)

Just as a dirty old pipe was a hallmark of the riff-raff, an expensive cigar proclaimed the aristocrat, or the bloated plutocrat. In his diary of the siege of Mafeking during the Boer War, that remarkable African Sol Plaatje wrote that the great British Empire was doing nothing to protect the besieged. They had been left shut up for three months, after all their rulers' boasts of speedy victory. 'Now they let us square the account while they lounge on couches in London City, reading their newspapers and smoking their half-crown (2/6) cigars' (p 95). Paul Lafargue, the French socialist and son-in-law of Marx, also pointed to the inequality of justice: an unfortunate who broke into a shop because his children were hungry was sent to forced labour in the galleys, while the speculator who inflicted hunger on a whole people could parade with beaming face, cigar between his teeth (*Textes*, p 154).

At any social level to be seen with a cigar was thus to lay claim to a certain status. A parvenu is described by the fastidious Joseph Conrad in one of his novels as 'a podgy, wealthy, bald little man having chambers in the Albany', where he carried on shady loan transactions. The furnishings were old and precious,

> and these objects made of the costly black Havana cigar, which he rolled incessantly from the middle to the left corner of his mouth and back again, an inexpressibly cheap and nasty object. (*Chance*, Part 1 chap 3)

Cigars made convenient social offerings, and could help to coax those who might be useful into a good humour. The diary of Sir Edward Benthall, a jute magnate of Calcutta, for example, shows him one day in 1940 entertaining to lunch the Labour Minister of Bengal province, H.S. Suhrawardy, who was being helpful by assisting the Muslim League to promote anti-socialist 'yellow' or company unions.

My guest had two helpings of each course and finished off with a large cigar which by 3.30 proved too much for him. After being revived with ice water, he decided it was time to get back to work and departed with many pleasant personal compliments. (Chakrabarty, p 201)

But Britain and the Western world were moving towards the era of self-proclaimed democracy and equality, of which the (perhaps suitably meretricious) symbol, the common denominator of all ranks, has been the cigarette. It had a medley of ancestors, not all easily distinguishable. Their common feature was to be smaller than cigars, and packed into some kind of wrapping paper. Braudel holds that they came into circulation in Spain during the Napoleonic Wars, and spread to France, with thinner kinds of paper being devised (Braudel, p 190). A rough-and-ready sort became familiar to British officers under the name of *papelito* (Bevill, p 128) – *papel* being paper. Other accounts assume a much earlier birth, and it would indeed be surprising if no experiments had been tried in earlier smoking history. Lighter kinds of tobacco, of the 'Turkish' variety, took the lead, and the Crimean War gave them a fillip, before British taste settled on Virginians. These came in along with large-scale manufacture. Spaniards commonly rolled their own cigarettes; in countries like Britain they could only be a success when machinery was invented to mass-produce them. A Wills factory was set up at Bristol in 1871; the Player's factory at Nottingham in 1888. Slot-machines multiplied in the streets.

There were conservative frowns, as with every innovation. In a one-act play of the inter-war years an old pipe-smoking night-watchman, seated at his brazier in the street, solemnly admonished his juniors that 'Cigs is vice'. Higher up in society they could be thought plebeian, or unmanly. 'Cigarettes were deemed effeminate', and in 1870 a popular writer explained the German victory as due to Germans smoking pipes, Frenchmen cigarettes (Jerome, *Life*, p 74). It was against the grain, in deference to his youthful sovereign William II, that Bismarck joined him in smoking a cigarette. Lord Frederick Hamilton was a memoirist who could look back on a time, before the 1870s, when cigarettes were despised and 'a pipe was unspeakably vulgar'; as a youngster he saw nothing smoked except cigars. Old drinking habits lingered on, especially in the universities. 'I am certain', he writes, 'of one thing; it is to the cigarette that the temperate habits of the twentieth century are due. Nicotine knocked port and claret out in the second round' (*Before Yesterday*, chap 11).

Sir Algernon West says the same, and adds that it was thanks to the introduction by the Prince of Wales of smoking after dinner that long-drawn-out tippling had come to an end. 'What it was in old days appears almost incredible . . . ' (p 73). A third testimonial comes from Lady Dorothy Nevill. Men were drinking much less at dinner, though women more. 'Cigarette-smoking after dinner has undoubtedly been a great factor in the cause of temperance. In old days such a thing would have been regarded with horror.' She adds that not long since smoking in Hyde Park had been 'absolutely unpardonable', and any smoking in a lady's presence a 'social crime' (pp 126-7). Why nicotine should have routed alcohol like this may not be clear, especially since to many they have seemed an ideally matched pair. However, reduction in men's intake of liquor narrowed a gap between them and women, and the cigarette helped to bridge it; if it could seem effeminate, so much the better for slender feminine fingers.

To get a torch burning, to light him on his wicked errand, Shakespeare's Tarquin struck sparks from the stone floor with his sword – a proceeding that might have been expected to raise the alarm all over the house. It is amazing that the needs of smokers, in addition to daily household requirements, should have taken over two hundred years to produce a modern match; two centuries during which huge strides were taken in the construction of ships, telescopes, cannon, none of them so necessary, at least for ordinary people. All that can be said for Europe is that if the task of striking a light had been left to Asia, it might have taken two millenniums.

Today it is hard to comprehend what obstacles the smoker of

old had to contend with. Even today a gusty breeze can be a troublesome one on a hillside or on deck; but to get flint and steel to cooperate in their duty, even under shelter, must have been much worse. Carlyle recalled early days in London with his Jane and the cheap kettles and pans they had to make do with.

> A tinderbox with steel and flint was part of our outfit (incredible as it may seem at this date): I could myself burn rags into tinder; and I have groped my way to the kitchen, in sleepless nights, to strike a light, for my pipe, in that manner. (*Reminiscences*, p 70)

How mighty has been the spell of tobacco, to compel sluggish, feckless mankind into such labours! Squire Brown made a virtue of necessity, when he was seeing Tom off to school and trying to think what advice to give him, by fiddling for a quarter of an hour with flint and steel 'till he had manufactured a light for a long Trichinopoli cigar, which he silently puffed' (Hughes, Thomas, chap 4).

With swarms of servants at their beck and call, the well-off did not have to get up before daybreak to light their own fires; and in the 18th century they were not smoking. When they took to the cigar, they did need some means of igniting one at frequent intervals, and still more so with the shortlived cigarette. Candles had been a convenient source, in the evening, but they were being banished by gas. It was time now for invention to respond, as usual, to the requirements of those with money and power, and make progress towards that artificial Prometheus, the match.

After various fumblings, it was in the 1830s that the 'phosphorus' or 'lucifer' match broke through the darkness. It had many stages to go through before it became a true blessing to the smoker and ceased to be a curse to the women employed in the manufacture. Vestas, Vesuvians, Flamers – all were adapted to different tastes or needs. 'Fuzees' came in early, large-headed long-burning things which reached London mainly from Germany and were hawked about the streets by boys, many of them vagrant or destitute, barefooted Irish and the like. Their wholesale cost was 4½ pence per thousand (Mayhew, pp 172-3), so that a boy able to gather a working capital of tuppence-farthing could set out with a stock of five hundred.

After all this it is odd to read in a modern Swiss story of a young goat-herd up in the Alps who sits down on a hillock to pull out his pipe, hoping his parents do not know about it, and lights it with the help of the sun's rays and a magnifying glass (Halter, p 118). Why had this simple expedient not occurred to thousands of better-tutored minds?

In the colony-owning countries nationalism had for long been fanned not only by sermons and other official propaganda, but by tangible benefits, not least of them tobacco, which could go far to reconciling the masses to burdens like war-taxation and conscription. Ireland was a colony, whose peasantry contributed multitudes of soldiers to the army, but benefited only in the smallest degree from its triumphs. Few in Europe needed more acutely the consolation that tobacco could bring. Even the British government admitted this, to the extent of allowing it to be grown in Ireland between 1779 and 1831.

Most Irish families subsisted chiefly on potatoes and sour milk, wrote John Stevens in 1690.

> They all smoke, women as well as men, and a pipe an inch long serves the whole family several years, and though never so black or fowl is never suffered to be burnt. Seven or eight will gather to the smoking of a pipe, and each taking two or three whiffs gives it to his neighbour, commonly holding his mouth full of smoke till the pipe comes about to him again. (O'Brien, G., p 140)

Things changed little as time went on. In 1766 a pair of English actors, footing it fromWaterford to Dublin, stopped at a miserable little 'hotel', or hovel, and were offered a filthy pipe which they guessed must be in use by the whole parish (Maxwell, C., pp 307-8).

How tobacco entered into Irish life could be seen in one typical way at the beginning of 1760, when Britain was at war and discontent was boiling over. Thomas Gray wrote to a friend with news he had heard from Dublin, where disturbances had broken out and there was tumult in the Irish Parliament.

> They placed an old woman on the throne, and called for pipes and tobacco ... beat the Bishop of Killaloe black and blue ... rolled my Lord Farnham in the kennel ... Then the horse broke in upon them, cutting and slashing ... (p 225)

Conditions were most primitive in the west. An observer said of an old-fashioned steward superintending workmen in Galway in 1824 that 'he smokes out of the same pipe and drinks whisky with the labourers', who called him by his first name (Maxwell, C., p 220). Tobacco, like whisky other than the illegally distilled *poteen*, continued to be a luxury, only consumed lavishly at festive times. Of these one peculiar sort, in the first half of the 19th century, was the 'faction-fight', or ritualised mass contest with quarter-staffs, possibly descended from old clan feuds. It began with the leaders of one band marching up close to the foe and throwing out a challenge: this was called the *wheel*, and every wheel had its counter –

> WHEEL: 'Here's tobacco and who dars smoke it?'
> COUNTER: 'I'll cut it. Let who likes smoke it' (to the accompaniment of a 'cut' with the fighting stick). (O'Donnell, p 19)

In all countries tobacco cost more because – as Carlyle saw in England – governments wanted to make it pay a good part of their expenses, chiefly on war or preparation for war. By 1850 about a thousand million cigars were being sold yearly by State monopoly in the far-flung Austrian dominions (Fairholt, p 323). In France since the Revolution the business had been managed directly by the government, instead of by licensed contractors as formerly. In the carefree days of the *ancien régime* snuff had sufficed a great many Frenchmen; but now the German poet Heine, much as he loved France, was conscious of 'a great metamorphosis' since 1789, and particularly since the second revolution in 1830, Frenchmen had grown depressingly serious. 'Their faces have lengthened, their mouths are pursed; they have learnt from us to smoke and to philosophise' (*Travel*, pp 185-6) – twin German habits. In this changed Europe even snuff might have a similar effect, judging by the Frenchman in Maria Edgeworth's novel:

'You would not think, to look at me, I was so philosophic; but even in the midst of my military career I have thought – thought profoundly. Everybody in France thinks now,' said M. de Connal, taking a pinch of snuff with a very pensive air. (*Ormond*, chap 15)

It must have cheered Frenchmen in some measure to know that their supplies were reaching them in part through an ingenious system of smuggling across the Belgian border; all the more so as the lawful commodity, thanks to the monopoly, was bad as well as dear.

A sagacious breed of dogs, called *picards*, are trained to cross the frontiers at different points, avoiding the high roads. These animals are large, and capable of carrying a heavy weight. A sack is slung across their shoulders, fastened by a girth, large enough to carry twenty pounds of tobacco or snuff.

They were highly trained, and made their journeys at night; many were intercepted and shot, but many others got through. All this showed the folly, our British informant commented, of excessive duties on an article 'that has long been considered as indispensable as bread' (Gordon, pp 229-30).

Holland was no longer in the forefront of European life, and its people seemed to have dropped into a permanent silence, as though feeling that talk was a waste of time that ought to be devoted to the prime business of life, smoking. A Scotswoman and her party, making a trip in a canal boat in 1819, scarcely heard a word spoken. They passed numerous gardens with summer houses, and towards evening saw groups sitting there,

smoking and drinking beer out of tall glasses, with the gravity of Red Indians – pictures of Dutch enjoyment. Conversation, they most surely never thought of, even a stray remark was rare among them. Words are not wasted in Holland. (Grant, E., p 124)

Germany was, if possible, even more heavily fumigated than Holland, as Coleridge had found. In the Napoleonic years following his visit tobacco-growing and curing expanded, which helped to make up for the exclusion of colonial produce, though it cannot have improved quality. And on the Wordsworths' continental tour in 1820 Dorothy found Darmstadt a dull place. Still, at the table d'hôte, 'The fumes of tobacco did not prevent me from enjoying a good supper among whiskered Germans and Prussians. Some were gentlemanly men – all civil' (vol 2, p 61). At Heidelberg she saw parties of students everywhere, not looking very scholarly –

> They wear whatever wild and coarse apparel pleases them – their hair long and disorderly – or rough as a water-dog – throats bare – or with a black collar – and often no appearance of a shirt. Every one has his pipe – and they all talk loud and boisterously. (vol 2, p 64)

George Eliot was less tolerant. Welcoming English amenities on her return from a visit to Germany in 1855 she noted in her journal: 'The taste and quietude of a first-rate English hotel were also in striking contrast with the heavy finery, the noise, and the indiscriminate smoking of German inns' (Cross, vol 1, p 271).

Borrow tells of an elderly gentleman who took a more amiable view of the Fatherland.

> 'It is good to be a German; the Germans are the most philosophic people in the world, and the greatest smokers . . . smoking has a sedative effect upon the nerves, and enables a man to bear the sorrows of this life (of which everyone has his share) not only decently, but dignifiedly. Suicide is not a national habit in Germany, as it is in England.' (*Lavengro*, chap 23)

Novelists knew that their German characters would be expected to smoke hard on every page where they appeared. A German officer serving with the British in the Peninsular War leads his men into an attack with sabre in one hand, meerschaum in the other; mortally wounded, he hurls his sabre at the enemy and crawls away into a corner to die, sucking at his pipe to the last breath (Grant, J., chap 44). In the London working-class scenes of

Henry James's *Princess Casamassima* there is a radical German cabinet maker, smoking 'a pipe with a bowl as big as a stove', a truly 'monumental' pipe, which he stows away in 'a receptacle almost as large as a fiddlecase' (chaps 14, 21).

All the same, some well qualified sniffers could not help thinking that the tobacco Germans were so fond of was poor stuff. Idolise Germany as he might, Carlyle considered Berlin an ugly, raw-boned city, like Manchester but with the smoke of factories replaced by 'that of bad tobacco, which penetrates all corners and sanctuaries' (Kaplan, p 389). And Jerome's Three Men ended their German tour, in a hotel at Bonn looking down on the Rhine, with some quaint reflections on the Germans as a young people whose future development would have an importance for the world –

> 'They are a good people, a lovable people, who should help much to make the world better ... '
>
> 'They have their points,' said George; 'but their tobacco is a national sin. I'm going to bed.' (*Bummel*, chap 14)

Spain before matches, on the other hand, was a country to be pitied. 'What Madrid most stands in need of', Gautier wrote,

> after water, is fire, wherewith to light its cigars; consequently, the cry, *Fuego, fuego,* is heard in every direction, mingled incessantly with that of *agua, agua.* (p 81)

Young rascals carried round small braziers containing coals and fine ash. Another aid that Gautier met with was the bit of smouldering rope dipped in brimstone and tied to a post in the street (p 261) – the same 'match' that old-time soldiers carried to fire their guns with. Before the end of the 1850s it could be reported that Spain was leading the world in 'the making of lucifer matches for smokers' (Bryant, W.C., p 174). Until then, chronic need promoted a mutual dependence among smokers, and it was something of a national boast that on the Castellana, the main venue of the Madrid promenader, the poorest man could take a light from a duke's cigar without ceremony.

One may choose to explain the Spanish passion for smoking as due to the long vacancies of life in a country unemployed by history – or to nervous irritability due to poverty, religion, civil strife. The best foreign writer on Spain in those days, Richard Ford, remarked that a Spaniard without a cigar in his mouth would be like a house without a chimney, a ship without a funnel. It seemed to him quite natural for Spaniards to want to 'steep in sweet oblivious stupefaction the misery of being fretted and excited by empty larders, vicious political institutions, and a very hot climate' (p 335).

After the restoration of the Bourbon monarchy in 1814, it was soon discovered that Ferdinand VII's cigars were more reliable than his promises.

> It was habitual with Ferdinand to offer cigars to those in his confidence or good graces: the *cigarros del rey* were easily known by their great size and excellent flavour. When in a good humour, he would send two or three boxes of them as a present to a favourite. (Anon., 'Resident Officer', vol 1, p 86)

He was also known on occasion to lull someone into false security by the gift of a cigar when just about to order his arrest (Ford, p 338).

But few of Ferdinand's subjects could follow his example so far as quality was concerned. Despite the possession of Cuba, government monopoly resulted in the tobacco sold to the public being notoriously bad; *Blackwood's Magazine* in June 1854 carried a humorous denunciation of it (p 674). Hence the active smuggling from Gibraltar, carried on in defiance of severe penalties, and entailing endless friction with Britain. Indeed when yellow fever paralysed Gibraltar there was panic among Spanish connoisseurs (Ford, pp 336-7). Yet to many other Europeans, Spaniards appeared not only to smoke as much as Germans, but to do very little else. Millions of them, a pair of French critics reckoned in 1853, spent at least eight hours daily smoking and chattering. 'En travaillant, en mangeant, en causant, on fume, on fume à la cour, on fume au cabaret' (Richard et Quétin, p xiii). And an English writer similarly regretted that his countrymen when they lived in Spain were soon 'Spanishised'; the climate 'reduces a man to the languid, lounging, smoking, idle, procrastinating Spaniard' (Thornbury, vol 1, p 125).

Smoking was universal, even in the best circles, though in 1835 a foreign resident reported that

> In those where civilization has made most advances, old habits and modern delicacy are in some measure reconciled by appropriating a room exclusively to the smokers. (Anon., 'Resident Officer', vol 1, p 242)

From this room some fragrance penetrated to the drawing room, when a soirée was in progress, and the clothing of all the gentlemen was sufficiently saturated in the fumes to satisfy ordinary noses. Much of daily life was passed, by men, out of doors, in the street, the café; above all, by Madrileños, in the Puerta del Sol, the old irregular plaza that formed the general rendezvous.

Gautier too found the city always full of loafers, muffled in their cloaks even in hot sunshine as they gravely discussed affairs – yellow-stained fingers protruding every now and then from a cloak to roll a crude cigarette, made with a bit of writing paper (pp 83-4). The 1835 commentator, after an account of the horrors of bullfighting (though Spaniards were entitled to say, he admitted, that there were always foreigners, including diplomats, in the audience), observed that when the spectators were not satisfied with the sport provided they all took out flint and steel and struck sparks. 'When this takes place at dusk, it has a singular and pleasing effect, resembling fireflies in a forest' ('Resident Officer', vol 1, p 320).

Touring in Spain, before railways began to roll, gave those who ventured on it a sensation of being unusually fearless travellers, braving bandits as well as discomforts. Wherever they bent their steps, the tobacco cloud, welcome or unwelcome, pursued them. It was densest of all perhaps in the Basque provinces, where tobacco was imported duty-free under the local *fueros*, historic privileges whose preservation was a principal motive of the Basques for supporting the old loose monarchy against Liberal centralism in the great Carlist War of 1833-9. This part of Spain was

> the Paradise of smokers. You smoke very good cigars in San Sebastian for less than a halfpenny each, if you buy them in quantity. The consequence is that smoking, a vice elsewhere in Spain, is here carried to ludicrous excess. The *aficionados* temporarily resident here make tobacco their 'meat, drink, washing, and lodging.' The cigar is never out of their mouths. (Hughes, T.M., vol 1, p 199)

Between the Basque provinces and the neighbouring territory a customs line ran, with the usual heavy duties and spirited smugglers. Ordinarily these and the *aduaneros* or customs men were sworn foes, wrote a visitor; but during Carlist risings, when both their professions were suspended, they would join hands and turn into 'the most desperate sort of guerrillas that can be met with' (Thieblin, vol 2, pp 67-8).

4

A Girdle Round About the Earth

[Afghans on the road are always] stopping to gossip, to drink, or to pray ... They seldom travel without their *chilim*, or water-pipe, at their saddle, for it is a punishment to them to pass a single hour without smoking. If they have not this indispensable article with them, they will make two little holes in the earth communicating subterraneously, fill one with water and one with tobacco, put a reed in the former, and, lying on their stomachs, smoke this primitive apparatus with as much pleasure as if it were the hooka of a nawab.

J.P. Ferrier, Caravan Journeys and Wanderings, p 383

A painted wooden statue of an Indian chief, some four feet tall, stands in the Green Bay (Wisconsin) Museum, with feathered headdress, a bundle of cigars under his arm, and an earnest expression, as of a missionary, on his face. It dates from about 1840; such effigies were placed in the street outside cigar shops, until about 1880 when they were expelled as an impediment to traffic. Such a form of advertisement was a natural one: Indians were the world's first smokers, and their survivors were as vigorous smokers as ever. Their pipes continued to play an important part in ritual as well as in daily life. In some tribal groups the big 'medicine pipe' was often used as a test of whether a member was telling the truth. It was handed to him by the headman with mysterious ceremonies: if he dared to smoke it, his word would be trusted.

Some changes took place, as new ideas crept in from outside. Comanche women, growing more independent, were jibbing at the traditional test of their virtue, which obliged them to take an oath while the husband puffed out smoke and invoked the deities of sun and earth; if a wife was lying she would fall ill and die. One thus challenged threatened that she too would smoke, and if her husband's suspicions were false *he* would die. He preferred to drop the matter (Bohannan, pp 202-3). Other inequalities of sex were less easily righted. During the rebellion of Riel in north-west Canada in 1885, a newspaper gave an account of the scene when Chief Poundmaker's band was striking camp. All the labour of dismantling tents and packing baggage was left to the squaws and youngsters, while 'Bucks lolled around, whiffing "Kinneekinick" from long-stemmed pipes' (Donkin, p 242).

As Europeans spread across the continent tobacco was one of their staple trade goods, and they might bring with them a better quality than Indians had known before, especially up north. Frenchmen on the Mississippi had a type of brown clay pipe for barter. Iron-bladed tomahawks were manufactured with a hollow stem and a tobacco-bowl above the blade. When Franklin's expedition, voyaging up the Saskatchewan River in the 1820s, came on a settlement of Indians and 'half-breeds', 'Governor Williams gave a dram and a piece of tobacco to each of the males of the party' (Franklin, pp 47-8).

If hostilities threatened, and a leader held aloft the pipe of peace, the gesture was usually respected by both red men and white in the mountain region (Hafen, pp 113, 124, 189). At Fort Laramie in 1850 a full-scale conference was held between the white Superintendent, with troops to back him, and the Sioux. A slow, solemn ceremony of circulating the pipe of peace took place – 'A large calumet, of red pipestone, with a three-foot stem and ornamented with bright-colored beads and hair', filled with the prescribed mixture of tobacco and kinneekinick (Hafen, p 292-3). A Cheyenne chief in those parts earned the soubriquet of 'Old Tobacco'. Two years later a group of Indian delegates were conducted from St Louis to Washington by Thomas Fitzpatrick, the famous frontier-man and Indian agent, and on 6 January, in full panoply, they were presented to President Fillmore at the White House. His wife and daughter were present, and the wife of Kossuth, the Hungarian patriot in exile. It was expected by the chiefs that the peace pipe ceremonial would be gone through; they readily gave way when told that smoking in the presence of ladies was considered by white men improper (Hafen, pp 305-6).

In the old South, meanwhile, Blacks were prohibited from smoking in any public place; freedom to smoke on the plantations must have been one of the few things that made life bearable. Many Blacks escaping from Kentucky, it was noted in 1826,

> arrive in Canada almost weekly, where they are free and work at raising tobacco; I believe they introduced the practice. One person will attend and manage the whole process of four acres, planting, hoeing, budding, etc., during the summer. (Guillet, p 151)

In the Civil War the commander of a Black regiment in the Federal army was impressed by his men's love of tobacco; it was the one luxury they pined for (Higginson, pp 42, 52, 57).

Contacts between Black men and Red, here and there in American history, were seldom harmonious, but an exception was an experiment that the Negro educationalist Booker. Washington took part in when he began teaching in 1879 at the Hampton Institute for Black students. He lived in a building housing 75 Indians, who had been admitted, and found them very responsive to a sympathetic approach, in spite of considering themselves a cut above white men, and far above Black. 'The things that they disliked most, I think, were to have their long hair cut, to give up wearing their blankets, and to cease smoking' (p 73).

Meanwhile, tobacco had been doing much from the outset to ease the toils and perils of pioneers from Europe; the New World's treacherous weed helped to draw into it the destroyers of its forests, and of a great many of its former inhabitants. When Robert Louis Stevenson followed his star across North America by emigrant train in 1879, all the way over the Ohio plains 'The fences along the line bore but two descriptions of advertisement; one to recommend tobaccos, and the other to vaunt remedies against the ague' (_Across the Plains_, p 11). One travelling companion was

> an amiable young fellow going west to cure an asthma, and retarding his
> recovery by incessantly chewing or smoking, and sometimes chewing
> and smoking together. I have never seen tobacco so sillily abused. (p 22)

(Stevenson himself, all the same, was an impenitent cigarette
smoker, in spite of his bad lungs.)

Voices of protest were lifted, too few to be effectual. Oliver
Wendell Holmes, through the mouthpiece of his 'Autocrat',
warned young men against pipe smoking; it might cost them 'a
brain enfeebled and a will enslaved' (Sims, p 150). A young man
on the towpath of the Erie Canal, who lived to be President Garfield, preached the same message to his fellow workers. 'Throw
whisky and tobacco overboard,' he urged one of them, who was
left to grumble to his chum – 'Jist think, Murphy; a boy on this old
canal as don't drink rum, or smoke, or chew, or swear, or fight –
would yer believe it, if yer didn't see it?' (Thayer, chap 13).

White America's addition to the world's stock of pipes was a
modest one: the corn-cob, to which an owner could none the less
become warmly attached. When Tom Sawyer was inspecting
Mount Sinai, on his marvellous balloon journey abroad, he was
deeply distressed to find his old corn-cob wearing out. No other
sort would do for him: 'a person that's got used to a cob pipe
knows it lays a long ways over all the pipes in this world, and you
can't git him to smoke any other' (Twain, *Tom Abroad,* chap 13).
(Incidentally, when the Korean civil war broke out in 1950 and the
northerners were marching triumphantly southward, a reporter in
the plane carrying General MacArthur to the scene of action saw
him, in the midst of anxious thought and discussion, get up to
rummage in his bag for a cherished corn-cob pipe, as though
turning to an oracle.)

But for a long time American taste was turned most strongly in a
very different direction, that of chewing. Whatever a poet might do
for it, chewing is unquestionably the crudest mode of taking
tobacco, and the cultural descent from the red man's pipe to the
white man's chew was a steep one. It is an aberration, understand-

able where smoking has been difficult, as for seamen in wind or rain, or dangerous, as for miners. And the only country where chewing became and long remained the favourite mode of nicotine-absorption was the USA. Had this not been so, matches might have been invented earlier, with the famous Yankee ingenuity for parent. Not surprisingly, chewing was one of the American practices least admired by foreigners. On New Year's Day in 1828 Frances Trollope, mother of the better-known novelist, boarded the steamboat _Belvidere_ at New Orleans for a trip up the Mississippi. Both the ladies' room and the main saloon were well fitted up, and the latter had a fine carpet – 'but oh! that carpet! I will not, I may not describe its condition ... ' She would rather have shared a cabin with 'a party of well-conditioned pigs ... I hardly know any annoyance so deeply repugnant to English feelings, as the incessant remorseless spitting of Americans' (p 12). And a few years earlier two Englishmen taking a steamboat trip from New York were among several hundred passengers of all sorts, 'all huddled together in glorious equality, smelling of antifogmatics, and in the most independent manner spitting and smoking almost in each other's faces', talking of nothing but money-making, and stupefying themselves all the time with drinks (Cather, p 23).

Later in the century a traveller during the Civil War found Nashville, the capital of Tennessee, a dirty town with a dirty hotel: its bar was closed by order,

> but the habitués still hang about the scene of their former pleasures. In the hall there are a number of broken shattered chairs; and here, with their legs stretched in every conceivable position, a number of well-dressed respectable-looking persons loaf all day long, smoking and chewing ... The floor is as dirty as successive strata of tobacco juice can make it. (Anon., 'Border States', p 152)

Piloting his river steamer on one voyage, Mark Twain ran into a big flood of the Mississippi, and describes an unappetising stretch along its fringe. They passed

> wretched little farms, and wretcheder little log-cabins; there were crazy

rail fences sticking a foot or two above the water, with one or two jeans-clad, chills-racked, yellow-faced male miserables roosting on the top-rail, elbows on knees, jaws in hands, grinding tobacco and discharging the result at floating chips through crevices left by lost teeth . . . (*Mississippi*, chap 11)

A pioneer of abolitionism, the landlady complained of by the inimitable clockmaker Sam Slick. She was always worrying about her carpets, with the result that he had

to go along that everlasting long entry, and down both staircases, to the street door to spit; and it keeps all the gentlemen a-running with their mouths full all day.

Once he had the bad luck to open the front door and spit all over a man's white waistcoat (Haliburton, p 31). Evidently this landlady refused to sanction spittoons, despite the remarkable skill acquired by chewers in ejecting juice into them from a distance. From it arose spitting competitions. Near the old schoolhouse in the silver-mining ghost-town of Calico in California a notice still hangs, recording a winning effort. But clearly the spittoons that covered the country were not always made use of, for in the miniature theatre at Calico a notice of bygone days requests smokers and chewers to spit on one another instead of on the floor.

Chewing found its way into Canada, and persisted as a backwoods habit into this century. A discouraging experience for Donkin, as a new Mounted Police recruit in the 1880s, came at a big wooden hotel in the pioneer township of Regina.

The solemnity which perennially reigns in a North-West hotel is beyond all words. Long-faced men sit silent around the stove, only varying the grim monotony by an occasional expectoration of tobacco juice. Sometimes they may break out and engage in the congenial pastime of 'swapping lies'. (Donkin, p 20)

Donkin was no doubt a supercilious Englishman. A typical comment on the inhabitants was inspired by the sight of the township of Carlyle on a mail-day, when many settlers had come in to collect their post; another attraction was a lawsuit in progress. 'The court of justice was an empty log-house, and tobacco-juice was freely squirted on the floor by the mob of settlers who crowded around in patched and seedy garments of homespun' (p 257). These caustic words find corroboration in a similar picture from a witness as unprejudiced as J.K. Galbraith, recalling the Scotch-Canadian settlement of his boyhood. At the end of a meeting in the school, to elect its trustees, 'there would be black tobacco-juice stains on the floors, some with a little rivulet spreading out from what had been the source . . . ' (p 86).

In America the habit could keep a sort of underground exist-ence in circles which considered themselves too civilised to give way to it under public gaze. Sinclair Lewis's likeable character George F. Babbitt came to the city from the farm. On a lakeside holiday he and his friend Paul were in high spirits at being able to get into rustic clothing again.

> They stood on the wharf before the hotel. He winked at Paul and drew from his back pocket a plug of chewing-tobacco, a vulgarism forbidden in the Babbitt home . . . They stood quiet, their jaws working. They solemnly spat, one after the other, into the placid water . . . A trout leaped, and fell back in a silver circle. They sighed together . . . (_Babbitt_, chap 11)

Chewing habits seem often to have made Americans champ on their cigars as well as sucking them; as Trollope's Mounser Green observed, it was like burning a candle at both ends. He was in charge of a visiting Senator Gotobed, and they were in his room at the Foreign Office together.

> It was quite clear that as quickly as the Senator got through one end of his cigar by the usual practice of burning, so quickly did he eat the other end . . . 'I'm sorry to say that I haven't a spittoon,' said Mounser Green, 'but the whole fire-place is at your service.' The Senator could hardly have heard this, as it made no difference in his practice. (_Senator_, chap 28)

Cigars spread their benediction further down the social scale in America than in Europe. They were cheaper, and people were better off. Making cigars by hand was a thriving industry until late in the 19th century, when mechanised manufacture ousted it; a hand-worker could turn out 40,000 in a year, costing 5 to 10 cents. As everywhere, a scale of prices enabled superior persons to mark themselves off. There is a story of a conceited young engineer coming into the store of a western township, when the West was still Wild, and demanding a 'good seegar'. He rejected a box of *Cincos*, a 'popular five-center of those days', at which the woman behind the counter produced a Colt revolver, and said they were quite good enough for the likes of him. He paid for the box and slunk out of town (Anon., *Calicut*, p 17).

But the cigarette was taking root in the USA too. From pipe to cigar, from cigar to cigarette, the trend was a good index of the accelerating tempo, and perhaps diminishing value, of life; by the early 1920s George F. Babbitt often smoked cigarettes instead of cigars, as fitting his role of a smart, up-to-date businessman who was leaving the old rugged generation behind (Lewis, *Babbitt*, chap 6). Snuff came lower in American taste, as in British since the 18th century, but in earlier days it had its devotees. In a Fenimore Cooper novel, *The Pioneers*, there is a New England housekeeper named Remarkable Pettibone, a middle-aged spinster with few and yellow teeth,

> a tall, meagre, shapeless figure, sharp features ... She took snuff in such quantities, as to create the impression, that she owed the saffron of her lips and the adjacent parts to this circumstance; but it was the unvarying colour of her whole face. (chap 5)

In eastern Maryland in the early 19th century a disgusting custom, as the traveller Pickering called it, prevailed, 'of girls taking a "rubber of snuff" – that is, taking as much snuff as will lie on the end of the forefinger out of a box, and running it round the inside of the mouth' (Guillet, p 300).

And in a novel of a century later Jeeter Lester, impoverished scion of Georgia tobacco planters, is left at last with a scrap of land, a family, and no more credit at the store, even for 'food and snuff and other necessities ... Jeeter did not know what to do.

Without snuff and food, life seemed not worth living any longer' (Caldwell, chap 7). His district no longer grew the crop, which had worn out the soil, but there had been a time when barrels of leaf dragged by mules or shoved by Negroes along the sand-hill ridges smoothed the tracks still called 'tobacco roads'.

All over Latin America it was the cigar that held sway, though there was a place for the pipe too. In Jamaica early in the 19th century Michael Scott's hero saw a band of captured pirates on trial, Spaniards and men of mixed race, all splendid-looking fellows –

> every Spaniard has a beautiful mouth, until he spoils it with the beastly cigar, as far as his well-formed firm lips can be spoiled; but his teeth he generally does destroy early in life. (chap 11)

H.W. Bates, the naturalist, made an enjoyable stay in mid-century on the Madeira River in Brazil, at the family farm of one John Trinidade, whose complex mixture of blood ranked him as a _mameluco._ He was famous for his tobacco and cigars, and his skill in preparing the 'envelope', made of inner tree-bark separated into thin layers (pp 160-2). During another halt Bates was able to watch the festive dances of Ega, while the more staid citizens, 'husbands with their wives and young daughters, all smoking gravely out of long pipes, sat in their hammocks and enjoyed the fun' (p 305).

In Paraguay under the dictator F.S. López, who reigned from 1865 to 1870, there was rude plenty until the terrible war with his neighbours wiped out most of the mainly Guaraní population. 'All classes and both sexes smoked continually,' wrote R.B. Cunninghame-Graham, who knew his Latin America well. 'The country-women, journeying in companies to market through the woods, smoked cigars as thick as an ordinary banana . . . A lady wishing to honour any of her guests handed him the cigar she was smoking.' An Indian country-wench would tuck up her skirt and rub one on her thigh, before handing it over to be smoked (_Dictator_, pp 17-18).

Over the Islamic world the potent and mysterious spell cast by nicotine was deepening from generation to generation. Alcohol being (not always effectively) forbidden, the faithful were 'immoderately addicted to other means of inducing a slight intoxication', the state of placid enjoyment, banishment of care, summed up by the Arabic word *kaif* (Lane, p 338). It may be permissible to guess that tobacco did more to reduce the East to torpor than poppy or mandragora could do. Living among Egyptians like one of themselves, during the middle decades of the 19th century, Lane concluded that smoking must have modified the national character, and the Turkish, by taking up too many hours of the day and fostering inactivity. Still, he pointed out that most of the tobaccos in use were mild, and in his opinion had 'a very gentle effect; they calm the nervous system, and, instead of stupefying, sharpen the intellect'. For the peasant too it was 'a cheap and social refreshment' (p 339). Back in England, with the Egyptian slave-girl of Greek origin, Nefeeseh, whom he eventually married, Lane kept his Eastern habits, often used his adopted name Mansur, loved his *nargeeleh* or water-pipe, would send for 50 mouthpieces, and always had a ready welcome for gifts of his favourite Egyptian tobacco (Ahmed, Leila, p 33).

Left behind by the West in nearly all material and intellectual achievements, Asia excelled in pipe-making. Apart from the water-cooled pipe prized under many names all over the Muslim lands, China had its bamboo-stemmed pipes, and the Near East its stems of cherrywood, rosewood, and others, long before Europe learned to exchange the clay pipe for the briar. Long stems needed frequent cleaning, which gave employment to many poor men in the streets of Cairo. In Burton's Arabia a water-pipe was called a *shisha;* in the holy cities of Mecca and Medina it comprised a large coconut-shell with a tall wooden stem, mounted on a tripod; the apparatus 'easily overturned, scattering fire and water over the carpets'. 'Snakes' or flexible tubes were the prime manufacture of the Yemen. Some men of rank owned Turkish *shishas* 'of admirable elegance, compared with the clumsy and unsightly Arab inventions' (Burton, *Meccah*, vol 1, p 296).

In the Ottoman dominions a right to smoke in public might be a badge of Muslim superiority over the conquered peoples. A Christian merchant in Bulgaria had to obtain a special charter en-titling him to move about freely, to ride a good horse, to carry a sword, to smoke with a long pipe (MacDermott, p 31). Smoking was firmly fixed in the habits of the governing élites. A grandee would have his pipe-bearer just as a European bigwig of old would have his cup-bearer. Everywhere the pipe played an indispensable part in official receptions. Sir William Gell on his tour of the Morea, or southern Greece, in the last period of Turkish power, had to pay a courtesy visit to the Pasha, in a grand, though – as always – ill-cared-for palace. He was received with solemnity, and the customary coffee and opulent pipes were set out. Gell and his party then handed over their present, a telescope; an unhappy choice, because the dignitary proved to be almost blind, but he civilly pretended to look out of a window through it, and 'pro-nounced it "Pek guazel", quite beautiful'. On taking leave they had to run the gauntlet of a throng of 'courtly slaves', 'insolent and rapacious chiboukshis or pipe-lighters', beggar boys, all wanting baksheesh (Gell, pp 142-7).

When Robert Curzon was in the Near East a little later hunting for manuscripts in old monasteries, he met the Pasha of Egypt, the celebrated Albanian-Turkish Mehemet Ali who ruled the country from 1805 to 1849. His first audience began with a flow of standard oriental compliments, after which coffee was served,

> in cups entirely covered with large diamonds. A pipe was then brought to the Pasha, but not to us. This pipe was about seven feet long; the mouthpiece, of light green amber, was a foot long; and a foot more below the mouthpiece, as well as another part of the pipe lower down, was richly set with diamonds of great value, with a diamond tassel hang-ing to it. (Curzon, chap 5)

Before his rise in the world Mehemet Ali had been a modest tobacco trader; it must have gratified him now to be able to display a pipe of these heroic dimensions, as he discussed with his caller the possibility of a railway across the isthmus of Suez.

Not all Europeans relished the compulsory fumigation on these occasions. One day in 1857 an English officer in Persia had to escort his Minister to an audience with the Shah, and then on a visit to another great man and his putative son – 'a lout of a fellow,' he recorded in his journal. 'After the usual infliction of tobacco smoke we drove home in the coaches of the King' (Hardy, 19 July 1857). Inveterate smoking was not, however, limited to Muslim dignitaries. A couple of years earlier, during the Crimean War, Lord Malmesbury, lately Foreign Secretary, heard a story from Lord Lansdowne, who had recently been a delegate at a diplomatic gathering in Vienna. He said that the others

> smoked a good deal, and one day M. de Bourqueney, the French Minister, proposed to adjourn for an hour for that purpose, upon which the Turkish Ambassador, who had not yet opened his mouth, jumped up and supported M. de Bourqueney's proposal. (Malmesbury, vol 2, p 185).

Still, ideas of propriety when smoking was going on might vary considerably. In 1878 Britain, by a neat piece of sleight of hand, took over Cyprus from Turkey. One duty of the first High Commissioner, General Wolseley, was to hold a banquet in honour of Rifaat Pasha, a Turkish minister sent from Constantinople to supervise removal of Turkish war material. 'After dinner, Sir Garnet offered his distinguished guest a cigar. The Turkish gentleman promptly filched fifty and rolled them up in his napkin, which he likewise appropriated, as His Excellency looked on with unbelieving eyes' (Lehmann, p 238).

An early celebrity among tourists in these parts was Thackeray, who in 1846 was given a passage to Constantinople on a cruise ship inaugurating a new P & O Company service. One of his sovereign experiences was a Turkish bath, in its native setting, accompanied by muscular pounding, brushing, soaping, and at last relaxation in the cooling-room, swathed in towels and turban.

> You are laid gently on the reposing bed; somebody brings a narghilé [water-pipe], which tastes as tobacco must taste in Mahomet's Paradise; a cool sweet dreamy languor takes possession of the purified

frame; and half-an-hour of such delicious laziness is spent over the pipe as is unknown in Europe . . . (*Cairo*, chap 7)

Thackeray was a man doomed to heavy brain-labour, for whom such a half-hour of glorious life would be a true escape into paradise. Penzer's book on the Seraglio, or imperial palace, gives details of the Sultan's three-room bath suite, the rest-room a small apartment formerly adorned with gorgeous hangings, Persian rugs, and low sofas. 'A bejewelled *nargileh* and coffee-set practically completed the furniture' (pp 205ff).

A year before Thackeray, in 1845, a foolhardy French officer, J.P. Ferrier, who had been in service in Persia, had set off to travel, most of the way alone, through Afghanistan to India. On the first stretch, inside Persia, he had the advantage of being with a foreign envoy, for whose benefit a *mehmandar* or guest-conductor went ahead daily to the stopping place and gave orders to the headman to requisition supplies. He then took his seat in the chief square of the town, with his pipe, while tradesmen (who were not going to be paid for their goods) flocked round, loudly protesting that they had no supplies. He smoked and listened in silence – 'for all the world he would not let his pipe go out. In Persia this is a very serious affair, to which great importance is attached.' At last he jumped up, seized his stick, and cudgelled the objectors into compliance (p 47).

At one camping place in Afghanistan Ferrier was well received, on the strength of an official letter he carried. Sensibly prudent, in view of the dizzy ups and downs of Afghan politics, the clan chief only opened his mouth, very briefly, three times.

> To make amends, however, for this extraordinary silence, he smoked his *tchilim*, water pipe, without quitting his hold all the time; his gurgle was the last thing that I heard when I fell asleep, and the first when I awoke in the morning. (p 241)

In a verminous lodging at Furrah he was honoured with a call by the governor, 'a short, fat man, with a kind and jovial face, filling his nose with snuff every moment' (p 388).

A British officer's account of central Asia about 1870, from Russian sources, speaks of snuff as in copious use among the roving tribesmen of what is now Uzbekistan. Sometimes it was a mixture of dried and powdered grass and tobacco, with some drops of sesame oil. Still, the water-pipe was the great thing, an odd sort with a wooden bowl, or sometimes a pumpkin skin, and no real stem. After dinner each man in turn took two or three rapid puffs, before handing the pipe on to his neighbour. He would then bend forward, 'in a state of ecstasy, or buried in his thoughts'. Their tobacco was very strong stuff, procured from Bokhara (Spalding, pp 75-7). Women seldom partook. A _barshi_ or minstrel was always an esteemed guest, and the first to be offered tea and pipe after a meal. He and his accompanist would go on performing all night, with 'momentary interruptions for a mouthful of tea or a whiff of smoke', until they were exhausted, almost unconscious (pp 96-7). It is not only in Europe that tobacco has ministered to the arts.

Indians in contact with their fiery white rulers must soon have learned that the 'hubble-bubble' was one of the few Indian things they could really appreciate, and had charms to soothe the savage breast. Thomas Metcalfe, Resident or virtual governor at Delhi from 1835 to 1853, lived in great state, with a daily routine rigorously followed. After breakfast, his daughter Emily tells us, his hookah was set up behind his chair on its solid silver base. Its tube was 6 or 8 feet long, its mouthpiece 'exquisitely wrought in silver ... The gurgle of the Hookah still rings in my ears' (Russell, R., pp 16-17).

Elaborate water-pipes were left, after the early 19th century, to the Indian leisured classes, among them the landowners and courtiers of Lucknow, whose other chief pastime was kite flying. They had refined modes of preparing tobacco, with subtle flavours imparted by additives, and hookahs of special design. Their chronicler was touched to hear on a visit to London that

> the Poet Laureate, Lord Tennyson, liked to smoke clay pipes and always kept a basket filled with them handy. He could only smoke one

for a few minutes, then he would have to throw it away. He would sit in this way all day, filling, smoking, and breaking up pipes.

Had Tennyson known of the hookahs of Lucknow, the writer concluded, he would have discarded his own poor makeshifts, and sent for one (Sharar, p 230).

Other luxurious smokers of the old school were the wealthy lawyers of Calcutta. One of the most eminent of these in later days, Sir D.N. Mitra, told me of rich Bengalis who when travelling by train would reserve a whole compartment, so as to be able to sit undisturbed with their hookahs. A younger Bengali, the physicist Dr Sanjay Biswas, told me of his grandfather, another lawyer, having a magnificent hookah in the old family mansion in Wellington Square in Calcutta, so designed that while the tobacco burned on the ground floor the smoke ascended to him on the floor above, passing through a sequence of seven bowls of rose-water. It must have left behind there all impurities, like Salome shedding her seven veils.

In India as at home Britons were turning to the cigar, which they could more easily go on consuming through the official day, or out of doors, and which fitted in better with the more strenuous habits demanded by Utilitarian philosophy. One of them, Prichard, fond of satirising his fellow countrymen, reports their floating about in the swimming pool on _mussucks,_ or inflated sheep-skins, as though riding on horseback. One man, for a bet, managed to float on his back, legs perpendicular, a lighted cigar in his mouth, with a _mussuck_ balanced on his feet and a small native boy on top of it (p 150). Sometimes the cigar had to support the _sahib-log_ or master-race through sterner tests. Prichard speaks of a local rising at a post where there were only two white men. They perched themselves and their rifles in a pair of trees, waiting. 'Each had five chuprassees [footmen] who stood five under each tree. One chuprassee carried a cheroot-box, one an earthen jar containing water, one a tumbler, one a bottle of brandy, while the fifth looked on' (p 124).

Arrival in India of the memsahib in larger numbers had a

blighting effect on the pipe, as well as on dalliance with Indian women. At Bombay a hookah continued to be allowed after dinner, but as late as the 1850s it was thought objectionable for young men to be seen smoking cigars while driving on the Esplanade in the evening, or lighting up near the bandstand, under the mango trees, as soon as it was too dark for them to be recognised (Kincaid, pp 158-9). In 1859 an English hotel there notified patrons that 'A bungalow containing a billiard table is set apart for smoking, which is not allowed in the house.' Even twenty years later 'Men smoked in private as if they were ashamed of it, going away into corners where ladies would not see them. Smoking in their presence showed rank bad manners' (Hobbs, p 68).

Tobacco was being cultivated commercially in many parts of India. Leaf for export to India became the chief product of the Jaffna peninsula of northern Ceylon. It was 'of a special quality, prepared by steeping in seawater, and peculiarly adapted to the tastes of the Travancoreans' of south India, and Malays (Silva, p 473). Trichinopoly or 'Trichi' cheroots (a word said to derive from the Tamil *shuruttu*, a roll, and meaning a cigar open at each end) were known everywhere. Indian brands benefited from higher duties imposed in 1910-11 on imported tobacco. Cheap American cigarettes suffered most from this, and 'enormous numbers of cheap cigarettes' were soon being manufactured in India (Thurston, p 211). Still cheaper are the *biris* bought by workmen and poor folk, diminutive cigars loosely rolled and sold in paper bags at street stalls, outside which may hang a length of smouldering string for buyers to light up at. Indians in higher walks of life often took to cigars or cigarettes from British example; those in government service might feel that they were thereby giving themselves a further qualification. Use of tobacco in India could be pronounced 'all but universal – men, women, and even children smoke' (Watt, p 796).

North-eastward from India, however, snuff held the primacy. A British frontier official in conference with the Mehtar or ruler of the Himalayan principality of Chitral, noticed that he broke off an hour-long speech now and then to rub snuff on his gums, in accordance with the Chitrali mode (Durand, p 116). An American couple in Tibet after crossing the Dang La Pass fell in with a set of very rough-looking Tibetans, armed and mounted, who wanted to stop them. 'They all used snuff, being very dirty about it, plastering it over the nostrils and upper lip.' 'Their behaviour proved less ferocious than their aspect' (Rijnhart, p 255). And a German interned in India during World War Two, who made a spirited escape and reached Lhasa, found a vigilant watch there against opium. Even tobacco-smoking was frowned on: 'though one can buy any sort of cigarette in Lhasa, there is no smoking in offices, in the streets or at public ceremonies.' When the monks took over control during the New Year celebration, sale of cigarettes was banned. This attitude promoted an intense fondness for snuff. Monks and laymen alike were proud of their own mixtures, and of their snuff-boxes; these were always produced when two men met, and pinches were exchanged. Sneezing was bad manners (Harrer, chap 9).

Compton Mackenzie ascribed 'the peculiar charm of the Burman' to his being 'an inveterate smoker from early childhood to old age' (p 308). And Americans on an early embassy to Japan, calling on the way at Siam, were amused by what they saw of feudal etiquette. When the prime minister's 'stogie' went out while he was walking on the deck of their ship, his younger brother had to kneel down and help to relight it. They were disgusted by the red mouths and black teeth of the Siamese, who had long ago taken to the Indian habit of areca- or betel-nut chewing; on their side the Siamese admired their visitors' accurate spitting of tobacco juice and the vessel's 'commodious spittoons' (Crow, p 69).

Further on in the eastern seas an English voyager, aboard a Dutch ship packed with Arabs, Malays, Chinese, noticed the captain going up on to the bridge 'in mauve pyjamas and a cigar' (Tomlinson, p 201). (During Holland's occupancy of Ceylon it had been said that Dutchmen there 'began their day with gin and tobacco, and ended it with tobacco and gin'; Boxer, *Dutch Empire*, p 233.) At the polyglot market of Ternate in Indonesia a vendor who had brought tobacco in a canoe sold him some handfuls, very cheap but potent enough 'to make all a hardened forecastle crowd wonder – after one pipeful each – whether smoking is not the worst of follies' (Tomlinson, p 201).

In China futile edicts against tobacco went on being issued until 1776, while cultivation steadily spread. It may be that the government was afraid of too much tobacco-growing leaving too little land for food. Population was swelling rapidly; and in 19th-century India cultivation of such profitable 'cash crops' did contribute to food shortages. On his embassy to China in 1793, in vain quest of a commercial treaty, Lord Macartney found smoking very common, among the élite class of mandarins and their landowning kin in particular.

> They almost all smoke tobacco and consider it as a compliment to offer each other a whiff of their pipes. They also take snuff, mostly Brazil, but in small quantities, not in that beastly profusion which is often practised in England, even by some of our fine ladies. (Cranmer-Byng, p 225).

By 1800 tobacco had spread into the vast grasslands of China's Mongolian provinces, so much so as to be reckoned, like tea, a necessity rather than a luxury (Fletcher, p 56).

Tobacco had entered China long before opium, and furnished it with a sort of introduction. In Taiwan, frequented by Portuguese traders, a mixture of tobacco and opium was smoked early; on the mainland it was first tried in the south-eastern commercial province of Fukien. Opium was exported by the Dutch from Java, and then in much larger quantities by the East India Company, with the British navy and smuggling to force open a Chinese market. The strongest protest came from the Taipings, in the greatest of many 19th-century rebellions, which convulsed the south and the Yangtze valley for two decades. In their opening years at least the Taipings were austerely puritanical; they had a religion of their own, a blend of Chinese and Christian ideas. 'The whole army', the British consular official T.T. Meadows wrote of them at the time, 'pray regularly before meals. They punish rape, adultery and

opium-smoking with death, and tobacco-smoking with the bamboo' (Gregory, p 18). Or a tobacco smoker might be paraded
through the streets and made to shout all the time that no brother
or sister should do as he had done (Teng, p 103). ('Sisters' were
women serving in the ranks of the Taipings, who in some ways
were remarkably forward-looking.) A smoker who persisted in
spite of warnings was executed. Eventually the rebels were worn
down by government forces, with some aid from foreigners,
among them the chain-smoking 'Chinese Gordon', the future
hero of Khartoum.

Bamboo stems were easily adapted to water-pipes, popular
there as in India. Out west, rich men liked to smoke what was
called 'water tobacco', advertised as washed in water from the distant Yellow River – it was said to be mixed with arsenic, and to be
dangerous if taken in quantity, whether along with opium or not
(Bird, p 503); rich men have always had some curious tastes. A
Dutch diplomat learning Chinese at Peking at the beginning of
this century carried away a picture of the Manchu dynasty's rule
nearing its end: a police station, a small building with half a dozen
rusty spears as symbols of authority, where three or four 'ancient
pensioners' sat over their teacups and water-pipes, wearing old
official hats with picturesque tassels (Oudendyk, p 25).

In China as everywhere the nimble cigarette was coming in.
Foreign firms were smacking their lips over the vast market they
hoped to supply. As trade spread inland from the ports, and into
the countryside, and familiarity with foreign products grew, 'cigarettes and cigarette advertising penetrated even to the farthest
provinces' (Eastman, p 167). A _Daily Worker_ correspondent on
holiday in the Cool Mountains of the south-west made the
acquaintance of the Jingpaw tribal people, keen smokers of both
tobacco and opium (Winnington, pp 221-2).

The Ryukyu or Lewchew islands, disputed between China and
Japan until the Japanese got firm control late in the 19th century,
had the distinction of being visited by two notable travellers from
Europe. Captain Basil Hall of the British navy, cruising on a mission of exploration in 1816, found the word 'tobacco' in use there,

and reflected that 'perhaps there is nothing which is expressed by the same word in so many different languages as this plant (vol 1, p 124). Himself a smoker, he was distressed at one village he looked in at to find his pipe missing from his pocket. Expostulations, chiefly by signs, had no effect; but an old gentleman handed him his own lighted pipe by way of consolation, and delivered a long address. Impatience being useless, Hall 'sat down amongst them, accepted the orator's pipe, and puffed away as well as the most experienced smoker of the party' (vol 1, p 48).

Every Ryukyu chief carried a fan and 'a short tobacco-pipe and pouch, inclosed in a small bag dangling at his waist'. At a feast that Hall and his officers were invited to,

> The short intervals between the numerous courses, were filled up with smoking, our pipes being filled and lighted by an attendant, whose sole business it was to run about with a small bag in his hand, and watch when anyone wanted tobacco, which was not unfrequently, as the pipes were so diminutive. (vol 1, pp 128, 163)

Goncharov, the Russian novelist, decided in the 1850s, shortly before his masterpiece *Oblomov* came out, to broaden his horizons by serving as diplomatic assistant with a small flotilla going out to the Far East. Its mission was to negotiate a trade treaty with Japan, a country still closed to the world as it had been for more than two centuries. He kept and later published a full narrative of his wanderings, *The Frigate Pallada*; he has the air in it of a good-humoured, easy-going individual, interested in all around him. He had read Hall, and did not altogether believe him, but he too found much smoking in the Ryukyus; the tobacco he thought good and strong, partly meant for chewing. An old man at the gate of a temple that he and his friends wanted to inspect would not let them in, but offered live coals for them to light their cigars with. At the chief town the governor came aboard, 'a tall, grey old man' with a red nose and 'strong evidence of debauchery on his face'. Behind him and his suite sat a boy of 16 'who constantly lighted his pipe for him', and was given the biscuits and other refreshments offered by the Russians (chap 12).

Tobacco had long been grown in Japan, and there is evidence of its popularity in literature. 'Tabako' is one of the few western words used by the writer Saikaku, who was born in 1642 (p 318 n). In a scene in one of his stories a group of young bucks are eyeing and commenting on the girls who pass by. One is very attractive, but poorly dressed; they are sorry to learn that she has to earn a living by chopping tobacco leaves. Another tale brings before us the type of gentleman whom a high-class courtesan of the later 17th century would admire – elegant, dignified, cultured. After his toilet 'he bids one of the girl assistants fetch his tobacco, which his attendant has brought along wrapped in white Hoshu paper' (pp 83, 140).

Goncharov's frigate had to make lengthy stays at Nagasaki, while the Japanese practised their arts of evasion and procrastination. Interpreters came aboard, showed curiosity about everything, and were plied with refreshments. Cigars proved too strong for their taste. 'They brought their tobacco out of their bosoms, pipes of palm wood with silver mouthpieces and a tiny pipe, as big as the smallest little finger of a woman.' A pipeful gave no more than three puffs, of a flavour like Turkish, but very weak (_Frigate_, pp 269-70). When the Russians were entertained ashore each was furnished with 'a lacquered, wooden pedestal with a pipe, tobacco, and a little clay brazier with glowing coal and an ashtray'; they found the miniature pipes hard to manipulate (p 302). As in Cairo, there was an itinerant profession of pipe cleaning; its followers played a flute in the street to announce themselves (Seidensticker, p 78). Tobacco has kept its place in literature; a modern Japanese poet writes of the day's memories merging into one –

> Like a film, a dim vision
> Through a boring day's tobacco haze,
> A sentimental movie. (Bownas, p 193)

At Manila Goncharov and some companions visited the Royal Cigar Factory, run on the model of the parent establishment at Seville. It was a huge, square two-storey building. In one long hall they saw and heard six or seven hundred Tagal women of all ages pounding tobacco leaves on low tables with round stones. 'What a mass of heads turned in our direction, how many eyes glanced at us!' Eight or nine thousand women were employed in all. 'It is said that they are strictly moral; all measures are taken for that', and there were very few men on the premises. Great numbers of cheroots of ordinary grades were made here – the sort everyone smokes, as the manager said, 'from India to America and all over the Indian and Pacific Oceans'.

Africa was taking to tobacco, in one form or another, as avidly as Asia. Mungo Park the Scottish explorer left home in 1795 on his first expedition to trace the course of the Niger; ten years later he was killed on the river. He found tobacco in demand wherever he went, more for smoking than for snuff. A typical note in his journal runs: 'The natives of all descriptions take snuff and smoke tobacco. Their pipes are made of wood, with an earthen bowl of curious workmanship' (p 214). Tobacco often served as a gift, which if not forthcoming might be insisted on. At Teesee when a present was called for in the name of the ruler, Tiggity Sego, Park offered 'seven bars of amber and five of tobacco'. The envoy surveyed them with a jaundiced eye, 'and told me that this was not a present for a man of Tiggity Sego's consequence, who had it in his own power to take whatever he pleased from me'. Without more ado his baggage was ransacked, and half of it looted (pp 59-60).

In the Muslim north Tunisia had been from the 18th century an exporter of tobacco, chiefly to Italy (Valensi, pp 153, 156). From Egypt the Nile provided an entry to Saharan Africa. Half-Arab Somalia was another gateway. When Richard Burton was setting off for some exploring in east Africa, his fellow passengers on the ship from Aden threw off their clothes as soon as it was out at sea, and reverted to loincloths. 'Mohammed filled his mouth with a mixture of coarse Surat tobacco and ashes – the latter article intended, like the Anglo-Indian soldier's chili in his arrack' (a pungent spice in raw native spirits) 'to "make it bite"' (*East Africa*, pp 21-2).

The captain was smoking a pipe made out of a goat's shank.

Few Somalis smoked, finding pipe tobacco expensive, but all chewed; this turned their gums black and mottled, but helped them to kill time, while their women did most of the work (pp 81, 220). Burton found the Bedouin or nomad Somalis

> kind and hospitable. A pinch of snuff or a handful of tobacco sufficed to win every heart, and a few yards of coarse cotton cloth supplied all our wants. I was petted like a child, forced to drink milk and to eat mutton; girls were offered to me in marriage . . . (p 88)

Burton's partner and then enemy J.H. Speke, in Uganda looking for the sources of the Nile, paid a formal call on the queen mother in her hut. He sums her up as 'fair, fat, and forty-five'. They conversed a while; beer, or *pombé*, 'the best in Uganda, was then drunk by the queen and handed to me and to all the high officers about her, when she smoked her pipe, and bade me smoke mine.' Musicians performed; the queen, 'now full of mirth', kept withdrawing and returning in a new costume. On her asking for medical advice he gave her some pills, and forbade *pombé* till the next meeting; this she confessed would be an ordeal. Speke did not take his own advice, but prepared for his next audience by smoking and drinking *pombé* all night (Speke, pp 247-8, 268).

African imports from Brazil were paid for with slaves, and part of Burton's duty when he was appointed Consul at Fernando Po on the west coast, in 1861, was to induce African rulers to halt their sales. In pursuance of this object he was despatched inland in 1863 on a mission to the king of Dahomey. A naval officer who had met this King Gelele had called him 'a very fine-looking man, upwards of six feet high, a great smoker but not much of a drinker'. On this hint the gifts conveyed to him by Burton included 'one richly embossed silver Pipe with amber mouthpiece, in morocco case' (Burton, *Dahome*, pp 21, 36).

At a ceremony in the capital Burton encountered

> the highest official of the empire, the senior Min-gan. His dress was a war-tunic and a Lagos smoking-cap; with pipe in mouth he rode a nag handsomely caparisoned, under a white fancy umbrella. He was numerously escorted, and was followed by a big drum, and by rattles,

discoursing hideous music. (p 185)

On another occasion there was a parade of ministers, in tattered motley, before the king, all with lighted pipes as badge of their privileged status. One sported a German student pipe, others had clays, 'mostly French, with monkey and skull bowls', or else native pipes. Officers followed, each with pipe and musket; the commander 'smoked with an air a pestilent Bahia cigar' (pp 244-5). There was one parade when 'the King's smoker stood up before the throne. He was a black youth, in an ochre-stained kilt, with a pigtail of sombre-coloured cotton, and he used a long stem ending in a bowl as big as a cocoa-nut. The office is one of the true African fantasticals . . . ' (p 282). Clearly tobacco had become very much a part of the rituals of royalty.

Further south a little earlier, near Luanda in 1854, Livingstone – suffering from soakings and fever – passed through a populous region, huts almost buried in the riotous vegetation. 'By and by the villagers emerged from their lairs, men and women smoking a long pipe and followed by crowds of children' (p 261). When Goncharov was in Cape Colony at about the same time, on his odyssey to the Far East, he was one of the group who, during an excursion ashore, paid a call, of courtesy or curiosity, on Ceyolo, a chief captured in the latest 'Kaffir War' and imprisoned. They were advised to take cigars as an offering. They found him with one of his wives, who were admitted in rotation to keep him company, reposing on a mattress. He sat up and shook hands, laying the gifts of cigars and tobacco down without looking at them (*Frigate*, pp 195-7).

But what was most eagerly sought by southern Africans was, apparently, snuff. (Perhaps there was a lack of flint and steel suitable for kindling a pipe, when a man was away from his fireside.) So an item of wear indispensable to a Kaffir of Natal, a missionary there wrote, was a small calabash snuff-holder, hung on a string; with it, if he could afford it, went an ivory spoon. 'The size of this spoon would astonish a Highlander.' Its owner filled his nose and inhaled slowly, while tears rolled slowly down his face.

The flowing of the tears is a necessary part of his enjoyment; and so completely is he entranced that it is almost impossible to induce him to move until the operation is completed. This excessive use of snuff has necessarily a great effect on the nerves . . . All classes and both sexes indulge in the excitement. (Shooter, pp 8-9)

A Zulu epic poem on Shaka, the founder of the military state of Zululand in the early 19th century, pictures him reviewing his famous regiments as they marched off to quell a defiant chief. Heroic songs were being chanted, as usual before battle, one of them about the ruler, the 'elephant' who tramples men down –

He asked for snuff from Macingwane of eNgonyameni:
Macingwane declared he had none.
Thus did he court trouble! (Kunene, p 221)

It sounds from this as if snuff had acquired a symbolic character, as a tribute to be extorted in token of submission, as war elephants were of old in India.

In their grand conflict in 1879 with the Zulu kingdom the British had some of the fighting race on their side, recruited into the Natal Native Pioneers. In a letter home an officer serving with them spoke of his men as good fellows on the whole, 'very fond of Natal rum' – less so of water, but not quarrelsome. 'They love snuff dearly; but, instead of sneezing, it makes them yawn. A few of them smoke tobacco, and a native compound called _dagga_' – hemp, an intoxicant (Emery, p 53). And when E.S. Grogan was making the first traverse of Africa from south to north, in 1898, in one part of German Tanganyika he saw villagers

wearing wooden tweezers on their noses; on inquiry we discovered that they injected snuff mixed with water, and then put the apparatus on to keep the concoction from wasting away at once. (Grogan and Sharp, p 118)

Finally, it was under tuition from Indonesian fishermen long ago that Australian aborigines – like the Andaman islanders – learned to smoke (Coon, pp 213-14). Their taste for it must have grown strong. A charge made by one of their descendants against white men is that the latter often got black women to sleep with them by supplying their husbands with tobacco (Lockwood, pp 160, 175). There is unhappily no link between the 'primitiveness', or closeness to Nature, of a race, and its morality, whatever Rousseau and his disciples may have supposed. In New Zealand the Maoris too, when tobacco came their way, took to it readily. A song current among the colonists in 1860-61, about an unpleasant native and how he was bayoneted and thrown into a hole, began –

> He wore a filthy blanket on the day when first we met,
> And held between his dirty teeth, a pipe as black as jet;
> His footsteps had a lightness, and his voice a fiendish tone:
> He was thinking of the plunder, when we were gone to town.
>
> (Scott, D., p 10)

Mark Twain viewed Pacific islanders with distaste, if not with hatred like this, when he cruised in the schooner *Boomerang*. 'As soon as we set sail the natives all lay down on the deck as thick as negroes in a slave-pen, and smoked, conversed, and spit on each other, and were truly sociable' (*Roughing It*, p 442). But Rupert Brooke praised the Tahitians for their polished courtesy. And R.L. Stevenson may have got to know the Pacific better than any other literary man, from long residence there in search of health. He noted the eagerness for money-hoarding of the people of Paumotu, and saw two men spend a whole day cleaning the copper sheath of the vessel he was touring in. They were entirely at ease in the water, 'working at times with their pipes lighted, the smoker at times submerged and only the glowing bowl above the surface . . . ' (*South Seas*, Part 2 chap 4).

It is pinpoints of faint light like this that History discloses to us in the far distance. How these two industrious islanders fared in life, what wives fell to their lot, how many years that schooner's copper held out, no one can tell, any more than – as Sir Thomas Browne asked – what song the Sirens sang. Almost all human records are made up of middles without beginnings or ends.

5

The Conversion of Women

Fie, this stinking tobacco kills me! would there were none in England! – Now, I pray, gentlemen, what good does this stinking tobacco do you? nothing, I warrant you: make chimneys o' your faces!

> Citizen's wife, in Beaumont and Fletcher, *The Knight of the Burning Pestle*
> (1613), Act 1 Scene 2

'Men have always smoked. With women it is just a habit', a conservative Briton wrote querulously to his newspaper, the *Bradford Telegraph and Argus*, (Bateman, p 61). Smoking drew a dividing-line between masculine and feminine, as did, among the higher ranks, the convention obliging ladies to leave the table after dinner, when serious drinking began. Such demarcations, to keep women in their place, were more needed in western Europe than anywhere else, because women always had much more freedom in western Europe to mingle in male society, to dance with men, to ride out hunting with them. This peculiarity must have done as much as any other factor to give western civilisation through the centuries its unique qualities, its aptitude for change.

Smoking became a badge of masculinity very quickly; though since it requires neither skill nor strength the logic of this is not obvious. Mr Rochester's cigar as he walked in the grounds with Jane Eyre 'breathed a trail of Havannah incense on the freezing and sunless air', and she learned to recognise it among all the flowerbed odours (Brontë, C., *Jane Eyre*, chaps 15, 22). Winifred in *The Forsyte Saga* comes back to her house and at once her nose tells her that her runagate husband Monty has returned. 'A male scent! A faint reek of cigars and lavender-water,' missing for the past six months (Galsworthy, *In Chancery,* Part 2 chap 13).

On the other hand, it may not have gone without saying that females of respectable degree in Europe, and England in particular, should suffer exclusion from the new felicity wafted across the Atlantic. After all, they needed it more than men as a relief from domestic boredom; and before custom hardened, some did take it up, if not nearly so many as the sour puritans would have us believe. Tobacco could be bought at the theatre, as well as apples and nuts, and William Prynne the hammer of the actors made it one of his complaints in 1632 that pipes were offered by the vendors to women. A religious writer in 1628, Samuel Rowlands, drew an alarming picture of the fashionably extravagant kind of merchant's wife, living above her station, discontented

> except (contrary to the modesty of her sexe) shee be halfe (at least) of the mans fashion: she jets, she cuts, shee smoakes, shee drinkes, and what not that is evill. (Lee, vol 2, pp 276-7)

It may be guessed that moral saws carried less weight than the fact that a pipe was a dirty thing, likely to soil clothes, and that a long clay one of the old pattern was a clumsy thing to handle. If cigarettes had been invented two or three centuries earlier, the outcome might have been different. No doubt curiosity could provoke some experiments. Louis XIV, who disliked smoking, was shocked to discover his daughters smoking pipes borrowed from officers of the guard. Much oftener, snuff would fill the blank in feminine life, less inelegantly than any pipe. George III's consort was nicknamed 'Snuffy Charlotte'.

In some circles women took up smoking promptly enough. Dutch genre paintings often show them puffing away along with men. In a bourgeois society like Holland's, relatively free from genteel posturing, it would be easier for women to get their share of the pipe than in England. By the 18th century this had spread further afield. Traversi, the Neapolitan artist, painted a group of merrymakers (now at San Francisco), one of them an old woman sitting at a table with the bowl of her pipe resting on it, a long wooden stem conducting smoke to her mouth. But pictures of this kind, often set in taverns, breathe a mode of life comfortable rather than fashionable; and lower down the scale there was a great deal of more disreputable smoking. By not smoking, a lady placed a distance between herself and her humbler sisters. Something like this has always been the prime motive force of social behaviour; it has induced women to submit to far more serious deprivations and unpleasantnesses.

'Ladies, when pipes are brought, affect to swoon', wrote a satirical poet (Brand, p 365). Not all did. Mrs Drake of early 18th-century Manchester, who headed the local Tory and Jacobite faction, in opposition to Lady Ann Blount, the Whig leading lady, 'preferred a tankard of ale and a pipe of tobacco rather than the new-fashioned beverages of tea and coffee' (Thomson, pp 150-1). In the north such traditional tastes could hold their ground, among conservatives, more tenaciously than nearer London; and in the Celtic lands more than in England. One very cold April evening in 1789 Lady Eleanor Butler, one of the two 'Ladies of Llangollen' – Irishwomen who lived together there for many years and grew into celebrities – entered a curious sight in her journal.

> A comfortable well clad old woman rode up the field with a pipe of Tobacco in her Mouth, the Puffs from which softened the keenness of the air and must make her journey over the mountains delectable. (Bell, G.H., pp 194-5)

But most females drawn to tobacco were not well clad. British fairground amusements included the sport of getting old women to grin through a horse-collar, the widest grin earning a prize. At a festivity provided by the Bishop of Killala (in north-west Ireland) for his flock in 1732, this prize was tobacco; there were others for dancing, singing, horse-racing (Maxwell, C., p 337). Less kind to the infirmities of age was the game of 'Aunt Sally', a wooden figure of an old woman with a pipe in her mouth, which competitors tried to hit with a wooden ball. She must have epitomised many generations of women, among whom the association of tobacco with age and poverty was very close, and by society treated with scant respect. It can be supposed to have deterred many younger women, even of humble station, from taking to the pipe.

Typical of the unrespectable was old Mrs Brown, into whose hands little Florence Dombey, lost in the London streets, fell; a rag and bone peddler, who seized on the girl's bonnet and frock and gave her rags in exchange. 'Mrs. Brown resumed her seat on the bones, and smoked a very short black pipe, mowing and mumbling all the time, as if she were eating the stem' (Dickens, *Dombey*, chap 6). Mr Rochester's servant, Grace Poole, in charge of his mad wife only consorted with her fellow workers for one hour daily. She would then descend to the kitchen, 'eat her dinner, smoke a moderate pipe on the hearth, and go back, carrying her pot of porter with her, for her private solace, in her own gloomy, upper haunt' (Brontë, C., *Jane Eyre*, chap 16).

Scotland and Ireland, deeper in poverty than England, abounded in old crones, many with scarcely more than a thin thread of tobacco smoke to tie them to human life. One who was somehow able to repel gloom was the wife of an aged man living in a hut on the bank of Loch Ness, who had only a few words of English but assured Boswell and Johnson that 'she was as happy as any woman in Scotland', and offered them a dram.

> Dr. Johnson was pleased at seeing, for the first time, such a state of human life. She asked for snuff. It is her luxury, and she uses a great deal. We had none; but gave her six pence a-piece. She then brought out her whisky bottle. (Boswell, *Hebrides*, 30 August 1773)

Thomas Carlyle's father was 'irascible, choleric, and we all dreaded his wrath'; but it softened his son's memory of him to recall that once or twice as a boy he was sent out to buy a quarterpound of tobacco to be given to some old women hired to pick potatoes. 'I love to think of it. "The little that a just man hath." The old women are now perhaps *all* dead; he too is dead: but the gift still lives' (*Reminiscences*, pp 6, 11). Thomas and his pious old mother, at home, used to smoke their pipes together (Froude, vol 1, pp 335-6); it must have been a fine scene. There was a coarse evil-smelling tobacco known as *mundungus*, with which the very poor had to be content; the old hag, for instance, in Scott's tale, whose hovel the inquisitive Lady Penelope and the wicked Lord Etherington visited in an effort to get at another woman's secret. She was in no hurry to reveal it, even when tempted with some silver; 'she sat down to her wheel, and seized, while she spun, her jet-black cutty pipe, from which she sent out such clouds of vile mundungus vapour' as would quickly have driven the lady away had her curiosity been less sharp (Scott, *St Ronan's,* chap 32).

Elsewhere Scott draws a more agreeable sketch, of a rustic holiday when the goodwife's mother,

> old Luckie Loup-the Dyke, 'a canty carline' as was within twenty miles of her . . . sat by the fire in the full glory of a grogram gown, lammer beads, and a clean cockernony, whiffing a snug pipe of tobacco, and superintending the affairs of the kitchen. (*Lammermoor,* chap 12)

Old women in northern Scotland were still smoking short clay pipes well into this century, Miss Joanna Gordon tells me, with a resulting frequency of cancer of the mouth. Possibly smokers who could not afford many fills liked to get concentrated smoke, just under their noses. Women still young enough to be active might prefer snuff because a pinch could be taken at any moment, in the course of work. Among them were English farm labourers' wives in some areas, like Oxfordshire in the later 19th century. 'All the women over fifty took snuff. It was the one luxury in their hard lives. "I couldn't do wi'out my pinch o' snuff," they used to say. "'Tis meat an' drink to me"' (Thompson, Flora, chap 5).

Jack Yeats, brother of the poet, tells in a reminiscent story of Ireland of how at one time he would go down to the quay and sit on an old broken boat, where he would be joined by a middle-aged man, and by a not-young woman who never spoke. He had a box of small cigars, and used to give one to this man, and after a while thought of offering one to the woman. 'She took it like a mouthful of spring water on a parching day,' but would never accept another, although 'She'd drawn away from it every breath and whiff there was in it, making it last, and living with it to the stump' (p 43). About this enigmatic figure there is something of a visitant from the Celtic twilight, as likely as not a princess or deer transformed by a magician.

Outside Europe a great many women were smoking. In the Levant, where so many cultures mingled, women of all sorts and degrees learned the art. Calling on an acquaintance in the Coptic quarter of Cairo, during his monastic researches, Robert Curzon was conversing with an old lady when a welcome interruption came with the entrance of 'the most lovely apparition that can be conceived, in the person of a young lady about sixteen years old', followed by two graceful black girls. She sat beside him on the divan, and was amused by his attempts at Arabic. 'I must confess that I was rather vexed with her for smoking a long jessamine pipe, which, however, most Eastern ladies do' (Curzon, chap 5).

Hill, forest, desert have always favoured some sort of freedom for women, if not freedom from toil. Garhwali women of the north Indian hills have all been smokers time out of mind. The 'Hottentot Venus' exhibited in Paris and London early in the 19th century attracted notice partly by her habit of smoking a pipe. Two of the parades witnessed by Burton in Dahomey were of 'she ministers and captainesses, who were muffled up, and who smoked like the men' (p 245). There were female regiments in the army. In most of western Africa women seem to have been free of any male embargo on their smoking. Nigerian market-women, even in the Muslim north, are commonly provided with short pipes as they chaffer over their wares. Gerald Durrell, the animal collector, was struck, while watching a fiesta in the hills, by the colourful costumes, and the long slender pipes, black with use, that most of the older women were smoking: lowland tribes preferred short stubby ones (chap 4). When the traveller Freya Stark visited a Kurdish encampment in Luristan in southern Persia, she was received by the absent headman's wife, who was smoking a short clay in her tent; she appeared sulky at first, but delivered a speech of restrained welcome (p 81).

Among American Indians there might be some ritual restrictions; the Piegans of the Plains had a 'Red Pipe', with spiritual as well as medicinal virtues, that no woman was allowed to touch (Thompson, D., p 365). Otherwise women were at liberty to smoke if they had anything to put in their pipes. Some had quite enough. An 18th-century witness who lived among the Creek Indians says that 'the women of the tribe were wont to make payment in tobacco for the privilege of whipping prisoners as they passed' (Hobhouse, p 238). This is one example among many of how women have worked off their pent-up resentments against their own masters by vindictive treatment of men from outside. More regrettably, they have oftener worked them off against other women. Daughters-in-law have frequently been the victims, as in Japan where among the poorer classes they are said to have been reduced at times to suicide by bullying, including blows with metal tobacco pipes (Diösy, p 256).

Paradoxically lack of social freedom, for women kept in purdah in Muslim countries, or something close to it in China, might make their lords more willing to let them smoke: nobody else could see them. But in China there could be women neither aristocratic nor poverty-stricken who were able to smoke in the face of the world. That fearless traveller Isabella Bird voyaged up the Yangtze in 1898 in a two-decker barge housing three generations of the family that owned it. Below was the grandmother, 'in blissful idleness and authority. The wife, a comely, healthy, broad-shouldered woman, with bound feet, worked and smoked all day', with the heavy tiller under her arm or chin (p 30).

An adventurer of the 1860s in the Yap islands of the Pacific found that the women of higher rank, who had 'perfect, luxuriant figures', like their men, were,

> passionate smokers. It almost seems as though the feminine sex, especially the young girls, are possessed by this habit learned from the Europeans. A cigarette is seldom absent from the lips of the beautiful and graceful smoker.

At a festive gathering the foreigner was puzzled by questions from the ladies which became embarrassingly pressing, and were enforced by 'certain indescribable caresses'. The king's youngest daughter, aged 15, came to the rescue by conveying to him that what was wanted was tobacco for rolling into cigarettes. 'With pleasure I handed the lovely child the desired weed. At this the bevy of ladies burst into joyful excitement; in a few minutes the tobacco was divided among them' (Tetens, pp 11, 13). In 1882 a London magazine had an imaginative picture of a young Maori couple on horseback, in European dress, he with a cigar, she in a riding habit and side-saddle, with a small pipe in her mouth (Scott, D., p 208).

Away from Europe, white women of good standing could throw off some of their own inhibitions, or male prohibitions. Among the first to become regular smokers were those who did so in the colonies. Ladies born in Bengal, in the opening years of British power, sometimes had their own ornamental hookahs, and smoked a preparation of betel-root instead of tobacco, or light Persian tobacco flavoured with herbs and spices. But an officer's wife staying with a Mr Cleland 'expressed astonishment' at the ladies of the family enjoying cheroots after each meal (Kincaid, pp 93-4).

A celebrated Englishwoman in the East was the Lady Hester Stanhope, a niece of Pitt, who settled in Syria, acquired some authority among the Arabs, and after losing it turned mystic prophetess instead. When Kinglake was making his tour in 1834-5 he called on her, near Beirut; she had known his mother. He encountered a gaunt-faced woman of about 60, in a large turban and flowing robe.

> A couple of black slave-girls came at a signal, and supplied their mistress, as well as myself, with lighted tchibouques, and coffee. The custom of the East sanctions, and almost commands, some moments of silence whilst you are inhaling the first few breaths of the fragrant pipe . . .

Then Lady Hester began with a few words about her guest's native Somerset; she very soon 'bounded onward into loftier spheres of thought,' leaving him helplessly behind (Kinglake, chap 8).

Soldiers' wives, or those who followed the marching regiments across the globe, had far more need than any fine ladies of the comforts of tobacco; they must often have owed a debt to it as deep as their men's, amid the bruises and bitterness of their lot. During the Crimean War, for example, someone on shipboard heard from the first mate the story of a recent voyage into the Black Sea. At Varna they took on board 'a cargo of soldiers' wives . . . the ladies *would* be always drunk, to the great destruction of all quiet in the ship . . . They also would be always smoking, to the great danger of setting the ship on fire' – but it was hazardous for any officer to interfere. 'The women's part of the ship was an independent Amazonian kingdom' (Anon., *Inside Sebastopol*, pp 52-3).

At home in Europe, and particularly in England, the 18th-century hostility of polite society to smoking survived far more tenaciously among women than men. Anything connected with tobacco could be deserving of respect only as a relic of the past. Scott made fun of the old-fashioned collections of family heirlooms treasured by

> all the old maids or magpies, who have inhabited the mansion for a century . . . the boatswain's whistle of some old naval uncle, or silver tobacco-box, redolent of Oroonoko, happily grouped with the mother's ivory comb-case, still odorous of musk . . . (*St Ronan's*, chap 10)

Of men still breathing and smoking, women were apt to be sharply condemnatory; religious revivalism made them all the more strait-laced. Military men were often the worst culprits, and the long-drawn-out wars against the Revolution and Napoleon multiplied their numbers and sapped their morals. One of their sternest critics was the Mrs Downe Wright of a novel by Susan Ferrier which came out shortly after the wars' end. 'I'm sure', she declared,

> they are to be pitied who have friends or relations either in army or navy at present . . . they are professions that spoil a man for domestic life . . .

I never knew a military man but what must have his bottle of port every day; with sailors, indeed, it's still worse; – grog and tobacco soon destroy them. (chap 71)

At times such diatribes sound like a general condemnation of the smoking sex. Trollope brings into one novel a riverside party where the ladies got soaked with rain. '"There's somebody smoking," said the Countess angrily ... "I never knew anything so nasty."' There was in fact a crowd of men smoking on the verandah, and it was not clear 'whether she spoke of the rain, or the smoke, or the party generally' (*Duke's Children*, chap 32). In other cases some professional antipathy might be at work. In August 1884 Engels, on holiday at Worthing, wrote to Laura Marx in Paris: 'Here we are ... in as primitive a place as the British seaside will admit of – the first lodgings we took we had to leave because the old Madame objected to smoking!'; evidently he viewed this as amazing perversity (Engels, *Lafargue*, vol 1, p 228). A few years later *Punch* published a poem complaining that women, having compelled smoking men to retire to the outside seats on buses, were now following them there and complaining again (Sims, pp 21-2).

Coleridge's son Hartley, amiable and talented but unpredictable, endorsed a letter to his friend Mrs Claude in 1841 by denying that it was, as she might suspect, 'The product of *six* pipes ... I only smok'd one pipe and a precious black one.' Another to her is headed: 'without a pipe in his mouth' (*Letters*, pp 247, 251). This suggests that she had been sermonising him on his bad habit. Many women did indeed try to rescue their friends and relations from it. Tennyson was showered with remonstrances by doctors and others about his incessant pipe smoking, and late in 1855 his wife Emily persuaded him to make a bonfire of his stocks; but he soon relapsed, and she could never really get him to give it up (Martin, R.B., p 398). Nevertheless, though a heavy drinker too, he lived to the creditable age of 83, and his friend Carlyle to 86. Jane Carlyle soon understood that to get Thomas to stop smoking was as impossible as to make him stop talking; she did manage to confine his pipes to his study, or the garden. But there is a touching story of their first wedded years when Jane, thrilled by letters from her absent husband, found a cigar stub in his room and smoked half an inch of it for the satisfaction of feeling close to him (Hanson, p 152).

Novelists made the most of the theme of tobacco as an apple of conjugal discord. Three days after their marriage Thackeray's Mrs Swigby was sparring with her husband

> because he would smoke, and no gentleman ought to smoke. Swigby, therefore, patiently resigned his pipe, and with it one of the quietest, happiest, kindest companions of his solitude. He was a different man after this; his pipe was as a limb of his body. (*Shabby Genteel*, chap 6)

Three days more and she had swept away the poor fellow's rum and water too. One of Douglas Jerrold's 'curtain lectures', or bedtime jeremiads, very popular in *Punch* in the 1840s, is delivered by a Mrs Caudle to a partner who has come home late; she overflows on the sins of drinking and smoking, and threatens divorce – 'I'm sure tobacco ought to be good grounds' (Sims, pp 71ff). In higher society such shafts may have been, as Trollope seems to have thought, less penetrating. One of his Deans is indignant with his son-in-law Lord George for being angry with his wife because she had joined in dancing the Kappa-kappa, the craze of the moment, and forbidding her even to waltz. 'Pish!' he ejaculates, 'I hate these attempted restrictions. It is like a woman telling her husband not to smoke' (*Popenjoy*, chap 49).

On the other hand, a good many lovers must have rashly vowed to give up smoking, a folly made fun of by W.W. Jacobs's nightwatchman in a story of two ship's officers infatuated with a girl who has got on board in the guise of cabin-boy.

> She 'appened one day to say she could never, never care for a man who drank and smoked, and I'm blest if both of 'em didn't give 'er their pipes to chuck overboard, and the agony those two chaps used to suffer when they saw other people smoking was pitiful to witness. (*'Question of Habit'*)

But many little love-tricks, signals of soft feelings, could be played by young ladies with nicotine for ally instead of rival. Some of these acquired the sanction of custom. In British India when the Orient was still thrillingly strange, 'Ladies worked fancy *hookah* rugs for their sweethearts', and deemed it 'the finest compliment they could pay a man when they took a pull at his hubblebubble. Ladykillers carried a spare mouthpiece, to substitute for the one they were using, when taking soundings . . . to see how they stood' (Hobbs, p 154). In Germany women embroidered tobacco pouches for their lovers. In England a little ceremony grew up which even Miss Matty of Cranford, a spinster very conscious of being a vicar's daughter and a gentlewoman, could bring herself to fall in with. She and two other ladies were invited to dinner by that rough-diamond bachelor Mr Holbrook, who did not scruple to shovel peas into his mouth with a big round-ended knife. 'After dinner a clay pipe was brought in, and a spittoon; and, asking us to retire to another room . . . he presented his pipe to Miss Matty, and requested her to fill the bowl.' She 'had been trained by her sister to hold smoking of every kind in utter abhorrence' – but appreciated the compliment, and did as requested (Gaskell, *Cranford*, chap 4). When cigarettes came in such civilities could take a new turn. A cynical reprobate in a novel of the 1860s, in want of a lady with money, breaks off a letter to a confidant with 'here is Milly, whose taper fingers have been making cigarettes for me all morning, come to propose a sail on the lake' (Lever, *Rent*, chap 11).

Some of the encouragements that Venus and Nicotine might combine to bestow on male ardour were of a less delicate sort, likely to deepen disgust with tobacco in any woman whose eyes fell on them. In a Turgenev novel the hero, a young Bulgar patriot in exile, had to consult a retired public prosecutor, up to all the tricks of the legal trade. This worthy listened to him attentively, 'looking at him sideways with his small, sly, tobacco-coloured eyes, and taking snuff all the while from a snuff-box which was embellished with a picture of a full-bosomed nymph' (*Eve*, chap 24). It belonged to a species of art that had been in flower since the springtime of tobacco, even in Calvinist Holland. An old French ivory tobacco-grater in the Wallace Collection in London has one of Jupiter's amours carved on its flat side. Mayhew roaming London came on street-sellers of snuff-boxes and cigar-cases with indecent scenes painted on them, for '"fast gents that has money to spare"', and a stylish shop in Oxford Street sold pipes whose broad bowls were decorated with seductive nudes. A good many later specimens have a place in the Irvine collection. In one, a draped but well-developed female figure reclines under a pipe-bowl, like a ship's figurehead. In another a short-skirted circus girl sits on the stem as if riding a pony. An equestrienne canters, side-saddle, on a white steed, her face towards the smoker. More up-to-date, a lady holding a tennis racket leans against a pipe's tall bowl.

Tobacco smoke might cast darker shadows when it came out of feminine mouths and noses, redolent of everything *demi-mondaine* and licentious. On 4 December 1855, *The Times* reported a case of *Crim. con.*, a suit against Sir Henry Seale, Bart., for adultery with Mrs Hawker, who was living apart from her husband in a villa at Clifton in Devon. Evidence was given by Hugh Pugh, porter at the local station of the South Devon Railway, that he had often seen Sir Henry getting off the train there and making for the villa, usually with a portmanteau and 'several little hampers or parcels', which Hugh sometimes helped to carry. One summer evening he saw the pair together in Woodover Lane.

> 'They were talking together there and smoking.'
> Mr Collier, QC, Attorney-General, for the defence: 'Who was smoking – one or both?'
> Witness: 'Both, sir.' (Laughter).

(Whether or not this scene of depravity helped to sway the jury's mind, the verdict was for the plaintiff, though with damages of only a meagre £100).

One final vignette: Oscar Wilde's poem 'The Harlot's House' conjures up a moonlit street, loud music, shadows flitting across the curtain of dancers, like puppets on wires – and

> Sometimes a horrible marionette
> Came out, and smoked its cigarette
> Upon the steps like a live thing.

In all this, men's double standards of sexual morality found a reflection in their attitudes to male and female smoking; and the implication that only women lost to all sense of shame could want to smoke was an effective menace to deter others from venturing.

A mid-Victorian curate was amused to see a friend 'covered with confusion at having put his betrothed into a smoking carriage' at the station by error (Kilvert, 9 October 1871). But it was the right of entry into the world's smoking places that normal women were beginning to demand – a right they were at last to secure just when it came out that cigarette smoking might be a death warrant. From filling men's pipes or rolling their cigarettes, they might well want to graduate towards something of their own to smoke. There were pioneers claiming this long before they had any notion of a right to vote, and before there was any feminist movement to band them together.

In early 19th-century Upper Canada, or Ontario, there were old women, stragglers rather than forerunners, enjoying their old clay pipes, but also some young girls who thought it smart to emulate them. A traveller's journal of 1826 records that while he was staying at a tavern some of these lasses would come in of an evening, and most of them 'took a smoke with the landlord and the landlady, passing the short black pipe from one to another' (Guillet, pp 299-300). George Sand had a big pipe, like some other women of the time, not all of them otherwise disreputable; but cigars, and still more cigarettes, made indulgence far easier, first in private, then in company, finally in public.

In exile in London the Italian patriot Mazzini was befriended by the Ashurst family of Muswell Hill. It included, he informed his mother, three sisters who smoked, and a fourth who came to have tea with him, bringing flowers – 'all capital crimes against English *mores*'! (Rudman, p 73). After the fiasco of his rising at Genoa his admirer and helper Miss Jessie White was 'arrested and kept in a Piedmontese jail, where her flaming red hair and her long cigars, in contrast with her fine, intellectual cast of features, must have mildly amazed her keepers' (Rudman, p 118).

Eccentrics sometimes led the way, as they often do. Another friend of Mazzini's, Jane Carlyle, acquired the taste from her un-balanced associate Geraldine Jewsbury. A letter of Jane's reports a hysterical scene with a Geraldine full of 'mad _lover-like_ jealousy', whom it took a long time to cajole into a better humour –

> with her hair all dishevelled and her face all bewept she thereupon sat down at my feet and – smoked a cigarette!! with all the placidity in life! She keeps a regular supply of these little things – and smokes them before all the world. (Hanson, p 307)

There might be a touch of exhibitionism in such behaviour, a desire to shock. A heroine in a late 19th-century play by Jerome K. Jerome and Phillpotts evidently intended to be shocking: she rode a bicycle, smoked a cigarette, and twice said 'Damn' (Jerome, _Life_, p 110).

Fashion of course had its oscillations. In a Pinero play of 1899 a not too ascetic duchess is smoking in her bedroom in company with a married friend, who is intrigued by her collection of sala-cious French novels (which the duchess says she only reads for the sake of their style); the caller remarks on what a pleasure ciga-rettes are, and regrets that women now seem to be giving them up (_Quex_, Act 3). But some far less frivolous women were turning to nicotine for relief. In 1883 Beatrice Potter (later Mrs Sidney Webb), launched on her social researches, was staying with a working-class family at Bacup in Lancashire, the town her grand-mother, a weaver's daughter, had come from. In a letter home she told how one evening her elderly host's wife, a fat jolly person, 'bashfully admitted that she "summat took a bit of baccy", where-upon I produced my cigarette-case and offered the company some "Welsh cigars".' Very soon Beatrice was able to report that she could now have her cigarette every evening, 'in a rocking-chair by the kitchen fire, having persuaded my friends that all Welshwomen smoke'. Her thrifty host accepted one, but after a puff or two put it carefully on the mantelpiece for next night (Webb, pp 135,137). In the years when British drama was being given new life by Shaw, Galsworthy, the 'Manchester School', and others, Neville Cardus used to see 'a delightful spinster who openly smoked cigarettes in the lounge of the Midland Hotel' (Cardus, p 46) Manchester's grandest establishment; this was Miss A.E. Horniman, who built the Manchester Repertory Theatre and in 1904 helped to build the Abbey Theatre at Dublin.

After 1918 the rising generation of women smoked much more freely, though 'a young lady in a small restaurant had a cigarette knocked out of her mouth by an irate elderly waiter'. They were not permitted to smoke on top of buses, and tended to choose Turkish cigarettes instead of the more plebeian Virginians (Graves, p 43). But before the end of the 1920s they were appearing in trousers, and buying 'smoking suits'. In France things had been moving in much the same way. Proust, or his narrator, never lost a vivid memory of 'a glorious girl' once briefly seen in a train, when he could not keep his eyes off 'her magnolia skin, her dark eyes, her bold and admirable outlines'. She opened a window, with an offhanded apology – next lit a cigarette, with a few similar words – and soon after got out (p 40).

Spain and its daughter countries treated women oppressively in many respects, but did not much object to their smoking, partly it may be because, as in the East, women had been kept for long in seclusion. Here too public displays might start with women less than completely respectable. A young English diplomat posted at Madrid met a wealthy banker who neglected his beautiful wife in favour of an opera dancer, because it was a feather in his cap to have snatched her from the arms of a duke. She was 'a tall, bony, muscular woman ... but she could tell a good story *un peu risqué* with effect and with unblushing audacity, drinking champagne and smoking cigarettes whilst doing so' (Hornby, p 36). But other women were not far behind as smokers, at least when under proper protection. A sightseer on the Valencian coast came on the spectacle of a host of bathers, all under big straw hats, men and

women on opposite sides of a cove, with armed sentries posted between, the men puffing away at their cigarettes even in the water.
On the night train to Alicante he shared a compartment with a
Spanish family and some engineers; the ladies joined in smoking
cigars, and 'the consumption of tobacco and dense fumes of
smoke became really terrific. To my English notions, the thing at
first seems scandalous, but the novelty is decidedly agreeable'
(Andros, p 62). And an American serving in the war of 1846 with
Mexico was captivated by the 'elegance and ease with which a
pretty señorita will handle and puff the delicate cigaritto' (Henry,
p 91).

For working-class women, as in Britain, tobacco could make up
for some of the comforts missing from their lives. When Dickens
went to Italy on a mission to find an old political prisoner, he had
no knowledge of Italian, but a small incident in an inn yard shows
how tobacco could help to smooth the way. A 'brisk little woman'
volunteered in pantomime to brush his shoes.

> As the little woman's bright eyes sparkled on the cigarette I am smok-
> ing, I make bold to offer her one; she accepts it none the less merrily
> because I touch a most charming little dimple in her fat cheek, with its
> light paper end.

Having looked up at the windows to make sure of the mistress not
being on the watch, she 'stands on tiptoe to light her cigarette at
mine' (*Traveller*, chap 17).

A far less decorous record survives from 1861, of a party at the
Swann Inn at Mühlebach, not far from Zurich, typical of one
aspect of the international revolutionary movement. Among those
present were the German rebel poet of 1848, George Herwegh,
now a self-indulgent dandy living at Zurich, and his wife and son;
Lassalle, the German socialist leader, killed soon afterwards in a
preposterous duel, and his patroness Countess Hatzfeld; an old
Garibaldian colonel in a red blouse; and a Russian Nihilist
woman. 'The women drank champagne and smoked big cigars all
night.' At dawn Lassalle was performing mesmeristic tricks, until
the Swiss poet Gottfried Keller rushed furiously at him. 'Women

wept, men swore, and so on and on – and out into the open air'
(Legge, pp 206-7).

Russia, like Spain, was a country long backward, with women
long shut up; but in the 19th century the higher classes were
emancipated to a surprising degree by the invasion of Western
manners and the rage for imitating them. It is tempting to spec-
ulate on whether old contacts with Turkey and the East made it
seem more natural that women should smoke. Liszt acquired a
Russian princess who liked to go off into the forest for a day's
hunting with a pocketful of cigars for company. Feminine smoking
was not without its enemies: in a Goncharov novel a lady grumbles
about her daughter going off for long rides with a wealthy count.

> That's not how we were brought up at all. But nowadays – oh, horror! –
> ladies have actually begun to smoke! There's a young widow living over
> the way there – she sits on the balcony all day smoking cigarettes.
> People walk by, drive past, and she doesn't care a bit. (*Old Story*, p 157).

Still, by the time Lord Randolph Churchill and his American wife
visited Russia in the late 1880s, they found most of the ladies
smoking, and at parties a reception room was dedicated to this
purpose – which, Lady Randolph observed, 'caused a continual
movement to and fro – taking off the stiffness of a formal party and
enabling people to circulate more freely' (Martin, R.G., vol 1,
p 203).

In the USA we can discern the same convergence as in Britain,
of rustic or low-class women who had always smoked and urban
women beginning to assert their right to smoke. R.L. Stevenson's
wife, Fanny Osbourne, was living at one time with her vagrant first
husband in a Nevada mining camp, where she picked up the scandalous accomplishment of rolling cigarettes for herself. At San
Francisco, while waiting for a divorce, she and her sister had to
nurse the ailing Stevenson in his hotel – conduct all the more outrageous since 'they were already subjects of gossip because they
dared smoke cigarettes' (Nickerson, pp 14, 73).

And not far away, in Hollywood, a powerful if mercenary re-
inforcement to the cause of freedom was destined to arise half a

century later. It may be said that the cinema trivialised feminism by whittling it down to such things; but as a symbol the right to smoke was far from meaningless. Advertisers, too, were aware of this symbol, and played on the association (Laplace, in Gledhill, p 140). On 19 July 1916, the *Sketch Supplement* had a full-page picture entitled 'The First Cigarette', young lady just out of her bath, loosely garbed in a towel, and rapturously puffing – a thrilling enticement to any flapper. It was the era of two world wars, far the most potent subverters of old rules and conventions and, in conservative eyes, morals. Thus in what came to be known as 'women's films' were to be seen self-assertive characters, played by serious actresses often known to be fond of smoking themselves. In the 1927 film *The Flesh and the Devil,* ending sensationally in a duel, the married heroine, Greta Garbo, and her lover gazed into each other's eyes at a range of six inches, until he lit a cigarette – she blew the match out for him – he claimed and received the kiss this somehow entitled him to. In a 1942 film that became famous, *Now, Voyager,* the male lead Paul Henreid put two cigarettes in his mouth, lit them, and handed one to Bette Davis. Soon all the romantic young men in America were handing lighted cigarettes to their young ladies – as ladies once filled pipes or rolled cigarettes for young men. Bob Hope, the comedian, parodied the scene, in *Let's Face It,* with eight cigarettes (Halliwell, p 642).

Ironically, while nowadays in progressive countries women, along with men, are being persuaded to stop smoking, in some backward countries they are being ordered, unlike men, to stop. One day in March 1979 a thousand women held a meeting at Teheran University, smoking cigarettes all through it, in protest at the Khomeini regime's threat to forbid them (*Guardian* 10 March 79).

In the long run, however, equal opportunity for women to *live* depends on their success in winning equal opportunity to earn a living. And they have had a long history of employment in tobacco business. They toiled on plantations as slaves. They found jobs in Holland in the curing industry. Most famous of all, generations of women at Seville, Spain's port of entry for all colonial goods, worked in the huge tobacco and cigar factory, until they grew into a legend, a sort of separate race like the gypsies. For tourists in 19th-century Spain a visit to it was compulsory, and they have left numerous descriptions of its inmates. Portraits like Prosper Méri-mée's *Carmen* (1845) conjured up an image of bold bad charmers; the reality looked very different to different eyes.

Gautier was struck at the outset by the din of chopping and grinding machines, turned, he says, by two or three hundred mules. Competing with them he saw five or six hundred women, smoking and making

> a perfect tempest of noise; they were talking, singing, and disputing, in the same breath . . . Most of them were young, and several very pretty. The extreme carelessness of their dress allowed us to contemplate their charms at our ease. Some of them had got the end of a cigar boldly stuck in the corner of their mouth, with all the coolness of an officer of hussars, while some – O Muse, come to my assistance! – were chewing away like old sailors. (pp 271-2)

Another witness heard that there were some 4,000 workers in the establishment. 'I never saw so many ugly women under one roof,' he declares; 'I speak of downright monkey ugliness: hardly one was good-looking' (Adolphus, pp 257-8). If so, some other in-quisitives were lucky to be spared the vision. A party was refused admission on the ground that the women – eight thousand, by this account – were going about their duties almost unclothed because of the intense heat (Andros, p 123). A young Frenchman, on the other hand, was grateful to the heat for disclosing the women (five or six thousand, he says) in ravishingly light attire, many of them youthful, lovely, amiable. 'Farewell, loves of a moment!' he exclaimed, writing his recollections four decades later, with some nostalgic regret we may guess to put a bloom on them. 'They will never see us again; but my heart, then twenty-three years of age, cherishes a still ardent memory of them' (Dauchez, pp 240-2). An Englishman was amused by the swarms of 'mischievous chattering girls, brimful of fun and gossip' (Thornbury, vol 1, pp 155ff). An

American, more matter of fact, was pleased to learn that each could turn out eight bundles of 51 cigars daily, and earn 8 *reales;* Seville being cheap, this sufficed for a livelihood (Wallis, p 227). Another American sourly termed the factory 'a vast seraglio to some dozen or two of old fellows, who strut round with cigars in their mouths . . . ' (Anon., *A Young American,* vol 2, p 161).

That was in 1831; we may hope that things had really improved by the time Havelock Ellis, the sexologist, always interested in things Spanish, wrote his engaging sketch. Undaunted by Baedeker's warning against the 'unpleasant and malodorous' premises, he was agreeably surprised at the spacious, airy rooms, each with an altar and full of industrious, decently dressed women and girls: 'a more restful and charming scene of labour, and one more typically Spanish, it could not be possible to find.' Equally, he found the workers' annual fair 'quite free from the vulgarities of an English bazaar. Every stall was presided over by a group of shy, gracious, beautiful *cigarreras',* in their best Andalusian attire (pp 88-9).

6

Religion Reconciled

It froze all day. The mountains all white. Went up the Cwm to
White Ash. Old Sarah Robert groaning and rolling about in bed.
Read to her Mark VI and made sure she knew the Lord's Prayer
by heart, making her repeat it. Hannah Jones smoking a short
black pipe by the fire, and her daughter, a young mother with
dark eyes and her hair hanging loose, nursing her baby and displaying her charms liberally.

Rev. Francis Kilvert, Diary, 8 February 1870

With all its near-universal popularity, only among peoples still
close to prehistory could tobacco receive its full, semi-divine
honours. In customs like the Red Indian offerings to the spirits
there must be a feeling, instinctive in ancient man and lingering
here and there into times nearer ours, of the unity or kinship of all
created things. Just as the North American tribesman shared all he
had with his fellows, he felt an obligation to share what he held
precious, like tobacco, with hills, or rivers, or the dead. Among the
Birhor tribe in the Behar hills of northern India, when a hunting
expedition fails the shaman studies a bunch of leaves and finds out
what forces are hindering success. 'These are usually identified as
the spirits of ancestors who died hunting. Once the shaman has
called out the names of these spirits the presiding chief offers each
a pinch of tobacco' (Coon, p 126). And tradition speaks of an
Englishman who conquered the Tinnevelly district of southern
India, and whose arrogant soul had to be placated by offerings of
brandy and cigars.

Tobacco fell on Europe like manna in the howling desert of the era of religious wars. Unquestionably it did not quieten the storm-winds; but these must have made it all the more welcome to individuals as an allayer of fears – fears of persecution, civil strife, and above all of hell. Satan's realm had suddenly grown far hotter; its breath could be felt on every rustling of the wind. To many conservative minds, at the outset, tobacco was bad because it was new; and churchmen wanted to see men and women as badly frightened as possible, not supplied with tranquillisers. Warnings against the spiritual perils of smoking were at least as numerous as those concerned with bodily health. They came from both Catholic and Protestant pulpits, alike confident of being in possession of all truth. There had to be sins for them to thunder against, and the really heinous ones, those of the rich against the poor, were always ticklish themes to handle. In Holland the Calvinist _predikants_, who had much in common with Puritans, roared loudest. One argument they resorted to was that tobacco was being cured and sold by Marranos, converts from Judaism to whom the taint still clung, and that they insolently employed Christian women and children (Schama, p 201).

In 1594 Thomas Allen, Lieutenant of Portland Castle, an associate of the black sheep Raleigh, was accused before a Commission on Atheism of infidelity, blasphemy, and absenteeism from church. One charge against him was that he 'did teare twoe leaves out of a Bible to dry Tobacco on'(Boas, p 87). And James I compared the obdurate sinner's rejection of Grace to a tobacco addict's excuse of being unable to shake off the spell. Puritans might well regard tobacco, at first so costly, as a form of aristocratic dissipation, wasteful of money and time; it had a reputation (as almost everything has had at some time or place) as a sexual stimulant. With their licence to generalise sweepingly, preachers could bracket it with practically every vice, great or small. Religion, justice, order, the three pillars of society, were all being set at nought, John White declared in his 1613 sermons (Wright, p 290).

Yet after all it was difficult (for some controversialists not quite impossible) to point to any text of Scripture that excommunicated tobacco; and some even among the clergy were soon ready to welcome its consolations. Bishop Fletcher, father of the playwright, is said to have died of immoderate smoking, in grief over the death of his wife (Lee, vol 1, p 29). One vicar was quick to see in the much-calumniated weed a fellow-worker for righteousness. Lamenting the decay of 'good fellowship' in his parish, he hoped to revive it by an invitation to 'wine and tobacco to all that would come to the vicarage house on Sundays after prayers' (Hill, *Bunyan*, p 353).

When civil broils broke out, Puritan austerity could find itself under fire not only from pleasure-loving Cavaliers, but from breakaway zealots on the other flank. Mystics and shamans have been known to make use of opium or similar intoxicants; tobacco offered a milder stimulant to sectaries, and was accepted by some of them as a means to 'heighten spiritual vision'. A millennarian named John Mason, looking to the speedy Second Coming of Christ and his reign on earth, fell into '"a kind of ecstasy"' while smoking. In New England Captain Underhill testified that he had received Grace, or assurance of salvation, 'while he was in the moderate enjoyment of the creature called tobacco' (Hill, *Upside Down*, pp 198ff).

Extremists of the sort known loosely as 'Ranters', moreover, liked to maintain that it was one of the good things bestowed by the Creator, disparaged only by purblind dogmatists. Baptists, who had continental Anabaptist – sometimes revolutionary – antecedents, were fond of smoking during their services. When Laurence Clarkson was being examined, by Parliamentary order, he declined to answer the allegations: 'As you were preaching you took a pipe of Tobacco, and women came and saluted you, and others above was committing Adultery' (Morton, A.L., p 135). George Fox, the first Quaker, records that when he was a prisoner at Charing Cross he had many visitors, among them one day a throng of Ranters, who 'began to call for drink and tobacco; and I desired them to forbear it in my room' (Morton, A.L., p 109). He was not a smoker, but when a youth offered him a pipe he felt obliged to put it to his mouth, for fear of its being said that 'I had not unity with the creatures' – proper respect, that is, for all God's works.

'Creature' was a term much in vogue, and signified everything, since everything was God's handiwork, like Man himself. A recrudescence of belief in the primal unity of the universe shows here; in times of upheaval and distraction it may be natural for religion to turn back to its primordial beginnings. A Ranter named Jacob Bautumley argued in a pamphlet of 1650 that God is in everything, and has no existence outside the creation. He is in 'this dog, this tobacco pipe, he is me and I am him . . . ' (Hill, *Upside Down*, p 206). From this pantheism a free-thinking shoemaker took a long step towards scepticism – 'When he heard any mention of God, he used to laugh, and in a disdainful manner say that he believed in *money*, good *clothes*, good *meat and drink, tobacco and merry company*, to be *Gods*' – but he had little good of them, because 'his God allowed him but eight pence or ten pence a day' (Morton, A.L., p 76).

1660 brought back the Church of England, but not its Calvinist-Puritan spirit. 'Within these 35 years,' John Aubrey, the antiquarian, wrote, ''twas scandalous for a divine to take Tobacco. Now, the customers of it are the greatest his majestie hath' (p 45). A learned Buckinghamshire parson was said to be so much given up to smoking, as well as toping, that when his tobacco ran out he would cut up a bell-rope and fill his pipe with shreds (Brand, pp 365-6). Nicotine was simply too powerful an enchanter to be banished, and the objectors had to come to terms. They could make use of it as a peg to hang moralising reflections on: a poem 'Smoking Spiritualised', attributed to the Rev. Ralph Erskine (born in 1685, one of 33 children), was long familiar from recitations and chapbooks to rustics of the north of England. All flesh is perishable, like tobacco; its floating smoke is like the vanity of earthly gear;

> And when the pipe grows foul within,
> Think on thy soul defiled with sin. (Dixon, pp 39ff)

Such rhymes were well calculated to throw a wet blanket on any smoker's relish.

A Puritan artisan named Wallington whose papers have survived used to carry ginger, cloves, pepper to church with him, to help him to stay awake through innumerable sermons; some pious people may have employed snuff for the same purpose. Less virtuously the young fortune-hunter in the 18th century comedy talks to his friend about how, when he goes to church, he tips the verger and gets the best pew, where 'I pull out my snuff-box, turn myself round, bow to the bishop, or the dean', and pick out the best-looking woman to fix my eyes on (Farquhar, Act 2 Scene 2). There was no longer any harm in a clergyman being seen with a pipe – any more than a glass – at his mouth. We see Dr Syntax on his celebrated tour regaling after the day's ride at a small country inn –

> The Doctor drank – the Doctor eat,
> Well pleased to find so fair a treat;
> Then to his pipe he kindly took,
> And with a condescending look,
> Call'd on the Hostess to relate
> What was the village name and state –

until the starveling curate, ill paid by a rich rector, dropped in, and was happy to be invited to a share of tobacco and beer (Anon., Canto 7).

George Eliot's gallery of clerical portraits includes worthy old Mr Gilgil, 'who smoked very long pipes and preached very short sermons'. His life, she hints, 'had its little romance, as most lives have between the ages of teetotum [top-and-whip] and tobacco' (_Clerical Life_, chap 1). But the Evangelical revival, led by Wesley and Wilberforce, brought a mood of austerity, self-denial, which could find one outlet in rejection of tobacco as a needless and therefore blameworthy self-indulgence. Like the Sabbath travelling that Mrs Proudie and Mr Slope of Barchester were so fond of inveighing against, smoking could make a convenient punchbag; all the better because the working class was always having to be rebuked for its wasteful pampering of itself.

Indeed, another George Eliot clergyman, Amos Barton, embodies the hell-fire doctrines brought back by the religious revival. This had failed to reach his parish of Shepperton, 'a terrible stronghold of Satan' for him to have to storm.

> Indeed, Mrs. Hackit often observed that the colliers, who many of them earned better wages than Mr. Barton, 'passed their time in doing nothing but swilling ale and smoking, like the beasts that perish'.

Mr Barton had no talent for simple preaching, and no sense of humour. At the end of a laborious exposition of Scripture, to children and aged pensioners, 'Mrs Brick rubbed her withered forefinger round and round her little shoe-shaped snuff-box, vainly seeking for the fraction of a pinch'. George Eliot feels that the minister would have done best to shake into it 'a small portion of Scotch high-dried'. Instead he braced her with the reminder

> Ah, well! you'll soon be going where there is no more snuff. You'll be in need of mercy then. You must remember that you may have to seek for mercy and not find it, just as you're seeking for snuff. (_Clerical Life_, chap 2)

Meanwhile at Cambridge Samuel Butler's young hero, or _alter ego_, fell under the sway of the Simeonites, or disciples of Charles Simeon (d 1836), the oracle of collegiate evangelism. Ernest felt that he must 'give up all for Christ – even his tobacco'. He bundled away all his pipes and pouches, under the bed, out of sight. 'He did not burn them, because some one might come in who wanted to smoke . . .' And by evening he had persuaded himself that smoking was only, after all, on a par with drinking tea or coffee; it was not forbidden by the Bible. He admitted to himself that St Paul would doubtless have forbidden it had he known about it.

> On the other hand, it was possible that God knew Paul would have forbidden smoking, and had purposely arranged the discovery of tobacco for a period at which Paul should be no longer living. (_All Flesh_, chap 50)

And with this ingenious casuistry Ernest set his mind and his nose at rest.

Theological trends were even more hostile to science, Darwinism, Biblical criticism. On the whole Britons and others, of the higher classes, found it easier to give up these heresies, so perilous to the social order, than their cigars. They could sacrifice freedom of thinking, according to Friedrich Engels, because they were frightened of socialism, and felt that church-going was needed to keep the masses away from it. Nothing, he commented, in a well-chosen metaphor,

> remained to the French and German bourgeoisie as a last resource but to silently drop their free thought, as a youngster, when sea-sickness creeps upon him, quietly drops the burning cigar he brought swaggeringly aboard; one by one, the scoffers turned pious . . . (*Socialism*, p 414)

Abstinence from tobacco on religious grounds was commoner among Dissenters than others in England, but even they, although some of their pastors as late as yesterday might need to be cautious about smoking in public, could do so privately with a good conscience. George Eliot's excellent old Nonconformist minister, whose Sunday evening supper was a bowl of porridge at the kitchen fire, 'afterwards smoked his weekly pipe up the broad chimney – the one great relaxation he allowed himself. Smoking, he considered, was a recreation of the travailed spirit' – though not one to be indulged in to the point where it might 'endear this world to us' overmuch. 'Daily smoking might be lawful, but it was not expedient' (*Felix Holt*, chap 13).

An English Methodist minister attending the 1888 Conference of the Methodist Episcopalian Church in New York, thought it very silly for a motion to be proposed 'that no one should be appointed a bishop who would not pledge himself to abstain for ever from the use of tobacco, both for smoking and chewing' (Kelly, p 198). But Scots might have stricter views. James Murray, first editor of the *Oxford English Dictionary*, was a Scot, a Dissenter, a lay preacher and holder of family prayers, who never touched liquor and never went to a theatre. 'No one dared to smoke in the house, and visitors would seek refuge behind bushes in the garden if they felt desperate for a pipe' (Murray, K.M.E., p 319). The established Kirk, however, was more liberal about liquor and tobacco, though for long it frowned on the stage. Early in the 19th century the Rev. John Lockhart could be depicted (in a small watercolour, at the Scottish Portrait Gallery in Edinburgh) with a touch of caricature, but no hint of censure, seated with a long clay pipe between his lips, throwing out a thick curl of smoke.

One of Dean Ramsay's anecdotes shows a Scots minister taking snuff in the pulpit, so generously that when the parish was snow-bound and supplies cut off his servant could come to the rescue by sweeping up the droppings on the pulpit floor (Ramsay, p 118). And from a hilarious little book of recent recollections about a preacher of the 'Wee Free' Kirk – theologically the most severe of Scottish Churches – up in the Highlands, we learn that 'Uncle George' smoked his pipes all through Saturday while composing his sermon. On Sunday when it reached its second 'main heading' the elders, seated below him in a half-circle, passed a snuff-mull round from hand to hand. 'They did not take their eyes off the preacher's face, but each, when his turn came, took the mull from his neighbour, and in his own way, ladled the snuff into his nose.' Each then produced a large 'snuff handkerchief'. This weekly idyll came to an end when a new elder, 'a young man with a tender nose,' uproariously sneezed (Phillips, A., pp 100-110).

In France the religious wars of the 16th century were chiefly brawlings within the feudal ranks. Where the Huguenots or Protestants belonged to the common people, they might appear to Catholics quite as wild as any English sectaries, and some of them just as viciously addicted to tobacco. Ravanel, a wool-carder by origin, became a leader of the Camisards, Protestant peasants of the Cévennes goaded into ferocious resistance by ferocious persecution. 'He was an old soldier,' writes their sympathetic English chronicler; 'his face was gashed with sabre-cuts, and he lived (we quote from a Protestant writer) "on nothing but brandy, tobacco, fighting and Psalm-singing"' (Tylor, p 93). Tobacco comes in an odder way into a tale of that dark time told by one of a pair of Huguenots who in 1700, seeking asylum abroad, made their way on foot to Paris, and got into Luxemburg. At an inn they were recognised as French, and someone said

> he would wager we did not carry rosaries in our pockets. My companion, who was taking a pinch of snuff, showed him his snuff-box, and said very imprudently, 'This is my rosary.'

This confirmed the man's suspicions: he followed them, to earn a reward, and at the next town denounced them and got them arrested (Tylor, p 16).

In Catholic countries it was very often snuff that the clergy took to; a justification given by some of them, or for them, was that it helped to soften the stings of celibacy. Laurence Sterne on his renowned journey through France was reproaching himself for giving offence to a 'good old monk', when the latter met him and the lady traveller out walking, and good-naturedly offered a pinch from his horn snuff-box. By way of apology Sterne presented him with his own superior tortoise-shell box. The trio had an amiable chat, at the end of which the monk, rubbing his box on his sleeve, begged Sterne to accept it in exchange. By its new owner it was always treasured, and it was with him on a later day as he sat by Father Lorenzo's grave ('The Snuff Box', *Journey*).

Catholic ways made a less good impression on the German historian Gregorovius, however, when he looked on at the festival of St Paulinus at Nola, near Naples, on 26 June 1853; the crowds, noise, pageantry were almost enough to stupefy him, and transport him back into pagan times. In the procession to the cathedral was a line of huge floats, or wooden towers, each contributed by one of the guilds, and carrying a tableau. One of these represented a war galley, fully equipped. 'On the bowsprit stood a young man in Moorish costume pleasantly occupied in smoking a cigar, on the starboard the figure of S. Paulinus himself kneeling in front of an altar' (p 117).

Complaints from Seville about priests smoking while actually on duty at the altar are said to have helped to provoke Urban VIII's bull of 1642, banning all smoking in church. In Spain this was not understood as extending to snuff; in her travels there in the next century Mme d'Aulnoy saw women doing a great deal of church-going, for want of anything more interesting, but clearly with wandering thoughts, and much need of support from snuff.

> In the church they all sit upon their legs, and are continually taking of snuff, and yet never smut themselves with it, as 'tis usual. For in this, as in all other things, they have very neat and dexterous ways of management. (p 218).

And Sir Compton Mackenzie affirms that in Seville Cathedral he saw a prelate who could spit over the heads of the pious women seated on the floor under his pulpit, and each time hit the same flag-stone with his tobacco juice (p 36).

Outside church the clergy might well feel even more free to partake. A 19th-century visitor to Spain, travelling by coach in a southern province, had for companion a priest who smoked cigarettes incessantly; the flavour of his own tobacco was lost in 'the musty odour of the vile rubbish of which these _cigarillos_ are composed' (Andros, pp 86-7). Richard Ford's classic guidebook to Spain contains a macabre scene in a miserable jail, on the day before the execution of a brigand nicknamed _Veneno_, or 'Poison'. A charitable society was collecting alms for masses to be said for the souls of criminals.

> There were groups of officers, and of portly Franciscan friars smoking their cigars and looking carefully from time to time into the amount of the contributions, which were to benefit their bodies, quite as much as the souls of the condemned. (p 208)

Far removed from Ranters or Camisards – and an index of the gap of centuries between eastern and western Europe – were the 'Raskolniki', schismatics, or 'Old Believers', who had a long history in Russia. They were religious conservatives, breaking away from an Orthodox Church they held to be corrupted by the modernising tendency adopted by it, or imposed on it in the later 17th century by the tsars. They repudiated all the novelties brought into Russia

by foreign trade and intercourse, outlandish costumes and manners and shaving of beards, and, perhaps most uncompromisingly
of all, tobacco. Peter the Great (1689-1725) was obnoxious as the
worst innovator, and as himself an unashamed smoker; all the
changes were for the benefit of the upper classes, they believed,
and were paid for by the reduction of the peasantry to serfdom.
'Old Believers' were numerous among the peasants who fled from
oppression to the open frontiers of the south-east, where they became Cossacks. Serving in youth in the Russian conquest of the
Caucasus, Tolstoy noticed that the frontier Cossacks could respect their tribal neighbours and foes, and hated them less than
they did the rowdy Russian soldiery billeted on them, who defiled
their cottages by smoking (*Cossacks,* p 179; pp 205, 218).

A minor sidelight on Orthodoxy can be found in what is related
by Count Vitzthum, Saxon envoy at the court of St Petersburg in
the early 1850s, about a dinner at the house of Baron Bode, a man
steeped in the most credulous piety. At the end of the meal he
gave his guests cigars, and while coffee was being served 'opened,
with an air of mystery, the Holy of Holies', a small chamber ornamented like a chapel, with ikons and lighted tapers, and in the
middle, in an open coffin, the mummied corpse of the saint
revered by the family.

> He crossed himself and bowed every time he came near the coffin. But
> the presence of this corpse among the living was a thing so familiar and
> of everyday occurrence that it seemed no profanation at all when we lit
> our cigars by the consecrated tapers. (col 1, p 1.24).

It is possible that some of those who defied the Sultan, who was
also Caliph, or Commander of the Faithful, by smoking tobacco
when it was still under a ban, were giving indirect expression to
heterodox ideas, both religious and social, that had been lurking
for centuries under the stagnant surface of Islam. If so, they could
find company within the clerical ranks. Islam had no 'priests' like
those of Christendom, but its *'uluma* formed a parallel to Europe's
canon lawyers, its dervishes resembled those humbler men of

God, the friars, and were much closer to the common people. 'The use of tobacco spread very rapidly in dervish circles, just as the drinking of coffee had done' (Keddie, pp 288-9). Their mystic dreams blended as harmoniously with the fumes of the pipe as metaphysical fancies did in Germany. Ordinary folk followed their lead, while the *'ulama'*, many of them in State service, took their cue from the government and reinforced its conservatism.

Here and there a lingering intolerance could still impede the free circulation of the pipe. Under one Pasha, or Turkish governor, of Egypt, Lane says, 'it frequently happened that when a man was found with a pipe in his hand in Cairo, he was made to eat the bowl with its burning contents' (p 338). Hostility was strengthened by the Wahhabi movement of the 18th century, a fanatical fundamentalism born in the Arabian deserts, and partly an anti-Turkish movement, from which descends the ruling family of Saudi Arabia. Wahhabis made up for their abstention by excessive coffee drinking. Their influence may have spread their prejudice among *Maghribis*, 'Westerners' or Moroccans. Burton had the uncongenial company of some of these when he embarked from Egypt in a sailing-boat to cross the Red Sea on his venturesome way to Mecca. They would not allow the young fellows of the Egyptian crew to smoke. 'These Maghribis,' he comments, 'like the Somalis, the Wahhabis of the desert, and certain other barbarous races, unaccustomed to tobacco, appeared to hate the smell of a pipe' (*Meccah*, vol 1 p 194).

Later on in his pilgrimage his dislike of Wahhabis was confirmed by encounters with some of them.

> Once a Wahhabi stood in front of us, and . . . showed his hatred to the chibuk in which I was peaceably indulging. It was impossible to refrain from chastising his insolence by a polite and smiling offer of the offending pipe. This made him draw his dagger without a thought; but it was sheathed again, for we all cocked our pistols, and these gentry prefer steel to lead. (vol 2, p 129)

Islam maintained its embargo in at least token form, since tobacco smoke is included, at any rate by the more devout, in the prohibition of all nourishment between daybreak and sunset during the month of Ramadan. Happening to be in Srinagar, the capital of Kashmir, in that month in 1945, I was aware that some Muslims were still smoking, in discreet privacy; some others were over-bold, until an enraged zealot ran wild with an axe and massacred half a dozen of them. However, during a recent holiday in Tunisia during Ramadan I saw no infringements, though a sharp sense of deprivation, manfully borne, was evident. This annual ordeal, by reminding smokers of how barren life without nicotine can be – especially for the less well-off, in a poor country, who have few other pleasures – must have done much to sustain its popularity.

Tobacco can have no share in Islamic worship, yet in some lands, Persia in particular, it has been a frequent accompaniment. 'The Persians', an English visitor named Fryer reported in the later 17th century, 'smoke tobacco in their most solemn assemblies, and for this purpose are provided with spitting-pots or *pigdans*' (Watt, p 796). At Isfahan two centuries later on a sacred anniversary Pierre Loti watched thirty men sitting in a garden and puffing at their water-pipes while listening with horror to the time-honoured story of the death of the Prophet's grandson Husain – in Shia belief, that of the mainly Persian branch of Islam, the supreme tragedy. At Teheran, the Shah being away in Europe, Loti was able to visit the palace and see the throne on which it was customary for him to take his seat on festival days and pretend to smoke a jewelled water-pipe with huge rubies on top symbolising fire (*Isfahan*, p 10, 27 May).

In an environment so well fumigated, the outward austerity of clerical demeanour might well, as in Europe, hide a milder inward disposition. Hajji Baba of Isfahan, when a tobacco vendor in the holy city of Meshed, had for his chief customer a dervish, a connoisseur content with only the purest leaf, who was 'not very exact in his payments', but did the Hajji good by recommending him to all his friends. Forbiddingly chilly of mien in public, over a pipe if no stranger was present 'he was the most natural and unreserved of beings' (Morier, chap 10).

Hinduism had no general pronouncement to make on tobacco, if only because it was too heterogeneous a creed, lacking any central authority. In parts of rural Bengal, down to at least the late 19th century, Hindus and Muslims, as well as different Hindu caste men, would share a hookah together, always a gesture of good will. But some conservative objectors there have always been. Early in this century Verrier Elwin, an Englishman who took up the cause of the Gond aborigines and lived among them for years, was eating in a small Hindu restaurant. When he asked the proprietor whether he thought members of different castes ought to eat together, the answer showed a fear of the slippery slope. 'My boy dines with low-caste. To-day, he takes tobacco . . . The day after, he elopes with girl . . . '(p 78).

Only Sikhism, an early modern offshoot of Hinduism influenced by Muslim monotheism, condemned smoking as totally as Islam did alcohol. Whatever its spiritual benefits, the ban may have done something to keep Sikhs as a community in a state of robust health and vigour, as they always seem to be. It was part of the self-discipline of a sect which for a long time had to fight for survival under Mughul power. Even in much later days, only ne'er-do-wells or feudal lords could venture to flout it. At the court of Patiala, biggest of the princely states under Sikh rulers in British times, cigar smoking was little concealed when the last maharajah but one, a notorious sybarite, was on the scene. Visitors to the Golden Temple at Amritsar have always been questioned as to whether they were carrying any tobacco. But time blurs all things, at least all self-denying ordinances. Today Sikhs are once again, as in their heroic age, in a militant mood; yet one is assured that not only students, but the Jat peasants of the Punjab, the backbone of the community, smoke cigarettes and (another sinful act) trim their beards. (It seems a trait common to all men to be able to say one thing and do another, with equal conviction.)). Europe has been the chosen home of Christianity and of war.

Eastward from India, smokers have had little to complain of in the way of religious meddling. There has been some disapproval among Buddhist monks, as in Tibet; but Burma has been one of the most Buddhist and most tobacco-loving countries. A diviner and healer of our day, Pak Damun, well known in his own corner of Java, makes no formal charge for his services, but is usually re-compensed with rice, or packets of cigarettes (Cederroth, p 166). Far Eastern religious attitudes have been more pragmatic or common-sensical than those of Europe or the lands in between. In Africa, too, vestiges of primitive religion have continued to show more clearly on the surface than where more sophisticated creeds have obliterated them. Antique cults were rational enough in their aims and calculations, if not in their methods. Men and gods each understood one another's wants, as today they can no longer do.

Gilbert Islanders in the Pacific until lately preserved skulls or skeletons in village shrines, for ancestral spirits – feared but also loved – to re-enter when they wanted to see how their descendants were behaving. A British governor once came on an old man, in a canoe at the waterside, with his grandfather's skull under his arm, blowing tobacco smoke between its jaws and mumbling amiably to it. His grandfather had been good to him, and he was returning his kindness in this way because be believed that in the spirit-land there was no tobacco to smoke (Grimble, p 114).

Spiritualism, more than a hundred years ago, was one of the pathfinders to a world standing on its head. 'Sloppy twaddle' was Mark Twain's succinct comment on a New York medium's answers to a string of questions, in the name of the spirits –

'What do you drink?' – 'We do not drink.'
'What do you smoke?' – 'We do not smoke.' (*Mississippi,* chap 48)

Conan Doyle, in his spiritualist crusade, borrowed from the scientist Oliver Lodge's book *Raymond,* about his dead son, the notion of 'transcendental chemists who could even make alcohol and tobacco for unregenerate spirits ... These were no doubt the nuisances who sent down false or jokey messages' (Pearsall, p 156). One such unregenerate makes an appearance in Aldous Huxley's mysticising novel *Time Must Have a Stop* (1944), a *bon viveur* who after death is agreeably surprised to find cigars still available. Anne Sexton, an American poetess in search of God, whom she conceives of as suffering the same alienation as mankind, confers on tobacco the ultimate accolade –

> God loafs around heaven, without a shape,
> But He would like to smoke His cigar
> And bite His fingernails. (Collins, p 33)

Under the frothy surface of our times the current has been in another direction. The writer W.H. Hudson, unsurpassed in prose-pictures of nature, was troubled by religious doubts in his boyhood on the lonely Argentinian pampas. One day an old gaucho, sitting on a bench outside the house, called him over. 'He remained silent for some time, smoking a cigar, and staring at the sky as if watching the smoke vanish in the air.' At length he asked the boy, as a son of educated parents, what was the difference between Catholicism and Protestantism. Hudson explained that Catholicism was a corrupt form of Christianity, Protestantism the true form. He went on smoking, and then rejoined that all religions are false; there is no such thing as a soul; when we die we are dead (Hudson, chap 23). For such a man, in such a place, it was as bold a speculative leap as any learned philosopher has ever taken.

With him and a great many others, it may be said that in the modern world, whose guides and leaders have been able to imprint so little rationality on it, tobacco has gone far towards taking the place of religion as the great consoler. An officer of Victorian times visiting a pious aunt at Glasgow was loaded with tracts to distribute among his soldiers. This was embarrassing, but the corporal he consulted pointed out that they could be torn up and made into spills for lighting pipes. He was able to write to his aunt and tell her that 'the light which dawned upon the soldiers' countenances when using her tracts was something wonderful' (Stuart, vol 2, pp 80-1).

Yet a word, or a heroic silence, on the other side, from another remoteness of the earth, deserves to be heard. A Frenchman in the Arctic got to know an old French missionary, living in a sort of man-made cave, on a diet of one daily meal of raw frozen fish. On one visit to the cave, or hole in the ground, he brought some gifts, from himself and others. Among them were cigars, which were rejected, and a pipe.

> He had had a pipe. Smoking it from time to time had been his only luxury. But my Lord Bishop had asked all his missionaries to make one supplementary sacrifice, and Father Henry had sacrificed his pipe. I protested; but I do not believe I quite got him to promise to smoke again. (Poncins, p 236).

7

At Rest, At Work, On the March

At the conference table a break for a smoke can be the start of a treaty . . .

Wherever men foregather, a good tobacco can ensure that ill-will goes up in smoke.

Just so does Balkan Sobranie spread its beneficent wisdom. In its long slow smoke, anger loses its venom. In its rare and magical aroma, argument loses its bite.

Through its smoke-rings all men can see a rosier world – and be at peace.

Balkan Sobranie advertisement, 1967

'It has been the companionship of smoking that I have loved, rather than the habit,' Trollope wrote (*Autobiography,* p 334). Smoking together, like eating together in older days, could go half-way towards turning men into friends; the curling wreaths of smoke above a pair of heads might seem allegorical of an inter-twining of thought and feeling. Tobacco could bring strangers into harmony, loosen tongues – less erratically than alcohol – and pro-vide a social emollient. A cigarette or a pinch of snuff provided, almost anywhere, a token exchange of gifts. Falling in with parties of Turcomans, for example, a traveller in central Asia found them friendly when they learned he was a Russian. 'Compliments would then be exchanged, the pipe passed round, and afterwards we would disperse in the most amicable manner' (Marvin, p 228). And 'In Mexico,' a visitor not very long ago discovered, 'cigarettes are cheap, but matches are not. If a man wishes to honor you, he lights your cigarette, and if you have given him a cigarette he must so honor you. When a match has kindled two cigarettes and is still burning, strangers will hurry up to take a light, bow, and pass on' (Steinbeck, p 65).

Such a gift has not always been welcome, of course; it may stir suspicion about motives. In Conrad's great novel *Nostromo* there is a scene between a scheming Latin American officer and a wary European doctor. As soon as they were alone together,

> the colonel's severe official manner changed. His eyes shone with rapacity and hope; he became confidential ... The doctor, watching every word, nodded slightly, smoking with apparent relish the cigar which Sotillo had offered him as a sign of his friendly intentions. (Part 3 chap 3)

There may be more humdrum reasons for caution. A journalist long ago commented on English reserve, and with it the reluctance to accept a cigar in a train, which might mean being drawn into an unwanted conversation, or having to pretend to enjoy a bad smoke (*Tobacco*, 15 January 1881).

A converse truth is that no article (except money) has been solicited as a gift through a greater number of more or less ingenious approaches or pretexts. 'My friend Joseph Fuller', the Sussex shopkeeper-diarist Turner noted in 1765, 'I must own is rather too fruitful in his invention to contrive some way to get a little liquor or a pipe or two of tobacco' (1 April 1765). Writers of fiction have played on this infirmity. One of the sketches of lower-class life with which 'F. Anstey' regaled middle-class readers of *Punch* in the 1880s revealed a couple of strangers in a third-class smoking compartment. 'I've been in America', says one, a trifle tipsy and impecunious.

> '*There's* a country now – they don't overtax you like they do 'ere!'
> 'There you '*ave* touched a point – we're taxed past all common sense. Why, this very tobacco I'm smoking is charged –'
> 'Talkin' of terbaccer, I don't mind 'aving a pipe along with yer myself.'

His companion, a small suburban tradesman by his looks, hands over his pouch with 'a happy mixture of cordiality and condescension' (*Voces*, vol 1, pp 12-13).

Earnest conversationalists have sometimes disliked smoking habits as making for interruptions. In one of the *Noctes Ambrosianae*, the rambling dialogues mostly composed by 'Christopher North' – Professor John Wilson – for *Blackwood's Magazine* at Edinburgh in the 1820s and 1830s, with himself as chief talker, North pauses for a moment in a political harangue. Tickler is impatient. 'I like to hear you speak right on without that botheration of the eternal cigar. This vice, sir, is the bane of all real flow of talk.' 'Nonsense,' North retorts, 'nonsense' – and goes on to talk nonsense about how happy and prosperous the country is under its present wise Tory administration (Wilson, John, vol 1, p 20, March 1825).

Much oftener, however, tobacco has been felt to promote talk; when ideas have been lacking, it could be turned into a kind of entertainment. Our foreigner in Madrid in 1835 found the *tertulia*, an evening gathering for light chat and lighter refreshments, a grand social institution. Every type of cigar contributed its quota of smoke – the Havana, the *puro*, the *pajilla*, the *papeleta* – until the circle was wrapped in an 'ambrosial cloud'. He could notbut admire

> the wondrous feats performed by the amateurs of the cigar, to attract the notice of the ladies, and excite the envy of their less intrepid companions. At one moment, one of these gifted beings discharges a column of blue smoke first down one nostril, then down the other.

Even eyes and ears could be vents for the expelling of smoke (Anon., 'Resident Officer', vol 1, pp 241-3). And Willy Sprott in an English novel of the 1850s was wont to entertain friends with a display of his repertoire, sometimes blowing soap bubbles filled with cigar smoke. 'He had reduced bubble-blowing to a science that the whole Stock-exchange might have envied' (Smith, Albert, *Pottleton*, p 149).

Smoking lent itself also to more easily acquired airs and graces, or attitudinising, which might make up for lack of higher attainments. R.L. Stevenson, when a young man, is said to have been a culprit, seeking notice by outlandish dress and frenchified manners, and trying to hold attention for his patter, when the company had heard enough of it, by taking a 'prominent position in front of the fire with his cigarette, more waved in semi-circles as he chattered than legitimately smoked . . . ' (Simpson, p 228).

Oscar Wilde was an exquisite of the same species as his Lord Henry Wotton, whom he shows us reposing on a divan made up of Persian saddlebags: we have glimpses through the window of laburnum and birds on the wing, while blue wreaths curl up from his 'heavy opium-tainted cigarette', and he converses aesthetically with his artist friend Basil (*Dorian Gray,*).

Lord Clarendon as Foreign Secretary in the 1850s and 1860s justified his reeking room at the Office with the maxim that 'The art of diplomacy is the judicious administration of tobacco' ('Alpha', pp 43ff).

Smoking has also played no inconsiderable part in the graceful pirouettings of diplomats, often as silly as any other kind of posturing. Late in 1847 when Lord Dalhousie was passing through Egypt on his way to India as Governor-General, the old pasha Mehemet Ali took pains to be flatteringly attentive.

> He went so far as to receive Lady Dalhousie in open Durbar, an unheard-of event even in these liberal days, and there she sat with her cup of coffee and a huge pipe about seven feet long, blowing a distinguished cloud, but blowing it the *wrong* way, and down the pipe instead of up it. (Dalhousie, p 19)

Perhaps it was the self-same marvellous pipe that Curzon had seen the Pasha himself smoking. When the celebrated Chinese minister Li Hung-chang, one of the pillars of the last dynasty in its declining years, was in Russia in 1896, the Finance Minister, Witte, gave an imposing tea party in his honour, and at the right moment suggested that His Excellency might like to smoke. 'He emitted a sound', Witte says in his memoirs, 'not unlike the neighing of a horse,' and two Chinese attendants bustled in with his pipe and tobacco, making a huge ceremony of them. He was trying to impress his host, who feigned indifference. In business talks later on Witte formed a very high opinion of the Chinese states-man's ability (p 88).

In India the hookah entered the charmed circle of social and official etiquette at many points. At Lucknow, capital of the East India Company's client king of Oudh, the British Resident made a great point of being treated on a footing of equality with the ruler. 'He was allowed the shade of an umbrella, the traditional symbol of royalty, in the presence of the King; and he smoked his hookah as of right before him' (Pemble, p 35). In 1837 Emily Eden, on tour with her brother Lord Auckland, then Governor-General, was present at a breakfast at the close of which hookahs were brought in for the King and Auckland, and a third for the Resi-dent, Colonel John Low – 'that his consequence might be kept up in the eyes of Lucknowites, by showing that he is allowed to smoke at the Governor-General's table'. A non-smoker, Auckland had arranged for no tobacco to be put in his pipe, but was chagrined by his failure to make it produce the proper bubbling sound (Eden, p 55).

Frederick William I of Prussia, father of Frederick the Great, was a military man careless of frills; he held a regular 'Tobacco Parliament' with his cronies, where all smoked and swilled and argued as they would. In grander kingdoms, and in Prussia too as it expanded, such familiarity could not be allowed. One cannot imagine Louis XIV puffing at a pipe in a circle of puffing cour-tiers; if he could have brought himself to do so he might have heard more common sense talked, and Europe might have been a better place. It was much later that European royalty conde-scended to smoke in company with its subjects; it was then taking a long step towards modernity and demagogy.

Tobacco has even been known to soften the acerbities of re-ligious controversy, the _odium theologicum_. Some hospitable but caste-bound Hindus were once holding a debate with missionaries on the doctrine of justification by faith. Among themselves such an exchange of views would have an accompaniment in the soft gur-glings of the water-pipe, but to this the presence of outsiders would be an obstacle. They got over it by giving the Christians tobacco to smoke in hookahs, while they themselves self-denyingly smoked pipes emptied of water (Macpherson, pp 66-7). This fine distinction, well suited to a contest in metaphysics, apparently satisfied all caste scruples.

Yet tobacco has also been to blame for much boorishness. An instance of the ill-mannered egotism that has too often disgraced the name of smoker comes out in a heartfelt complaint by a war correspondent about the hardships of getting up in camp, in cold air, with water nearly freezing – washing in a small tent with three occupants – and cursing 'those fellows who sat smoking so late last night, and converted your horsehair mat into an ashbox and spit-toon' (Hardman, pp 57-8). It has sometimes, however, happened to the smoker to be the target of aggression, instead of the culprit. A Baron von Falkenhausen told an English friend of a duel he had been compelled to fight with a bully who rudely assailed him for smoking in a public place in the company of ladies. Though a tiro with the pistol, he managed to shoot the ruffian dead (Whitman, pp 77-8).

Boorishness in high places came under Thackeray's censure of George IV, whom he accused of cheating his brief favourite Beau Brummell out of a snuff-box, and ignoring him when he fell into penury (*Four Georges*, p 114). And E.M. Forster in youth had an unpleasant meeting with Scindhia, Maharajah of Gwalior and uncle of the much smaller princeling whose secretary Forster was. The three met at Ujjain and

> passed a most ignoble evening . . . a slipshod dinner was served, and I remember that when it came to smoking and I wanted a match Scindhia bounced the match-box at me on the tablecloth although he was near enough to hand it. (p 83)

Most of the toil by which the human race has kept itself going, on a (justifiably) unwelcoming planet, has been disagreeable or monotonous or noxious. Industrial revolution, whatever its other effects, made labour far more crampingly irksome, employers more despotic. Without the consolation of tobacco, and its too frequent companion alcohol, one may wonder whether human beings could have been induced to submit to such servitude, or could have endured it so comparatively long. 'Tobacco', wrote a very censorious economist,

> is very largely consumed by the male and female labourers indiscriminately; hundreds of men and women may be daily seen inhaling the fumes of this extraordinary plant, by means of short and blackened pipes. (Gaskell, P.)

But low wages and war taxes might make the coveted sedatives hard to buy. Moreover they might sometimes turn into stimulants, helping to breathe into the workers enough human spirit and hardihood to make them capable of thoughts of resistance; something that even sympathisers could not condone. In Mrs Gaskell's *Mary Barton*, published in 1848, there is a scene of Manchester trade unionists gathered to listen to a delegate from London. Before starting, the delegate

> inquired whether it would not be agreeable to the gentlemen present to have pipes and liquor handed round, adding, that he would stand treat ... These poor fellows ... gleamed up at the proposal ... Tobacco and drink deaden the pangs of hunger, and make one forget the miserable home, the desolate future. (chap 16)

In 1834 the tobacco workers themselves had founded a union, which has lived to celebrate its 150th anniversary.

There were sometimes good reasons for smoking at work to be banned, as in mines. In industry there was a general dislike of it on the part of employers, like the autocratic London ironmaster Ambrose Crawley, who in Charles II's reign set up a large metalworking factory on the south side of the Tyne, with workers' housing on the premises. His 'Law Book' or regulations allowed no one to be out after an early curfew hour. 'Smoking was forbidden at all hours for men and women alike, although the practice had become common by the late seventeenth century even among women in the country districts of the west of England' (Nef, p 220). And Sam Slick, the clockmaker, tells a tale which sounds as if it might well be true, about a shrewd Yankee boss putting a notice over the entrance to his mill; '"No cigars or Irishmen admitted within these walls"; for, said he, "The one will set a flame a 'goin' among my cottons, and t'other among my gals"' (Haliburton, p 70).

In some branches of industrial work concessions had to be made, to render life bearable, if brief. At Manchester Thomas Carlyle saw 'huge sandstone grinding-cylinders, turning with inconceivable velocity (in the condemned room of the Iron Factory, where "the men die of lung disease at forty", but are *permitted to smoke* in their damp cellar, and think that a rich recompense!)' (*Reminiscences*, p 356). On occasion the same smoking privilege might be granted as a means of conciliation. In 1871 when the English engineers went on strike for a nine-hour day the employers collected blacklegs at home and abroad; Brussels was placarded with advertisements inviting them. Many foreigners came, and were lodged in the factories. Some quickly grew dissatisfied, among them 120 Germans in Sir William Armstrong's works whom the managers could not subdue. They were offered smoking rights, but in this case nicotine failed to work: these Germans joined in the nine-hour agitation, and had, along with many others, to be shipped home (Jefferys, pp 76-8).

Conversely, withdrawal of a right to smoke could be used as a means of disciplining workers. An old book on show in the Maritime Museum at Hull gives advice on its open page to officers on fishing vessels, about how to deal with work-shy lascars, Asians employed as cheap labour. 'In genuine shamming and shirking, rest in bed on slop diet, above all no tobacco and no companionship, will soon tire out a malingerer.'

Workers in England have won a reputation by their insistence on tea-breaks. Some of those in Australia have secured a 'smoko', or break for smoking. Charlie Chaplin as a factory hand in *Modern Times* (1936) tried to treat himself to a private 'smoko' by sneaking off to the lavatory, where he had just struck a match on the seat of his trousers when a huge intimidating picture of the manager's visage appeared on a screen, and a stern voice ordered him back to his machine. George Orwell's *1984* appeared thirteen years later, and one may wonder whether its television-screen in every dwelling, and its *Big Brother is watching you*, owed anything to this episode. There were in any case capitalist as well as Stalinist watchers keeping an eye on 'the little man'.

A smoke in the midday 'dinner-time' was one of the best things in a workman's day. We hear the house painters in *The Ragged-Trousered Philanthropists* engaged in a rambling debate about the existence of hell, and kindred matters.

> Most of the hands had by now lit their pipes, but there were a few who preferred chewing their tobacco . . . Wantley was one of those who preferred chewing and he had been spitting upon the floor to such an extent that he was by this time partly surrounded by a kind of semicircular moat of dark brown spittle.
> 'I'm a Bush Baptist!' he shouted –
> A person of unspecified religious views (Tressell, p 154).

A hundred years before, about 1800, a boy called Samuel Bamford, who was to grow into a prominent Chartist, used to accompany an uncle, a cottage weaver, going to Manchester to hand in the cloth he had woven and collect next week's material. They then repaired to the 'Hope and Anchor' for a lunch of bread and cheese, or cold meat, with ale, 'to which my uncle added his ever-favourite pipe of tobacco'. His employer's man in charge of the 'putting-out' business often dined there, in the parlour, and would end by coming in to 'take a glass of ale, smoke his pipe, and chat with the weavers' (Harrison, p 216).

A very different sequence fell to the lot of a district officer at Bannu, in the far north-west of India, during the fearful blaze of summer when white women disappeared to a hill-station to get cool.

> Men cease to live, but exist as breathing automata, who perform daily at fixed hours a certain set of movements . . . Rise at 4 A.M. . . . Noon a substantial breakfast . . . which, with the post-prandial cheroot, carries the day on to 2 P.M. when – oblivion until 5 . . . (Thorburn, p 105)

But most men and women have found tobacco most congenial not during work, or after work, but instead of work. Pierre Loti in Persia was pleased by the sight of muleteers sprawling in the sun and smoking 'comme des gens qui ont le temps de vivre', like people who have time to live (*Isfahan*, 24 April). Another French-man, Marx's son-in-law Paul Lafargue, was a trail-blazer of the philosophy of leisure, and wrote a pamphlet on *The Right to be Lazy*. Capitalists were ransacking the world for profits, he complained: 'they go among the happy nations who are loafing in the sun smoking cigarettes and they lay down railroads, erect factories and import the curse of work.' Wages ought to be raised, he contended, to compel employers to lighten labour by improving machinery. 'Plowing, so painful and so crippling to the laborer in our glorious France, is in the American West an agreeable open-air pastime, which he practices in a sitting posture, smoking his pipe nonchalantly' (pp 47-8, 61).

A traveller in times gone by – and this is true in other ways in our time too – was losing his familiar moorings, and might well have good reasons for feeling apprehensive; his pipe or cigar-case could be a reassuring presence. An early 19th-century explorer of South America, Charles Waterton, came under some understandable re-proaches when he rejoiced at the thought that since Dutch William's days 'the custom of smoking amongst genteel English-men has nearly died away with them; it is a foul custom; it makes a foul mouth, and a foul place where the smoker stands' (p 202). He failed to see that for countless grateful wayfarers it has been their *vade mecum*, by land, by sea, and by air.

Supply, quality, price of tobacco have been a prime factor in their well-being. A knowing Englishman in an old novel, for example, warns a newcomer to his hotel at Coblenz not to buy cigars from the waiter at two groschen each: they can be got in the Platz for three groschen a dozen – and on no account to go in for any of 'those vile Swiss ones' (Lever, chap 2). Carlyle presented his friend Irving, setting off from Glasgow to London to embark on his career as a prophet (not a much wilder one than Carlyle himself often was) with a bundle of first-rate cigars. Irving was no smoker, but agreed to try one now and then on the coach roof, where he was to sit day and night. Unluckily he left them behind in the coffee room where they had bidden each other farewell before a very long parting (Carlyle, _Reminiscences_, p 232). It may have been a bad omen for Irving's mission.

One of the longest of coach journeys is narrated by Mark Twain, who in 1861 joined his brother, appointed Secretary of the new Territory of Nevada, on the run to the far West. For the last stage, across the mountains, they took with them a few blankets, and, as sole luxury, five pounds of pipe tobacco. The stagecoach was always rushing up and down steep slopes, with everybody and everything being tossed about, including a heavy dictionary which kept hitting someone and 'spilling tobacco in our eyes, and water down our backs'. But there were compensations.

> Nothing helps scenery like ham and eggs. Ham and eggs, and after these a pipe – an old, rank, delicious pipe – ham and eggs and scenery, a 'down grade', a flying coach, a fragrant pipe and a contented heart – these make happiness. It is what all the ages have struggled for. (_Roughing It_, pp 46, 58, 139)

No fever for speed possessed Coleridge, by contrast, when he planned a bizarre journey from London to Bath to perform his reluctant duty of marrying Sara Fricker, who was not the woman he was in love with. After exhausting all excuses for delay, at the end of 1794 he informed her brother-in-law Southey that as stage-coaches often had accidents he was going to come by goods-waggon, evidently chosen as the slowest thing on wheels, at two miles an hour.

> I shall be supplied with Bread and Cheese from Christ's Hospital and shall take a bottle of Gin for myself and Tuom, the Waggoner! – Plenty of Oronoko Tobacco – Smoke all the Way . . . Wrapped up in Hay – so warm! There are four or five Calves Inside – Passengers like myself – I shall fraternize with them! (Lefebure, p 156)

Needless to say Coleridge missed the waggon, and Southey had to come to London and march him off.

In motion as at rest, tobacco smoke was as much a plague to some as a delight to others. In 1832 a horse-drawn carriage on rails, from Dundee to Newtyle, gave a woman an exciting new experience, but a dandy annoyed her with the fumes of his cigar, and 'A labourer sat behind him with a cutty pipe stuffed with pig-tail. The smoke and smell was almost insufferable and I was almost chocked [sic]' (Tennant, p 227). Innumerable such complaints were to pursue the railway in its world-circlings: 'It is a pity', Tolstoy (an ardent smoker) wrote to a friend in February 1870, 'that one can only get to your place after passing a sleepless, cigarette-smoky, stuffy railway-carriage conversational night' (Maude, vol 1, p 322).

But Sir Denison Ross, the famous linguist, had a different grievance to voice after a train run from Detroit to Chicago, while on a lecturing tour in 1931, which in other respects was extremely comfortable.

> If I could only have come by decent pipe tobacco, life would have been complete. It wasn't kept in America, where they smoke mixtures: in that dry climate they turn to powder at once. How I longed for Player's Navy Cut Mild! (p 220)

A travelling smoker in the Muslim East could seldom lack for company. At the end of 1823, preparing for his Greek venture, Byron drew on his old knowledge of the East and got his agent at Zante to buy 'smoking implements, it being the custom to offer pipes to visitors of dignity'. He had already ordered a hundred quills to make mouthpieces, besides another hundred for pens – not many of which he was to live to use (Moore, D.L., p 397). And Burton on his less warlike way to Mecca, masquerading as the pilgrim Haji Abdullah, sometimes smoked his water-pipe on camel-back among his Beduin companions as they jogged slowly in the midday heat. Their usual pipe was of coarse wood, with a soft stone bowl, though in Arabia a shortish thick clay stem was also used, with a capacious bowl. 'It contains a handful of tobacco, and the smoker emits puffs like a chimney' (*Meccah*, vol 1, p 144). Few pilgrims cared to smoke on the march, in the roasting wind.

> The first thing, however, called for at the halting-place is the pipe, and its delightfully soothing influence, followed by a cup of coffee, and a 'forty winks' upon the sand, will awaken an appetite not to be roused by other means. (vol 2, p 63)

On a night march smoking could be far pleasanter, and men would go to great pains to be able to enjoy it, far greater than they would put themselves to for any number of more useful objects. A journalist accompanying a pilgrim caravan bound for the great shrine at Meshed in north-east Persia had a slow, tedious forty miles of it. To light the water-pipe on horseback, resort was had to charcoal in a small wire basket, on a string a yard long. Tinder was kindled with flint and steel and put in the basket, which was then whirled round and round to bring the charcoal to a glow. All night 'meteor-like trains of sparks' floated in the air (O'Donovan, p 96).

Near the outset of Pierre Loti's ride across Persia to Teheran, five armed men joined his party. It was night, and there was uneasiness about them until they were discovered to be an escort detailed for his protection. They were on foot, so he and his people rode on slowly, sharing cigarettes with them – two smokers to each cigarette, in accordance with the local rule of politeness (*Isfahan*, 21 April 1903). At times strangers might be inconveniently pressing – Ferrier's tent at one stopping-place in Afghanistan was crammed with ragged visitors, who added to the unbearable heat under the impression that they were hospitably keeping him company; they would snatch the tube of his water-pipe before he could take three whiffs, and hand it round among themselves until the tobacco was burned out (Ferrier, J.P., p 276).

A British explorer in Arabia not many years ago, however, was impressed by the readiness of his Arabs to share and share alike among themselves. They all had a craving for coffee.

> Some of them smoked, and this was their only other indulgence. No one ever smoked without sharing his pipe with the others; they would squat round while one sifted a few grains of tobacco from the dust in the bottom of a small leather bag which he carried inside his shirt next

to his skin. (Thesiger, p 38)

For getting about in India all kinds of conveyance had to be made use of, and tobacco proved itself a travelling companion suited to all situations. A young officer who was joining his regiment, the 15th Hussars, stationed in the south, in 1845, had to make a long night journey in a pony trap, with a wild horse. Near the edge of a lake it bolted; he jumped out just in time. Luckily, he says, 'I found I had got my cigar case all right, so I lit a Trichinopoly, sat on the bank and smoked whilst I waited for the driver – whom I had sent off to knock up a neighbouring village' (Wale, p 70). And a district officer, one of the more scholarly sort, on tour in Orissa in 1877 in a *palki*, or palanquin, came to a *nullah* or pool swollen by heavy rains, and had to halt and send back for an elephant. He 'sat boxed up', he writes, 'smoking a pipe amidst the warfare of the elements, with the shivering bearers crouching under the trees, smoking one cigar of mine among them and the rain rattling down on the palki roof' (Beames, p 267). Without the pipe he would have been a pitiable object; as it was he was able to while away the time by improvising verses in French, descriptive of his plight.

After a day's mileage has been covered, under whatever skies, and a meal good or bad devoured, to countless wayfarers a smoke has seemed their fitting reward, and any delay in procuring it a grievance. Thus in Goldsmith's comedy the eloping heroine Olivia is delayed at a roadside inn, while the landlady bustles about the rooms, each in the old style with a picturesque title of its own. 'What! Solomon; why don't you move? Pipes and tobacco for the Lamb there. – Will nobody answer! To the Dolphin; quick. The Angel has been outrageous this half-hour' (*Good-Natur'd Man*, Act 5).

So a restful end to his day is every traveller's petition. One such fell to the lot of an English tourist settling down in a guest-house at Cartagena, with a pair of like-minded Spaniards.

> We had three beds in the same room. All three having undressed, lit a long cigar apiece, and went to bed. The lamp was put out and the glow-

ing cigar ends were all we could see of one another. I observed 'Quando se pone la luna las estrellas se ven' ['When the moon sets the stars appear'], which was received as a brilliant sally by the company. (Cayley, vol i, p 33).

For the Frenchman in the Arctic, already quoted, things were less easy; he had to help to build a snow-bedroom before he could lay himself down in it. Poncins learned that if he and his Eskimo friends halted at 6 pm, it would be near eleven before they could lie back on their furs 'and enjoy the bliss of a cigarette'. And next morning all the work would have to be undone again (p 98).

Two men in boats, on two very unlike rivers, recorded end-of-day memories in contrasting minor keys. Jerome dwelt on the hardships of boating on the Thames and camping in rainy weather, such as finding after supper that your tobacco is too damp to be smoked, and being left with no recourse but to drink your way to bed (*Three Men*, chap 9). Joseph Conrad's mind turned back to a night on the Upper Congo, in 'a wretched little stern-wheel steamboat' he was in command of. Everyone else was asleep.

> I was glad to be alone on deck, smoking the pipe of peace after an anxious day. The subdued thundering mutter of the Stanley Falls hung in the heavy night air . . . A great melancholy descended on me. Still, the fact remains that I have smoked a pipe of peace at midnight in the very heart of the African continent, and felt very lonely there. (*Last Essays*, p 17)

On sea as on land, not everybody relished the neighbourhood of the pipe. One who did not was the hero of a novel from the Highlands, on his way to the Peninsular War. No sooner was he aboard than 'The smell of tar, grease, bilge-water, tobacco, and a hundred disagreeable odours, assailed him . . . ' (Grant, J., *Romance*, chap 5). And late one autumn day in 1848 Lord Cockburn, the Scottish judge whose diaries of his circuit journeys were published after his death, reached Inverness through ceaseless torrents of rain. He was thankful that he had not gone instead by boat to Fort William, which would have doomed him 'to have either received all the splash of this day on the deck of a steamer, or to have escaped it by the worse horrors of a small cabin crowded by wet men stinking of tobacco' (p 220).

But ocean floors must be littered with testimonies to the attachment of numberless seafarers, as warm as any landsman's, to tobacco. Men on a troopship bound for India in 1845 caught a shark whose stomach contained parts of a shoe and a straw hat, and a steel tobacco box and pipe (Pearman, p 26). Such boxes were popular with seamen, the Dutch especially, and often had slots for pipe and flint and steel, and some rude ornamentation (Fairholt, p 227). Fondness for a smoke came to be deemed a sailor-like attribute, much played on by advertising in the great days of the British navy. 'Capstan's Navy Cut' cigarette packets had a virile face on them, inspired perhaps by King George V's 'Bounty', which any sailor could earn by wearing a beard like his sovereign. 'Popeye the Sailor', that great advocate of spinach, was never without a short pipe in his rugged mouth.

During the Crimean War an Englishman was crossing the Straits from Constantinople to Scutari, in a caique, and enjoying himself.

> Oh, what luxury! the first real luxury since I left England – a summer sun and a smooth sea, and a view only too beautiful. Lying on one's back with a hot sun and a cigar is perfect happiness. (West, p 136)

A less carefree time befell the Hussar we have just met in south India, when a decade later he was on board ship for the Crimea with a troop of cavalry. The decks were littered with hay, and a general order was read out forbidding smoking except in one corner. Five minutes later, his memoirs relate, 'I found one of my hopeful recruits sitting on a truss of hay smoking his pipe – five minutes more and we had him in irons' (Wale, pp 83-4).

Largely because of the fire risks of tobacco, chewing became so common a habit at sea that about 1800 a phrase was in use: 'making dead men chew tobacco', which meant fraudulently keeping dead crewmen's names on a ship's books, and pocketing their pay. But chewing had the drawback of causing more spitting. Mr

Falcon, first officer in a Marryat story, was very particular about the snowy whiteness of his decks, and had ingenious ways of penalising any who sullied it. He installed 'spitting-pans' here and there, and an offender who neglected to use them had to go about with one of them strapped to his chest, for his messmates to use, as they did with great relish. A youngster detected with a quid in his mouth, in breach of rules, had it pulled out with a pair of tongs, like a bad tooth (*Peter Simple,* chap 14).

On merchant ships, American at least, officers too might be chewers. In 1911 Miss Fountaine, the butterfly huntress, was sailing from Florida to Cuba with her Syrian companion. They slept on deck, the second class premises being too dreadful, and some of their belongings were blown overboard. Next morning 'a terrific cyclone' came on.

> Our small boat was torn from its moorings, but the captain, calm and collected, walked to and fro shouting his orders, coolly chewing his tobacco. Needless to say, I was almost beside myself with terror, but I held Khalil's hand the whole time and he was full of courage. (Fountaine, p 186)

All told, no men of the waves could be more irrepressible smokers than some Pacific islanders were learning to be. Coming in to the island of Hatiheu one day, when heavy surf was beating on the rock-bound coast, R.L. Stevenson was startled by his boatmen's casual bearing.

> As we came abreast of the sea-front, where the surf broke highest, Kauanui embraced the occasion to light his pipe, which then made the circuit of the boat – each man taking a whiff or two, and, ere he passed it on, filling his lungs and cheeks with smoke. Their faces were all puffed out like apples as we came abreast of the cliff foot, and the bursting surge fell back into the boat in showers (*South Seas,* Part 1 chap 7).

8

Pipe and Drum

21.3.1918 4.45 am. Awakened by a terrific bombardment all along the front. No doubt 'Der Tag'. Everyone sleeping peacefully. Had a look outside hut. Idea confirmed. Thick fog. Retired to bed. Smoked a pipe.

5.15 am. Threw a boot at Crawley and ordered 'Stand To'.

Diary of Brigadier F.E. Spencer (Imperial War Museum)

In the Imperial War Museum in London is the Brobdingnagian pipe belonging, before 1914, to the Baden Lifeguard Grenadiers, with ceramic bowl and ornately carved wooden stem two-and-a-half feet long. Such a ceremonial object or fetish may be taken as symbolising the close relationship of hundreds of years between Nicotine and Mars. War has been a fusion of all man's evil qualities with many of his good ones; and tobacco has been the faithfullest companion of the soldier, on the march, in the trench, over the bottle. It may be asked whether modern warfare with its intense psychological strains could have been kept going if tobacco had not been available as a tranquilliser, comforting without putting men out of action as alcohol too easily does, and relieving the general boredom as well as the periodic tensions of their vocation.

Smoking habits must have reached civil life partly through the men in arms, and their example, first in Europe and in course of time in the remotest places. It is said that Hessian troops brought to Scotland by its German king in 1746 made themselves liked, by being under better control than the British soldiery, and that this won esteem for the rappee or black snuff they used (Chambers, p 259). A century later the British army was bringing tobacco to the high Himalayas; a former Edinburgh student, Harka Gurung, has talked to me of how Gurkha soldiers brought back the cigarette-smoking habit from the army, and how it spread to the whole population of Nepal, women as well as men. A soldier came home with a bag of cigarettes, and everyone he met on the way to his village counted on being given a handful.

An appetite for smoke has often figured in stereotypes of the warrior. A former British private, looking back on life, recalled an old Corporal Churchill, in Ireland about 1831, stopping for breakfast with his party of sappers at an inn at Cookstown. After eating he reposed on the horse-block outside, and his 'smoking machinery', a pipe with tin cap and black chain, was speedily in action (Connolly, vol 1, p 247). Alfred de Vigny speaks of a group of his fellow officers in Paris during the excitement of the 1830 revolution, and the imperturbable coolness that all officers, not only English, cultivated. Their captain distributed cigars, and they began smoking, 'walking up and down in a calm silence undisturbed by any thought of the situation; no one deigned to speak of the day's hazards, or of his duty, but each perfectly understood both the one and the other' (Vigny, p 175).

From very early in modern warfare we catch sight here and there of tobacco; it was taking the field about the same time that gunpowder was spreading from cannon to musket. Its role was one of many things that James I signally failed to appreciate: England's victories had been won without tobacco, he grumbled, and dependence on it could only be enervating for the soldier. It was argued by some in Holland, too, that 'by inducing deep melancholia the habit rendered men unfit for military service' (Schama, p 203). And an overfondness for smoking was one vice alleged against officers sent to Ireland in 1598 to quell the rebellion of Tyrone: they were accused of embezzling army pay in order to buy rich apparel, liquor, and tobacco (Ridley, p 334). In 1600 Charles Blount, Lord Mountjoy, became Lord Deputy or governor there: he looked a delicate valetudinarian, but proved ruthlessly efficient. Fynes Moryson, the globe-trotter, 'thought his abundant use of tobacco helped to avert the ill effects of Irish provender, bogs and climate' (Calder, p 105).

In at least the first stages of the English Civil War an easy-going smokers' freemasonry peeps out in an anecdote of the time in 1643 when Prince Rupert was threatening Bristol. He sent a trumpeter or herald to the town, whom the garrison suspected of being a spy, but who only wanted to meet a certain Parliamentary officer and tell him that his friend the Earl of Cleveland, serving with Rupert, would be glad of a pound of tobacco. The man he sought was not on hand, but Colonel Fiennes chivalrously sent a pound on his behalf, and Colonel Popham another (Firth, p 44). Smoking might also be a bond between high and low, as well as friend and foe. Speaker Lenthall told John Aubrey a story he had heard about Sir Thomas Morgan. At the capture of Dunkirk in 1658 from Spain by the Anglo-French forces, the great Marshal Turenne and, he thought, Cardinal Mazarin, the head of the French government,

> had a great mind to see this famous Warrior. They gave him a visitt, and wheras they thought to have found an Achillean or gigantique person, they saw a little man, not many degrees above a dwarfe, sitting in a hutt of turves, with his fellowe soldiers, smoking a Pipe about 3 inches (or neer so) long. (Aubrey, p 143).

Tobacco was becoming a necessity of Europe's life, especially when the continent was at war; an army might almost be said to march on its nose. It was one of the commodities that Dutch shipping carried to German and Baltic ports during the Thirty Years War (1618-48), which by degrees engulfed most of Europe, to be distributed inland to the many forces in the field. In the English Civil War requirements of troops quartered on a district might be burdensome, as they were for villages round Newark, which was held by the Royalists. An item in the Upton parish constable's accounts for March 1645 reads: 'Paid for tobaco and tobaco pipes for Captaine Ashton when he quartered heare . . . 2s. 4d.' (Anon., *Newark*, p 20).

In Restoration England smoking was forbidden on English warships, 'except over a Tub of Water' (Mackenzie, p 153), but finds in Tobermory Museum on the island of Mull – from the wrecked ship of a flotilla sent to the west coast of Scotland after the revolution of 1688 to make it clear that William and Mary were now on the throne – include a clay pipe. William III's arch enemy Louis XIV, though no smoker, took care that every soldier should have his pipe and briquet, or lighter, and his endless wars made smoking a permanent habit of the French army. Napoleon had a special pipe designed as a prize for grenadiers who distinguished themselves (Jakovsky, p 48); pipes could also be a treasured possession in the ranks.

Napoleon's rash occupation of Spain in 1808 provoked rebellion and brought a British army on the scene. Most of its soldiers were doubtless sorry to find themselves there, and the comfort of the pipe clearly meant much to them. A private's diary entry gives a hint of how they managed to survive: 'Weather unfavourable and harassing. Winter fast approaching. On piquet every other night we make large fires and contrive to stupify [sic] ourselves with brandy and tobacco' (Wheatley, p 9). They could scarcely have been of much service if the French had suddenly turned up. Nor could their fellow-sufferers of the German Legion who, they noticed, spent all their leisure hours round the camp fires. 'Cooking, smoking, eating and drinking form their only amusements', and left them 'heavy-eyed, sallow and dull in every action of sense and body' (Wheatley, p 7). At Salamanca the French commander Junot had taken up his quarters in the house of an old nobleman. 'Junot', Wellington told his young admirer Lord Stanhope years later, 'though of humble extraction, affected great refinement and *hauteur*. One evening he smelt tobacco smoke, and expressed himself as much annoyed by it as if he had not himself been trained at a *tabagie*', or tobacconist's – and shouted for the culprit to be arrested at once (Stanhope, p 248).

At the end of the battle the soldier who had been in Spain was feeling much less comfortable when he gazed round him at the frightful scene of carnage. 'I looked down, I recollect, to take a pinch of snuff and thought of the old ballad, which I had seen somewhere . . . "But 'twas a famous victory"'. (Wheatley, p 67). (It was not a ballad he was remembering, but Southey's poem – written a long time before he was made poet laureate – of an old man telling his little grandson about the battle of Blenheim. The boy asks what they were fighting about, and what good came of it. His grandfather is puzzled – ' "Why, that I cannot tell", said he, / "But 'twas a famous victory." ')

British soldiers in Havana, meanwhile, on their way home from the war of 1812-14 with the United States, paid a visit to 'old Woodville, the famous cigar-maker'. He was an Englishman from Portsmouth, said to have had to emigrate and change his name because of some smuggling affair.

> We found the old man ill in bed, but able to sit up and speak with us. He wore an immense long white beard, reaching down nearly to the bed as he sat up. Yet this old man had a young black wife, and a whole fry of young mulattoes running about the house like as many little pigs . . . We bought each a considerable quantity of his famed cigars. (Surtees, p 405)

When the Crimean War (1854-6) brought resumption of full-scale warfare in Europe after the post-Waterloo lull, military consumption of tobacco (or desire for it) swelled. This conflict had a naval side too, in the Baltic, on which a patriotic English chaplain gives some sidelights. On the deck of his man-of-war one day he watched a bullock being slaughtered, marines being inspected before a landing, 'a large assembly of seamen smoking . . . Just abaft the foremast, a group of officers, with every variety of pipe, from the proud meerschaum to the jet black inch and a half of clay, were telling us the story of the Hango massacre.' Moving up in line to attack Sveaborg, the fortress protecting Helsinki, the squadron came under enemy fire: 'an officer with white kid gloves and a cigar, lounged carelessly on a rock' – when the British cannonade suddenly opened, though there was little but trees and rocks to aim at (Hughes, R.E., pp 219, 249).

Never did the tried and tested incompetence of British army management show more glaringly than in the Crimea. Shortages of everything, extremes of privation, were the result. Twenty years after, Kilvert the curate heard an old soldier talking of the horrors of the 1854-5 winter. 'Tobacco was more precious than gold. If a man was lucky enough to have a pipe he doted on it as if it were God Almighty coming down upon him.' He could only allow himself a few whiffs at a time. 'If I had had tobacco I could have done with one meal a day. The French soldiers were in plenty while we were starving' (Kilvert, 10 March 1874). When the order to charge reached the Light Brigade, most of the officers and men were standing about with their horses. 'One or two of the men had lighted pipes, and were told to put them out at once, and not disgrace their regiments by smoking in the presence of the enemy. Lord George Paget, who had just lighted a cigar, felt embarrassed. Was he setting a bad example?' On learning from his excited commander Lord Cardigan of the order to attack, 'he thought it was permissible to keep his cigar, and noticed that it lasted him until he got to the guns' (Woodham-Smith, p 237). It brought him luck; he was a survivor, one of the last to get back.

No such heroic folly was to be expected from officers of the allied Turkish army. A *Times* correspondent with the force on the Transcaucasian front described a lavish distribution of decorations; everyone supposed to have been in action expected one, whether he had in fact done anything or not. Many went to *chibuk-jis*, pipe-bearers of senior officers, a service for which reliable men were needed.

> An officer of any rank, when his troops are going into action, has his carpet spread upon the ground they are about to leave, dismounts from his horse, squats down, calls for his pipe, wishes his men God speed, and endeavours, more or less successfully, to deaden terror by the soothing influence of tobacco. The chibouque-jee, compelled by respect to stand behind his master, is, of course, far more exposed to danger. (*The Times*, 18 February 1856, p 9)

Before much longer tobacco was on its way to establishing itself as a regular responsibility of the commissariat, and was supplied to those who wanted it in fixed quantities, at cut prices; the military system thus became a tributary of the tobacco industry. So when German troops were pouring into France in 1870 a general order fixed the daily rations that they were entitled to levy from the districts where they were quartered. Each man's allowance included 750 grammes of tobacco or five cigars (Best, p 351). Barrels were placed in the streets of German towns, with an appeal to the public to donate tobacco for the fighting men (Graves, p 74).

Spain, another large inhaler of smoke, took part in no wars, colonial excepted, between 1814 and 1898, but it had a plethora of civil wars and revolutions to put a premium on tobacco. In the first and most violent conflict of that period, in the 1830s, Liberals in power and Carlist rebels vied with one another in ferocity. Cabrera, a Carlist guerrilla chief, is said to have earned his men's respect by his extreme brutality. 'None smoked the *cigarillo* more coolly than he while giving the verbal order to shoot a score of prisoners, none saw them pass on the road to death with an eye of colder indifference' (Hughes, T. M., vol 1, p 254). General Elío, Carlist commander in the third conflict – in 1873 – was a man of less repulsive character. This veteran of the cause had lived long in England, where he learned English manners; he wore very simple, barely military garb. 'Under the enemy's fire', a foreign observer wrote,

> old Elío is inimitable. The greater the danger the more he smokes; and the more he smokes the more serene he becomes, quietly smiling as he looks over his spectacles, and slowly and distinctly, without the slightest hurry or appearance of excitement, giving his orders. (Thieblin, vol 1, pp 66-7)

When Russia and Turkey clashed once more in the Balkans in 1876-8, cannon smoke and tobacco smoke hung over both camps like thunderclouds. Archibald Forbes, the well-known war correspondent, was there, and got to know some of the Russian officers. When a Russian assault was being launched in 1877, he writes, 'I shook hands with Andreiovich, as with a smile in his eye and a cigarette between his lips he lingered one moment to give me a message in case he should not come back. And he did not come back . . .' Forbes 'fervently hoped' that his friend had been shot dead, because the Turks slaughtered all enemy wounded, often with barbarous tortures; Russian officers carried daggers to use on themselves (p 197).

An Anglo-German, Captain von Herbert, was serving as a volunteer with the Turks, and his memories of the campaign and of the long drawn-out siege of Plevna by the Russians are strongly flavoured with nicotine. They show too how this could blend at times with the fragrance of love. In the small town of Widdin he was directed to the local businessman, an Austrian Jew with a charming daughter not averse to kisses, and laid in a stock of '2000 good cigarettes and a pound of smuggled Servian tobacco, the best tobacco I have ever smoked'. At Plevna he would walk into the town on freezing winter nights, to be met by an amorous young woman who devised 'extraordinary ruses' to evade her father's watch. 'At midnight, at three in the morning, in the early dawn – whatever the hour – she was at the place of tryst, and always had something to give me – a cigarette, a drop of brandy, a loaf' (Herbert, pp 61, 232, 292-3).

His Turkish fellow soldiers were as keen smokers as himself. During the siege a general, Adil Pasha, happened to come to Herbert's sector of the trenches, to give orders, and before vanishing into the fog asked him for a light; he was left reflecting on 'What a passion these Turks have for their cigarettes! I knew men who smoked a hundred a day.' One sergeant got the name of 'Tütünjü', or Tobacconist, 'by reason of his having a large quantity of – probably stolen – cigarettes and tobacco in his possession' (p 214).

A war correspondent might be as much in need of a refreshing interlude as the men whose deeds he was immortalising. During the Chilean Revolution of 1891, for example, the inevitable *Times* man was on a government warship when its captain Moraga steamed towards the port of Iquique, bent on attacking rebel transports there. 'This seems to me', he wrote, while the ship dashed onward through the darkness,

> a somewhat desperate venture, what with chains, booms, submarine mines or torpedoes, etc., to say nothing of the forts . . . but Moraga is

resolved to sink *something* . . . It occurs to me that a cigarette and B. and
S. (possibly my last in this vale of tears) would not be amiss, and not
being officially tied to the deck, I obey instinct and descend to the
saloon, profiting by the occasion to jot down these notes. (Hervey,
p 201)

Europe was marching towards the mastery of the globe, and
colonial wars, multiplying as the century wore on, provided
another spacious arena for tobacco to show its power. This went
back to the early days of colonial conquest. In the museum of the
old French mission station of 'Ste Marie among the Hurons', in
Ontario, there is a cartoon from the 17th century of soldiers, with
some doggerel verses which – being French – could not forgo the
chance of a classical allusion:

> Quand nous sommes remplis d'humeur mélancholique,
> La vapeur du Tabac ranime nos esprits;
> Lors de nouvelle ardeur entièrement surpris,
> Nous veincrons le Dieu Mars en sa fureur bellique!

The Canadian Mounted Police had as its mission to keep order on
the western prairies then being opened up; J.G. Donkin's remarkably well written memoirs of his time with the Police show him as a
disgruntled man throughout his years of duty, in his opinion ill-
rewarded, when his closest friend was his pipe. 'Tobacco was our
only solace', he wrote of four winter days in the ramshackle old
fort at Qu'Appelle. To be roused at 4 am by starlight for a 40-mile
ride was a fearsome ordeal. 'Men grow savage in such cold as this',
and – a further embitterment – 'You cannot smoke, for the juice
freezes in the pipe stem' (pp 53, 57). By contrast an evening of
benign weather could be bliss of the highest degree.

> Prairie chicken and fried ham, and excellent tea made us feel at peace
> with all mankind, and jokes were cracked without reserve. Then I un-
> rolled my blankets underneath the waggon, lit my beloved pipe and fell
> into a meditative reverie. There are two things for which one never
> loses a craving on the prairie – tea and tobacco. (p 169, cf p 255)

Nicotine has owed a good part of its charm to its ability to blend perfectly with either tea, coffee, or alcohol.

In India military operations went on sporadically until 1858, and on the edges of the country never ended. Hot or cold, wherever the soldier went his smoke went with him. It did a great deal for British morale, and a little for relations within a multi-racial army. When the great fortress of Bhurtpore was under siege in 1825 an observer noticed, as many did on other occasions, the good feeling between British soldiers and Gurkhas. 'A six-foot-two grenadier of the 59th would offer a cheroot to the little Gurkha . . . the latter would take it from him with a grin', and the big man would stoop to let him light it from his own (Mason, p 382). There was not much good will of that kind between Tommy Atkins and the ordinary Indian sepoy.

Looking back on the first Burma War (1824), an officer remembered loitering with his comrades one day, after the capture of a jungle stockade, 'under the cheering influence of a cigar, which, to a sub. of those days, was almost meat and drink. Indeed, we most of us looked upon _the weed_ as an indispensable necessary of life.' But he had come to realise since then how harmful was 'the practice of puffing away all day at the rate of thirty, forty, or even fifty cigars a day', along with 'copious potations of _brandy pawney_', or brandy and water (Doveton, pp 169-70).

One evening in January 1826, during that same contest, another young officer, a Scot named Pennycuick, was strolling with some companions near a village, 'walking along very composed each with a segar in his mouth', when a stampeding herd of buffaloes ran into them – 'I believe never were a set of British officers more completely put to the rout' (Diary A). Many a soothing whiff has been still more rudely interrupted. When Pennycuick was on a march during the first Afghan War in 1839 a soldier was killed, another wounded, by marauders. 'So far as can be ascertained', he noted in his diary, 'the two men had fallen to the rear through fatigue and were sitting by the road smoking their pipes when they were suddenly fired upon by two or three men armed with matchlocks' (Diary B, 2 April 1839).

Late in 1848 when the army was besieging the town and fort of Multan in the Punjab, there was much grumbling among the men – as in the Crimea – about shortage of supplies. Tobacco was cruelly expensive. Private Waterfield wrote bitterly later on:

> The officers had plenty of everything for themselves, so they didn't care if a soldier lived on old gun carriages. We could get neither tobacco nor vegetables. There was some leaf tobacco, but it was full of saltpetre. (pp 70-71)

More fortunate was a young staff officer when he called one day on his commander, Outram, and

> found him in his shirt sleeves and a pair of old military pantaloons sitting on his bed smoking a cheroot . . . I had hardly seated myself when he offered me a cigar which I thankfully accepted, they are scarce enough in camp . . . The General never ceased smoking and he was most liberal with them. (Smailes, p 86)

Waterfield was mistaken, it seems, in supposing that all officers were well supplied.

In that same year, 1848, when the conquest of the Punjab was on the agenda, a junior officer attached to one advancing column had the duty of sending forward the baggage, after camp was struck in the small hours; tiresome work, because the servants were always sitting down to smoke their hookahs. At last he was free to move off, and at daybreak after a spell of marching enjoyed the reward he had earned – 'a full-length recline on the sand, and a fragrant weed' (Anon., 'Subaltern', p 20). After the battle of Gujerat in the following year, and shortly before his own death, he was astonished to see that 'several men, whose legs had been taken off, lay smoking their pipes and chatting to their comrades, as unconcernedly as if nothing had happened' (p 159). From another colonial campaign we hear of a wounded Russian officer quietly smoking his pipe while his arm was being amputated (Baddeley, p 405).

Tobacco smoke might float over Indian battlefields where the white man had no place. In 1819 Gulab Singh, a lieutenant of

Ranjit Singh, the Sikh master of the Punjab, cornered a rebel, Mian Dide, in the Jammu hills south of Kashmir. He refused to surrender, and seized a chance to cut down an attacker who had brutally killed his old father; then he 'calmly puffed on his hookah and hurled insulting epithets at Gulab Singh. He even challenged him to a personal duel' (Singh, B.S., p 8). His displaying a pipe was itself an insult to the tobacco-hating Sikhs. At last he was shot. (Gulab Singh lived to be the first and – if possible – worst Maharajah of Kashmir, sold to him by the British.)

French soldiers meanwhile were having long years of fighting in Algeria, where they learned some reasons for not smoking. Setting out on a night march through enemy-infested country, with only dates for food, they would be warned that 'the smoke of tobacco is smelt a long way off: there are some men who can smell it at two or three leagues distance' (Castellane, vol 2, p 76). When Spain in turn tried an attack on Morocco, in 1859, its gunmen soon had to be equally abstemious, for a less sensible reason, a commissariat resembling the British in inefficiency. 'The soldiers, hungry and deprived of their _cigarrito_, which they prize above food, were not in the best of humours to-day', an English war correspondent wrote (Hardman, p 140). By that time the French conquest of Vietnam was under way; Catholic missionaries had undertaken to instigate a rising of their converts, in support of the invaders. 'Monsignor Pellerin and Admiral Genouilly had been smoking Manila cigars together on the (aptly named) flagship _Nemesis_' – but there was no sign of the promised revolt (Hodgkin, p 132).

In 1879 a Welshman, Private Cook, was writing home from Zululand about the horrors of Isandhlwana, one of Europe's few grand defeats in pitched battle. 'Myself, Jack Price, and Harry Lewis are all right, but we thought it was all up. I hope we shall all live to have a pipe of tobacco yet' (Emery, p 99). One contingent was trapped by the Zulus and suffered a long siege in an old mission station. After it was over a corporal wrote home about the hardships endured. 'I have seen 25 s. [shillings] offered for a small stick of tobacco weighing 1¼ oz., so you can see by this how everything was . . . The column left in a churchyard that we made there twenty-five men and four officers, and a fearful lot are walking about like skeletons' (Emery, p 213).

In 1882 Sir Garnet Wolseley was commissioned – by a Liberal government, headed by the peace-loving Gladstone – to attack and occupy Egypt. His great coup was the night march across the desert which led to the victory of Tel el Kebir on 19 September. It started at 1.30 am, with no blowing of bugles and trumpets, in a strange silence, 'more like dreamland than reality . . . Strict orders had been given that no lights were to be shown, not a match struck, no pipes or cigars lighted' (Atteridge, p 303). After the brief battle – duly celebrated by the poet laureate, Tennyson – thirst was so intense that some wounded men were driven to drinking the blood of wounded camels. No thirst could dry up the longing for a smoke.

> One rifleman, encountering dead Egyptians that were slowly roasting in their clothing, drew a pipe from his pocket and lit it from human flames, commenting: 'By — I never thought I should live to use a dead Egyptian for a light to my pipe!' (Lehmann, p 329)

Unperturbed by any such details, Wolseley was seated on the low parapet of a bridge, with a cigar. 'While engaged in a kind of tobacco debauch – six in a row – he smilingly received the reports of his commanders' (Lehmann, p 331). General Gordon, too, was a heavy smoker and hard worker, with little interest in food: he was satisfied with a dozen raw eggs to suck. In China he had shown that – unlike most military leaders – 'he conceived it the duty of a commanding officer not only to direct but personally to lead the critical assaults, smoking a cigar and carrying only a light cane' (Trench, pp 36, 42).

Tobacco meant nearly as much to Conan Doyle, and military affairs always fascinated him; the Boer War drew him to South Africa. In a prisoner-of-war camp he visited one man was raving; another 'sat in a corner with a proud dark face and brooding eagle eyes. He bowed with grave courtesy when I put down some money for cigarettes. A Huguenot, or I am mistaken' (*Memories*, p 160). In captured Pretoria he joined some bearded old burghers smoking on a bench, and craftily told them – hoping it would reach enemy ears outside – that Britain was not tired of fighting, as they supposed, but wanted the war to go on as long as possible, so that as many Boers as possible could be killed. 'The old fellows all grunted and puffed furiously at their pipes . . .' (p 184).

Another warlike Briton, who was to be one of his country's most distinguished smokers, was out there too, seeing things from the other side of the fence. Winston Churchill made his escape from a Boer prison camp in Pretoria by scrambling over the wall at night. As he did so his waistcoat was entangled for a moment in some stonework.

> In this posture I had one parting glimpse of the sentries still talking with their backs turned fifteen yards away. One of them was lighting his cigarette, and I remember the glow on the inside of his hands as a distinct impression which my mind recorded. (Martin, R. G., vol 2, p 167)

A patriotic writer made a collection of Boer War episodes from soldiers' letters, all throwing into relief the unconscious heroism of Tommy Atkins, with comments dwelling very often on how much tobacco meant to him. 'Turn to the supreme comfort which Atkins has amid all that befalls him; and who can fail to guess it? It is his pipe. We find it ever in his cheek, or his cheek crying for it' (Milne, p 40). A Gordon officer, crippled in a charge, limps to a rock where he can smoke and cheer on his men. A soldier with both arms broken is found lying with his eyes fixed on a cigarette case, inscribed 'From Alice to Fred', two paces away, that he cannot reach (pp 111, 153). Altogether the book's moral would seem to be that war and wounds matter nothing, so long as a man can get his smoke. Tobacco has stepped into the place once held by religion.

1914 came, and for four years soldiers crouched in opposite trenches, offering up the same prayers and wafting them towards heaven on the smoke of the same weed. In the two world wars problems of supply and rationing of tobacco, for armies and civil populations, had for the first time to be tackled in earnest. On the

German side additives had to be found, as in the packet preserved in the Imperial War Museum stamped 'Kriegstabak-Mischung No. 184 75 Gramm.' (In Charlie Chaplin's 1918 film *Shoulder Arms* – all the better loved because more anti-war than anti-German – Private Chaplin captured a whole regiment of Germans, and then humanely bestowed cigarettes on them. Their little martinet of a colonel snatched these and flung them on the ground; to his men's delight, Chaplin put him across his knee and spanked him.)

During the 1914-18 War the British public subscribed enough money to provide the men at the front with 232,599,191 cigarettes. 'The cheap cigarettes ("fags") were as much a part of the life of the trenches as the barbed wire, and one of the main army chaplains was named "Woodbine Willie" after a cigarette' (Briggs, p 260). Other funds were raised by sale of ashtrays, tobacco jars, etc, made out of shell-casings. Men eagerly looking for gift parcels from home often hailed most joyfully those containing tobacco. But disillusion was sometimes in store. Jerome K. Jerome, too old to wield a bayonet but driving an ambulance, was one who discovered that parcels from home were often opened and the contents purloined.

> Out of every three boxes of cigarettes that my wife sent me, I reckon I got one. The French cigarettes, that one bought at the canteens, were ten per cent poison and the rest dirt. The pain would go out of a wounded soldier's face when you showed him an English cigarette. (*Life*, p 226)

Not all soldiers could count on families as eager and well able to supply them as young Charles Wedgwood, son of the first Baron Barlaston. In February 1915 he was writing from the mess of the 20th Lincolnshires to ask his father to go to 'Dunhills *the* pipe sellers off Picadilly Circus' and get him 'a really nice pipe'. 'You need never feel shy about asking me for money', his father wrote to him from Africa in 1916; 'I have lots of it and it is all at your disposal – even for pernicious cigarettes should you think them necessary to your position in life' (7 June 1916, Imperial War Museum). At the front there were few who did not think them necessary.

After the poet Wilfred Owen joined the army his requests for items from home make it clear that he was not one of the few. 'Players' were his favourites. Early in 1917 he was sending thanks from an Advanced Horse Transport Depot, and emphasising that 'The Cigarettes are the most essential of all, because the stuff sold out here is abominable, except Turkish, which are cheap and good' (p 433). To his mother he wrote in October 1918: 'Am looking out with hungry eyes for your parcel. None of my rich relatives consider 20 cigarettes worth my life. They'll have a murderer's curse . . . Meanwhile you have a martyr's blessing' (p 583). On 29 October the end seemed near. 'It is rumoured that Austria has really surrendered . . . The new soldiers cheer when they hear these rumours, but the old ones bite their pipes, and go on cleaning their rifles, unbelieving' (p 590). The end *was* near, but so was his own; he was killed on 4 November, very close, like the German soldier at the end of *All Quiet on the Western Front*, to Armistice Day.

One of Siegfried Sassoon's experiences was of a night patrol, or raid; he was crawling round the muddy edge of a shell-crater, hearing the enemy guns, and 'miserably wondering whether my number was up; then I remembered that I was wearing my pre-war raincoat; I could feel the pipe and tobacco pouch in my pocket and somehow this made me less forlorn' (p 27). As he wrote in one letter from a dugout, indulgence in them could be overdone; he had sore feet from tramping along gluey trenches, and 'trench mouth': food tasted 'filthy'. Probably he had been smoking too much lately in his 'cramped little den', he concluded (p 30). Another lesson dawned on him as he sat in the Olympic Hotel at Liverpool and watched diners who 'ordered lobsters and selected colossal cigars', topping off with oysters and stout – the lesson that some non-combatants were 'doing themselves pretty well out of the War' (p 109).

War can be heroic, but it has always needed an element of play-acting and attitudinising to keep it going in the right spirit. A British recruiting poster showed Tommy Atkins coolly lighting his pipe under fire, with the words ''Arf a mo Kaiser'. Officers were still expected to lead charges, against barbed wire and machine guns now, with the sang-froid of aristocrats going to the guillotine, who perhaps floated through some French minds when the moment came to go 'over the top'. At Verdun in 1916 a French colonel was coolly smoking a cigar as he led a suicide charge in the style of a parade-ground drill (Horne, p 173). He may have needed it to steady his nerves, and equally to advertise his calm demeanour and invite his men to emulate it.

In March 1918, in one of the last German offensives on the Western front, during the final furious minutes of the artillery prelude,

> A German officer tried to light a cigar. Three times the blast of mortar-bombs falling short blew out the match . . . Zero hour had arrived . . . A Jäger lieutenant happily smoked a long green huntsman's pipe as he marched at the head of his men. (Moore, W., p 56)

In distant theatres other soldiers were fighting, with even less notion than those in Europe of what they were fighting about, but they too at times with one eye on the mirror of fame. A British officer with the Indian forces in the extraordinary campaign in German East Africa – now Tanzania – wrote of visits to the hospital to see his 'chaps'.

> They seem as usual happy and plucky. A Pathan swaggered in the other day, a cigarette in his mouth and his coat over his shoulders. The M.O. asked him if he was badly wounded. He replied 'It is nothing.' The M.O. asked 'Is it usual to speak to a sahib with a cigarette in your mouth?' He replied 'No Sahib but I cannot take it out, I have lost both my hands.' When they examined him they found both his arms broken. (Lewis, H. V., 25 April 1915)

World War One had an epilogue in the Allied intervention, and civil war, in Russia. On one of the scattered fronts, in Siberia, Admiral Kolchak was the 'White' or anti-Bolshevik leader. His forces were mostly foreign, and on the other side they made up a song about the miscellaneous aid he was receiving from abroad –

> Uniforms from England,
> Epaulettes from France,
> Japanese tobacco,
> Kolchak leads the dance.

The final stanza ran –

> Uniforms in tatters,
> Epaulettes all gone,
> So is the tobacco,
> Kolchak's day is done. (Leyda, p 145)

By the end of 1919 his forces had crumbled away, and he himself
was caught and executed.

World War Two had for prologue another Spanish civil war, with
massive foreign intervention, chiefly by Germany and Italy on the
Franco or fascist side. Franco had also an army of wild tribesmen
from Morocco, who were frequently made use of as death squads.
'I can never forget', wrote an American reporter, 'the first time I
saw the mass execution of prisoners.' Seven trucks brought their
loads of exhausted men on to the main street of a town. They were
given cigarettes, while Moorish soldiers set up a pair of machine
guns. 'The two guns suddenly roared in staccato, firing short, lazy
bursts of ten or twelve rounds at a time . . .' All the six hundred
captives were massacred (Payne, p 414).

And an eye-witness in Ronald Fraser's collection of memories
of individuals caught up in the conflict speaks of other murders of
prisoners or fugitives by Moors – under Christian orders – and six
bodies lying behind a barracks. 'One of the corpses still had his
pipe in his mouth' (p 157). Another was in a crowded prison cell at
Seville after its capture by the fascists, when a warder called the
names of three who were to go out and be shot.

> I'll never forget the last one, he couldn't have been more than sixteen or
> seventeen, and he was rolling a cigarette. He went on rolling it until it
> was finished, got up and turned to us: 'I wish you all better luck', he
> said, and went out. (pp 275-6)

As in all wars, amid the atrocious things happening were oases of relative calm, where tobacco could be more its natural, peaceable self. A Cambridge student in the International Brigade lived to write of one such interval, following the recapture from the fascists of the university buildings at Madrid, as

> a period when we were as happy as I think men can possibly be in the front line of a modern war. We were under cover from the deadly cold that so far had been our worst enemy, we had leisure to talk and smoke in physical comfort, and, greatest pleasure of all, it was safe to take our boots off at night ... Here we discussed art and literature, life and death and Marxism during the long day, and as the evening drew on, we sang. (Knox, p 190)

During the tension of the Munich crisis in 1938 it was observable in Czechoslovakia that people were smoking a good deal more than usual; and this must often have been repeated, in many threatened lands. In Germany when war broke out in 1939 demand for tobacco soared, despite a higher tax; one factor as in Britain and elsewhere was that more women now wanted to smoke. Supplies were inadequate and uncertain throughout the war; some of the fluctuations of this problem can be traced in the regular conferences held by Goebbels, Minister for Propaganda, who took it very seriously. The Fuehrer might be a non-smoker, but this was one direction in which his subjects were not prepared to follow him. At the outset Goebbels frowned on the idea of a 'smoker's card' as bad for public confidence, but by May 1940 he was having to call for steps to prevent queues from forming outside tobacconists' shops (Boelcke, p 10).

A year later he made it clear that the question must be tackled more energetically. 'The working people are complaining that they are getting less tobacco than anyone, because most of the time when they finish work the tobacconists are already closed.' Some firms were said to be buying in bulk for their canteens, and people were talking about rationing. A commission had been sent to Greece to negotiate purchases. Cigarette production was stated to have risen by 50 per cent over the peacetime level. The army pointed out that it was economising: men who wanted tobacco had to give up their claim on chocolate. All this was not enough, and Goebbels wound up with a further call for action. 'Useful as a universal stopping of smoking may be from a health point of view, at the present moment it would be highly inappropriate' (pp 165-6). By 1942 ration cards had become inevitable.

In occupied territories withdrawal of tobacco could be used as a punitive measure. When there were demonstrations in Prague on the national day, 28 October, in 1939, Goebbels proposed to make the punishment fit the crime. For instance, if the Czechs boycotted the cinemas for a day, all cinemas should be closed for three months. 'If they proclaim a short-term tobacco strike, they are to be told that for a number of months tobacco supplies earmarked for the Czechs will be sent to the German front' (p 2). In long-besieged Leningrad all military rations were dwindling in the later months of 1941. Besides food, soldiers and sailors were entitled to 10 grammes of tobacco or 20 of *makhorka* (the inferior local species) daily (Erickson, p 727). It is remarkable that in a city on the edge of famine people had to be urged to give up their tobacco ration in exchange for chocolate or sugar, and that the attempt failed.

Terrorist methods employed by the fascists in Spain were practised on a vaster scale in Russia by the Nazis. An eye-witness describes a mass execution – a huge grave, bodies crammed together into it, some still alive and stirring –

> an SS-man sitting on the edge of the short side of the pit, his legs hanging down into it; on his knees lay a submachine gun, and he was smoking a cigarette. The people, entirely naked, walked down some steps which had been dug into the clay wall of the pit, and then slid across the heads of those who lay there until they reached the place which the SS-man had pointed out to them . . . (Stern, p 223)

On sea as on land, tobacco had its place in the *matériel de guerre*. In August 1942 a convoy making for Malta came under heavy Axis air attacks, and the tanker *Ohio*, whose oil was vital to Malta's survival, was badly damaged. Thirty or so of its crew, sent off in a launch, 'took it in turns to smoke thirteen cigarettes contributed by Pumpman Collins, the only ones remaining amongst them, then all dropped off into a dreamless sleep. When they awoke they were in Malta.' The *Ohio* was towed in just in time before sinking (Shankland and Hunter, pp 165-6). Malta itself was suffering from every kind of shortage; to a great many, the most distressing of all was that of tobacco, which was strictly rationed: two weekly packets of cigarettes or tobacco to each man between sixteen and sixty. 'It was a commonplace feature of Maltese life to see up to a hundred or more people sleeping out the night on the pavement outside the tobacco shops when an issue was due the following morning' (p 44).

As World War Two neared its end the need to smoke intensified. One of the most vivid moments in the film *Mein Kampf*, put together from Nazi propaganda films, belongs to the German offensive in the Ardennes in the winter of 1944. Assault troops are pushing through a burning township; a gaunt-faced soldier stops to break open greedily a captured pack of American cigarettes, pushes one into his mouth and lights it, before hurrying on. Whether he lived long enough to smoke the rest of his packet is a question as unanswerable as most of history's queries.

Tobacco has not seldom served as a medium of exchange, when money has been lacking or – usually in wartime – has lost its purchasing power. It was so in Germany in the later stages of World War Two.

> The wartime dearth of consumer goods – especially in the countryside – robbed money of its attraction as an exchange medium, and farmers traded eggs for cigarettes (at the rate of one for one), pounds of butter for packets of pipe tobacco, and pounds of meat for ten cigarettes. (Grunberger, p 268)

In March 1944 a woman from a White Russian family living in Germany, Marie Vassiltchikov, was working for the Foreign Office, and being drawn into the anti-Hitler plot by Adam von Trott, who was to be among the victims of Hitler's revenge. The department had been evacuated to a rural backwater, and on 22

March her diary recorded:

> Worked late, as piles of photographs and office supplies have arrived from Breslau and we are now trying to find a car to tow the stuff up the hill. The A.A. [Foreign Office] has a special supply of cigarettes to bribe the locals into carrying loads for us, as there is hardly any transportation. (p 154)

When more volunteers were needed for the firing squads at Auschwitz, they are said to have been paid five cigarettes and 200 cc. of vodka (Craig, p 38).

And when Hitler was at last driven to put an end to himself, all the other occupants of his bunker at Berlin at once began to smoke: 'now the headmaster had gone and the boys could break the rules. Under the soothing influence of nicotine, whose absence must have increased the nervous tension of the past week', they could begin to contemplate their future (Trevor-Roper, pp 235-6). With the Allied occupation 'American cigarettes became the standard of value in the European black market . . . Many Americans in Europe during the years 1946 and 1947 made fabulous profits' (Roberts, p 272). It was one manifestation of the American hegemony now being inaugurated.

When the guns fell silent in Europe, elsewhere battles were still raging. In Burma a British officer was exhilarated by being given the 3rd Rajputana Rifles, his first real command after 14 years in India. He had a splendid adjutant, who, he says, 'never let me move off without seeing that my cigarette case was full – I smoked in those nervy days.' Evidently there was no shortage of tobacco, and as one result he had a problem with his mules, taken over from a British regiment. 'These mules were all nicotine addicts – Thomas Atkins, always fond of animals, had indulged them with ration cigarettes which they gobbled up.' On this diet they had grown 'desperately thin, extremely jittery', and very cantankerous (Prendergast, pp 231,243).

Meanwhile, a sufferer from the Japanese invasion of China was the progressive writer Wen I-to, forced to join in the westward exodus from Peking and the coastal cities and seek shelter in the town of Kunming in the south-west. Multitudes of refugees crammed the place, rents shot up. Hot water replaced tea except on rare occasions, and the previously chain-smoking Wen found cigarettes almost unobtainable (Spence, p 277). In Tokyo another writer, Kafu, was suffering from the effects of a war he regarded as an unpleasant nuisance. Already in its second year, returning from a search for comfort among chorus-girl acquaintances in the quarter where he felt most at home, he noticed long queues outside all the tobacconists'. Later, amid winter snow, he heard the warning of a coming American raid, and the anti-aircraft guns began to boom.

> On edge, I brewed some of the coffee that is among my treasures and was quite unstinting with sugar. Then I filled my pipe with Occidental tobacco, another treasure, and had a leisurely smoke. I wanted my last moments to be happy. (Seidensticker, p 167)

In March 1945 his house was destroyed in a raid, with all his library and other possessions; diggers among the ruins discovered a few mementoes – an old tea-bowl, a seal, his grandfather's pipe (p 169).

In 1943 things were painfully improving for the revolutionary movement in Japanese-occupied Vietnam, but new plans and decisions ran into difficulties of communication. So two women undertook to carry messages rolled up in cigarettes, and replies came back from the central committee in the same fashion (Hodgkin, p 313). But composing his manual for guerrilla fighters in 1961, Che Guevara gave full weight to the more ordinary purposes of tobacco.

> A customary and extremely important comfort in the life of the guerrilla fighter is a smoke . . . a smoke in moments of rest is a great friend to the solitary soldier. Pipes are useful, because they permit using to the extreme all tobacco that remains in the butts of cigars and cigarettes at times of scarcity. (p 58)

Innumerable soldiers must have suffered painful longings for a cigarette, or remembered for years an unexpected gift of one from fortune, or sighed to see a last remaining one wither so quickly into ashes. Once at least a soldier had to agonise over its too long life. He was on sentinel duty, when the general happened to ride up and caught him with a cigarette. He dropped it on the ground, where it lay smouldering. In thunderous silence the commander sat on his horse, his stern gaze riveted on the culprit, until at long last the cigarette burned out.

9

A Ministering Angel

... the deep perpetual groan of London misery seemed to swell
and swell and form the whole undertone of life. The filthy air
came into the place in the damp coats of silent men, and hung
there till it was brewed to a nauseous warmth ... strong-smell-
ing pipes contributed their element in a fierce, dogged manner
which appeared to say that it now had to stand for everything –
for bread and meat and beer, for shoes and blankets and the
poor things at the pawnbroker's and the smokeless chimney at
home.

Henry James on a public house in winter,
The Princess Casamassima, chap 21

It was a maxim ascribed to the Symbolist poet Mallarmé that
everyone should keep a little cigarette smoke between himself and
the world, as a curtain. And tobacco has been, for countless
legions of human beings, a palisade against every species of harrowing situation, malady of spirit or body or pocket. When Hamlet
counted up the ills that flesh is heir to, he little realised what a
panacea had just been bestowed on humanity, to assuage if it
could not heal them.

Henry James's distinguished medical man Dr Sloper, having
lost his only son in infancy, was anxious for his daughter to turn
out really intelligent; but by the time Catherine was 18 it was clear
that though a good child she was not going to be clever. 'He was a
philosopher: he smoked a good many cigars over his disappoint-
ment, and in the fullness of time he got used to it' (*Washington
Square*, chap 2). And in Virginia Woolf's novel Mrs Ramsay is
sorry for poor old Mr Carmichael, shuffling and useless and

miserable, treated with contempt by his wife. 'Had he money enough to buy tobacco? Did he have to ask for it? half a crown? eighteen-pence. Oh, she could not bear to think of the little in-dignities he must have to suffer' (*Lighthouse*, Part 1 sec 8).

Whole classes, not individuals alone, might suffer these priv-ations. On 10 November 1819, a Reform meeting was held at Dundee to protest against the 'Peterloo massacre' of reformers at Manchester; the radical landowner George Kinloch presided. No flags fluttered, no banners waved; instead, broken kettles and tea-pots, empty pipes and snuff-boxes, hung from poles, emblems of 'luxuries which poor people could no longer enjoy' (Tennant, pp 135-6). A William Heath cartoon of 1829, entitled 'Pastoral', showed a recumbent shepherd with his flock, and a romantic lady asking where his pipe is. 'I left un at home Marm,' he returns sadly ' – cause I got no *Bacco*.'

One of the criticisms made by Engels in the 1840s of the work-houses, where the poor were being shut up out of sight, was that 'tobacco is forbidden' (*Working Class*, p 284). Again, in his annals of the English farm labourer Richard Jefferies wrote of one old fellow, mouldering away in such an abode, that during his first winter he was buoyed up by hope of getting out in the spring, and finding odd jobs. 'Nothing else enlivened it except an occasional little present of tobacco' (p 310). A century later George Orwell made a brief stay in a workhouse, in the casual ward for tramps. It was piercingly chilly, too cold for sleep, and the tobacco he and the rest had smuggled in was in the pockets of their clothes, removed from them for the night. All next day they were locked up, tight-packed, in a dreary stone-floored eating-room. Orwell's chum from Glasgow, Scotty, had nothing to smoke, his tin of cigarette-ends picked up in the streets having been confiscated. Orwell was able to give him the makings of a smoke. It was not illegal, but they 'smoked furtively', pushing their cigarettes into their pockets, like schoolboys, when they heard the 'tramp major' coming (*Down and Out*, sec 35).

There was always worse poverty in Ireland, under the beaks and claws of the English landlords. In the later 17th century, for example, the economist Sir William Petty was struck by how little, except tobacco, Irish villages bought from outside. 'Tobacco in short Pipes seldom burnt, seems the pleasure of their Lives, together with Sneezing: Insomuch, that 2/7 of their Expence in Food, is Tobacco' (Calder, p 282). It is significant that he reckons it as part of their nutrition.

But in many regions of the earth poverty was the work of Nature, rather than man-made; a communal spirit of sharing good and ill was an alleviation. On his eastern tour Kinglake and his guide Mysseri came on an encampment of desert Arabs who seemed to have nothing more to live on than wild grasses. They flocked round 'begging like spaniels for bits of the beloved weed' – proof of true penury, 'for poor indeed is the man in these climes who cannot command a pipeful of tobacco'. They got him across the Jordan on a raft of inflated skins, and he slept on the bank, while they sat round a fire near by. 'They were made most savagely happy by the tobacco with which I supplied them, and they soon determined that the whole night should be one smoking festival.' They had nothing better than a cracked bowl for a pipe, and passed it round, each taking a fixed number of whiffs (chaps 14, 15).

Accident as well as poverty may come between the would-be smoker and his smoke, a blow of fate that few can have been spared. One of O. Henry's lively tales of the old West begins at a frontier store where cowboys have gathered to buy stocks of tobacco, only to learn that the pony-waggon bringing a consignment across the prairie has not arrived; the storekeeper's life is at some risk until he reassures them that it will soon turn up. And on his journey through Africa in 1898 Grogan had a bad night in Dinka-land, when salty water brought on a bad fit of vomiting. Several of his men had injuries, the cook-boy was ill. His last two tins of tobacco were mouldy and unappetising, and when he tried to smoke, mosquitoes 'settled in clouds on the rim of my pipe waiting their turn for a space on my epidermis' (chap 20). Reading such heartrending accounts, one can hardly wonder at the British of that epoch priding themselves on their dogged endurance.

Smokers have too often been cheated of their comforter, when most in need, by some mishap like illness. An English officer abroad in 1902 was having to take quinine for fever and neuralgia. 'Usual day', says his diary. 'Wish to goodness I could smoke, but know from old experience that it is absolutely out of the question yet, it would probably make me sick straight away' (Strickland, 7 February 1902). In May 1917 Wilfred Owen was down with fever, and wrote to his mother from hospital: 'I don't smoke. No, I could no more smoke a cigarette than any unborn chicken' (p 463).

Another unfeeling barrier between the smoker and his longed-for relief has been the prison gate. In older times in Europe tobacco might be allowed, or winked at, if the prisoner had the where-withal to pay for it, or kind friends outside – on whom he might often be dependent for food as well. The poet George Wither, an officer of the Parliamentarian army, when thrown into jail after the Restoration was solaced by his pipe as well as his prayers. During the long drawn-out 'Douglas Cause', the greatest *cause célèbre* of the Scottish law courts in Boswell's time at the bar, moving letters were read out from Lady Jane Douglas to her husband Sir John Steuart, in confinement as a bankrupt. She sent him her last half-crown to buy 'a little rappee', or snuff, and urged him to put his trust in Heaven (Pottle, p 339).

In British India a good deal of this old laxity lingered on. In 1929 the famous Meerut Conspiracy Trial, a government attack on trade unionism, started; it lasted more than four years. One of three Englishmen accused, along with a score of Indians, was a journalist, Lester Hutchinson, who was later on a Labour MP and wrote a book about the trial. He discovered that smuggling into Indian jails could be arranged, with the help of money, with 'astounding facility . . . drugs, tobacco, liquor, and the service of catamites' (p 68). But in Britain, the cutting off of tobacco and alcohol had become one of the fixed penalties incurred by prisoners. It was so in army punishment cells as well. Number 10 of the regulations issued by the Horse Guards (ie by the commander-in-chief, Wellington, a foe to tobacco) on 8 November 1844 specified that: 'The use of Tobacco, in any form, as well as of Spirituous, or other Liquors, by a prisoner, is peremptorily prohibited.' Alliteration lends the concluding words a fine sound as of a roll of drums.

Official vigilance in jails steadily increased, with tobacco very high on the forbidden list. No exception was made in favour of political prisoners. The Irish nationalist O'Donovan Rossa was caught when a piece of chewing-tobacco given him by a fellow convict slipped out of his mouth. It was best to swallow such a thing if a warden came near. But a pair of wardens might forestall the attempt by seizing a man's throat from front and back (Priestley, *Prison*, pp 201-2). It was regarded as a remarkable concession when Sir Roger Casement, a former consul with distinguished services in Africa, was allowed to smoke in Brixton prison before his trial and execution for treason in the summer of 1916. (In this century smoking has been allowed in British jails, and prisoners have been paid small sums for their work, about equal to half an ounce of shag weekly – 'just enough to keep the appetite alive and not enough to satisfy it'. Further quantities have been obtained through the 'barons', convicts who smuggle things in through bribed warders; to these men the smaller fry quickly fall into debt, and became their 'serfs' (Priestley, *Jail*, pp 48-9). Considering the villainous condition that British prisons have been left to get into in recent years, there clearly ought to be a more liberal policy, perhaps a free ration of wine and cigarettes for all who want them.)

In the period ending in 1867 capital punishment for offences often trivial was being softened into transportation, for any term up to life, to Botany Bay. The 'First Fleet' set out in 1787, to begin the building of Australia. Before crossing the ocean convicts might have a long spell in the 'hulks', old disused vessels moored in the Thames as detention centres.

> The great emblem of desire and repression in hulk life, more than sex or food or (in some cases) even freedom itself, was tobacco. Possession of tobacco was severely punished, but the nicotine addict would go through any degradation to get his 'quid'. (Hughes, Robert, p 141)

Even savage and repeated floggings could not deter some men, for whom the comforter had been turned into a tormentor. One who sailed in the First Fleet was John Wisehammer, at the age of 15 sentenced to transportation for seven years for snatching a packet of snuff from a shop counter in Gloucester. Those who survived the voyage were subjected to the ban until their terms ran out, and tobacco was responsible for many of the innumerable floggings inflicted on them in the meantime. However, a humane Scottish governor, Alexander Maconochie, broke with custom by allowing men to grow patches of tobacco and smoke it (Hughes, Robert, pp 72, 210).

The Russian political exile Herzen recalled in his memoirs how he used to smoke on the sly as a youngster, purloining tobacco and wrapping it in paper (p 52). In 1834 he was arrested in Moscow, after an epidemic of arson had put Nicholas II's police regime on the alert, and presently taken to the old Krutitsky monastery, which had become a police barracks. He was searched, but allowed to keep his tobacco pouch; lying on the bare bedstead in his cold cell, with overcoat for pillow, he lit his pipe, and a candle. This revealed that the ceiling was covered with vermin. 'Not having seen a light for a long time, the black beetles hurried to the lighted patch in great excitement, jostling one another, dropping on the table, and then running wildly along the edge of it' (p 167).

It appears from Solzhenitsyn's picture that Stalin – a robust pipe smoker – did not forbid smoking in his labour camps, but it was far from easy to obtain anything to smoke. Hence possession of a cigarette or two made their owner, for the time being, a privileged person, with favours to confer on nicotine-starved mates. One morning in the file being marched off to the day's work Shukhov saw his team-mate Tsezar smoking a cigarette, and longingly hoped to be given the fag-end, though too proud to ask for it as another sufferer was doing. 'Every nerve in his body was taut, all his longing was concentrated in that fag-end – which meant more to him now, it seemed, than freedom itself.' Given it at last, he seized it eagerly. 'The smoke crept and flowed through his whole hungry body . . .' (_One Day_, pp 28-9). Another day, desperate for a smoke after eating his porridge, Shukhov managed to borrow a pinch of loose tobacco, just enough to make one cigarette, rolled up in a bit of newspaper – to be repaid out of some cottage-grown leaf he hoped to buy tomorrow from another man. 'A sweet dizziness went all through his body, to his head, to his feet', like a drink of vodka (p 74).

In Mussolini's relatively humane jails the tobacco position seems to have been similar. Gramsci told his sister-in-law Tania, in a letter from Turi prison on 9 November 1931, that the inmates were accustomed to take turns at smoking, three men to a cigarette, each smoking one-third of it: the fag-end was kept for re-use. He himself found this disgusting, and preferred to make his own very small cigarettes (he asked her for some paper for this). Matches were cut in two, lengthwise, with a needle. He was consuming 40 per cent less tobacco than before his arrest; the result was that he could not concentrate so well, and was reading and thinking less (pp 236-7).

Tobacco-hunting could be an education for men and women under lock and key; it fostered qualities of courage, organising skill, mutual trust, and willingness to share. A vision of all this comes from a prisoner-of-war camp at Soltau in Hanover, in World War One. Daily as dusk fell a surreptitious stir broke out, of inmates flitting about and wares changing hands – principally

> tobacco, cigarette paper and matches, three strictly forbidden commodities ... I do not think a single cigarette was smoked in those days without being put out several times for fear of detection, then lovingly re-lit and probably passed from mouth to mouth like a Red Indian's pipe of peace. (Eeman, p 179)

One refinement of modern political life can be seen in the use of tobacco as a bribe to secure information from prisoners, a method at least less barbarous than the revival of torture which is likely to be remembered as a hallmark of the 20th century. A recorded experience from the USSR is of seven women in a cell, and of Larissa being summoned one morning for interrogation. She went off, crossing herself three times, and came back cheerfully with a lighted cigarette. One of the others reproached her.

> 'What can you know or understand, you non-smoking little runt',
> Larissa turned on Nisa.
> 'And is the cigarette good?' I asked.
> 'Divine.'
> 'And your opinion of yourself, what's that like?' I continued. 'Also
> divine?' (Joffe, p 99)

Many a prisoner, on the other hand, who owed what taste of tobacco he might get to the charity of a fellow creature must have remembered it with gratitude for the rest of his days. During the Indian Mutiny, for example, various princes of the lately deposed royal family of Oudh were confined in the banqueting hall of the palace at Lucknow, where they had been wont to carouse. They sat in gloomy silence, only lit up by a gleam of pleasure when Colonel Inglis gave them a donation of cigars (Hibbert, p 240). When the Cultural Revolution in China landed the communist writer Ding (Ting) Ling in jail, she felt little inspiration. She did complete one story, about one of the prison guards, 'friendly in a clumsy way, who occasionally would offer her a cigarette and re-minisce about his past exploits' (Spence, p 262).

And finally, an exceptional class of prisoners, very numerous in the East, consisted of women shut up in harems, from the Sultan's seven hundred concubines in Constantinople downward. For them the hubble-bubble, as Europeans called it, must have been a blessed sedative in their twilight existence. As a paradise forbid-den to Christians, the harem had an itching interest for them. Paintings like 'A New Star in the Harem' were in demand – the owner's latest acquisition lying on her back on a divan, the tube of a costly water-pipe in her hand. Far less appetising was a brief view Thackeray got of some inmates of the Seraglio, evidently older ones whose charms had waned, 'with their _cortège_ of infernal black eunuchs'. Strangers were kept at a distance, but from what he could see of them, muffled up, they

> looked just as vulgar and ugly as the other women ... The poor devils
> are allowed to come out, half-a-dozen times in the year, to spend their

little wretched allowance of pocket-money in purchasing trinkets and tobacco. (*Cairo*, chap 7)

Old age is another kind of lock-up, with only one exit. Lovers of tobacco always seem to have felt more and more need of it, with advancing years, to make up for other comforts lost and the altered aspect of the universe. Old women above all, when alone and bereft of almost everything else, have clung to it. In Ireland in July 1818 Keats saw a crone, whom he dubbed 'the Duchess of Dunghill', carried in a sort of hutch on two poles: 'a squalid old Woman squat like an ape . . . with a pipe in her mouth and looking out with a round-eyed skinny lidded inanity . . . she sat and puffed out the smoke while two ragged tattered Girls carried her along' (Keats, p 126).

Old people smoking have not seldom inspired similar sensations of disgust. A stanza of a Victorian ballad runs –

> Don't ever marry an old man
> I'll tell you the reason why
> His lips are all tobacco juice
> And his chin is never dry. (Day, p 136)

Still, we have more animated pictures of age and tobacco in unison, brightened by social participation. In Allan Ramsay's pastoral play of 1725,

> While the young brood sport on the green,
>   The old anes think it best,
> With the Brown Cow [beer barrel] to clear their een,
>   Snuff, crack [chat], and take their rest.
> > (Act 3 Scene 2 Prologue)

A tranquil memory comes to mind of a visit to Carlow Cathedral, one Sunday in the autumn of 1978, and a young couple reclining in the churchyard among the graves, spooning and smoking. They made an unstudied tableau of life rising superior to death. But death and tobacco have met in situations of every colour, from grotesque or heroic to elegiac or jocular. In 1679 the Scottish primate Archbishop Sharp, just before his murder by Covenanters, opponents of the episcopacy brought back by the Restoration, was on the road to St Andrews, and made a pause at Ceres in Fife to enjoy a pipe at the manse. When, a few hours later, the assassins were rifling his pockets and his coach, they came on State papers, pistols, and a tobacco box, from which a 'humming-bee' flew out; the more superstitious of Sharp's enemies took it to be his 'familiar', or attendant demon.

J.G. Lockhart's narrative of a visit to Glasgow contains an incident of a gentleman who took out in company 'a remarkably beautiful old chased silver snuff-box' and offered him a pinch, adding '"you shall have your finger in the box that was found in my grandfather's waistcoat-pocket after he was hanged."' This reminded Lockhart of 'a common saying that "a man is scarce of news when he tells you his father danced a jig upon nothing" ' – but it turned out that the grandfather was a 'martyr' of Bothwell Brigg, the Covenanter's' rising in 1679 (Lockhart, *Peter*, p 324).

Funeral as well as nuptial ceremonies have been a burden to many of those responsible for them, and tobacco like alcohol has often been obligatory. In a German story of the last century a poor woman dies, after a long struggle with difficulties. Her son Paul, much affected, is brought up against the fact that he is short of money for the funeral expenses, among which will be a thaler each for ten bottles of port, and two thalers for a box of cigars (Sudermann, p 201). In traditional societies death has often worn a sociable air, and nowhere more than in the Celtic lands. Three nights were taken up by the funeral wake of 'King Corny', the great magnate of Connemara in Maria Edgeworth's *Ormond*; and as a guest related, there was 'plenty of cake, and wine, and tea, and tobacco, and snuff; everything handsome as possible, and honourable to the deceased, who was always open-handed and open-hearted, and with open house, too' (*Ormond*, chap 17).

By the time of a Highland wake in 1740 dancing had been given up, but friends and relatives sat round the corpse, with plenty of whisky and snuff to sustain them, and there were ghost stories for the older, country games for the younger (Grant, I.F., p 368).

Smollett describes a wake, not much later, in a Highland castle, accompanied by deep drinking. In the morning there was a gargantuan breakfast, washed down by ale, brandy, and whisky. 'Finally, a large roll of tobacco was presented by way of dessert, and every individual took a comfortable quid, to prevent the bad effects of the morning air' (*Humphrey*, p 232).

There is the same determination of mourners to enjoy doing their duty, if on a more modest scale, in Scott's *Bride of Lammermoor*, when two old women are left in charge of a corpse, not without some shivers at the thought of the Devil putting in an appearance to claim the soul. '"But ne'er mind, cummer!"' the bolder spirit exclaims – '"we have this dollar of the Master's, and we'll send doun for bread and for yill, and tobacco, and a drap brandy to burn, and a wee pickle saft sugar – and be their deil, or nae deil, lass, we'll hae a merry night o't"' (chap 23).

Contemplation of death as a coming event has found a natural likeness in the eddying and vanishing of puffs of smoke. Joseph Conrad, or his spokesman Marlow,

> knew a man once who came to my rooms one evening, and while smoking a cigar confessed to me moodily that he was trying to discover some graceful way of retiring out of existence. I didn't study his case, but I had a glimpse of him the other day at a cricket match, with some women, having a good time. (*Chance*, Part 1 chap 7)

Possibly the cigar was of a quality to dissuade him from so drastic a method of giving up smoking. And one of Stevenson's old men tells how his father, near death, walked round the garden with him, smoking and meditating.

> It was his last pipe, and I believe he knew it; and it was a strange thing, without doubt, to leave the trees that he had planted, and the son that he had begotten, ay, sir, and even the old pipe with the Turk's head that he had smoked since he was a lad and went a-courting. (*Otto*, chap 3)

A tobacco glow, for want of better lantern, has lighted countless human beings the way to dusty death. Some aliens have seemed to European spectators to have no need of it for comfort, and to fill their last moments with smoke merely from habit. A Spanish priest in the Philippines, talking of the native temperament as phlegmatic and fatalistic, maintained that fear of death was unknown to them; 'they talk about death, even in the presence of the dying, without any concern. If condemned to the scaffold, they exhibit equal indifference, and smoke their cigar with wonted tranquillity' (Alatas, p 58). Marquesan islanders were obsessed with death, Stevenson believed, but had no dread of it; suicide he heard was common. He was told of an old man of Hapaa who caught smallpox during an epidemic and

> had his grave dug by a wayside, and lived in it for near a fortnight, eating, drinking, and smoking with the passers-by, talking mostly of his end, and equally unconcerned for himself and careless of the friend he infected. (*South Seas*, Part 1 chap 4)

But most 'civilised' men have needed something to compose their minds, especially when their lives have been forfeited not to age or sickness but to the justice or injustice of their fellow men. One of a party from a yacht wrecked in the archipelago in Conrad's novel *The Rescue*, captured by tribesmen and expecting death, is a Spanish gentleman, d'Alcacer. He resolves to ration the cigarettes he has with him strictly. At length, sitting by himself in the dark, he ponders –

> A cigarette was only to be lighted on special occasions; and now there were only three left and they had to be made to last till the end of life. They calmed, they soothed, they made an attitude. And only three left! One had to be kept for the morning, to be lighted before going through the gate of doom – the gate of Belarab's stockade . . .

After deliberation he agrees with himself that one of the other two may properly be smoked now, and lights it from the embers of the fire, under the night sky (Part 6 sec 4).

Walter Raleigh, sent to the block by a king whose son would before long follow him there, was perhaps the first of a terribly long line of political prisoners whose last moments have owed some relief to tobacco. 'He took a pipe of tobacco', according to

Aubrey, 'a little before he went to the scaffold, which some formall persons were scandalized at, but I thinke 'twas well and properly donne, to settle his spirits' (p 47). In such a situation chewing and spitting, or snuffing and sneezing, would be a solecism; even a pipe seems less than perfect, an artificial thing interposed between the immortal leaf, as it might have been plucked in the Garden of Eden, and the too mortal lips. Far better the cigar or cigarette which has been the last favour extended to those about to die in later years, the last admission of a common humanity.

A man whose execution at Oran in Algeria the poet Thomas Campbell witnessed in 1835 was an army deserter. He came out unflinchingly to face the firing squad of a dozen soldiers. 'He threw away the cigar he had been smoking, and I could see its red end fading into blackness, like a foregoing symbol of life's extinction.' The speech he was allowed to make was 'more piercingly and terribly touching than I ever heard from human lips' (Campbell, vol 2, pp 187ff).

When Conrad chose a Spaniard for *The Rescue* and its test of nerves, he must have had in mind the special gift that Spain has shown for breeding men equal to such ordeals, whether as sacrifice or as killer. In the first Carlist War, in the 1830s, the best Carlist forces were organised in Navarre by a leader named Zumalacárregui, who seems to have been endowed with a touch of true genius. He was not wantonly cruel, like Cabrera, but for him too the demands of war were inexorable. A foreigner in his camp tells of how, when some prisoners were about to be executed, the general noticed that one of them, a schoolmaster, was looking for a light, for a last smoke. He took his own cigar from his mouth and handed it to this man, who lit one from it, returned it with a polite bow, and prepared to die (Ford, p 339).

In 1839 the civil war ended, leaving in power General Espartero, head or figurehead of the more advanced of the two Liberal or anti-Carlist factions. In 1841 a rising of the more right-wing party broke out in the army. It was a fiasco, but furnished some martyrs for the 'Moderado' cause. One was the youthful chief Diego de León, who in his last hour was a giver instead of, like so many others, a receiver.

> [He] rode in an open carriage out of the Toledo gate of Madrid flaunting the crimson uniform and flamingo plumes of his old Princes hussars, and distributed to his executioners the cigars which may now be admired in the military museum.

His testament, written in the condemned cell, was soon widely read (Christiansen, p 108).

On 20 April 1963, Julian Grimau was led out into a prison courtyard. He had been on the Republican side in the civil war, and at his farcical trial proudly admitted having been a communist for 27 years. Even in fascist Spain there could be respect for a chivalrous tradition. Grimau was given a cigarette to smoke, and shot.

In the wars of South American independence from Spain a young poet, Melgar, of a distinguished Peruvian family, joined the cause of freedom. Years later Sir Clements Markham heard the story of his death from his brother. He was captured, condemned, and led out to be shot. A priest in attendance was commissioned to whisper to him an offer of pardon if he would betray his comrades' plans. He grew agitated, and reproached the priest for dangling temptation before him. 'Then, turning to his executioners, he said, – "Will anyone give me a cigar, for the love of God." One was handed to him. He smoked about half, and then threw it away. His countenance had again become calm and unruffled. He gave the signal to fire, and in another moment had breathed his last.' In Markham's time a song about his death was still sung by the ladies of Arequipa (Markham, pp 57-8).

In face of an end like this it may be not irreverent to recall Lear's words –

> Upon such sacrifices, my Cordelia,
> The gods themselves throw incense.

And after all, when these words were first spoken Shakespeare's auditors were puffing at their pipes. But for simple pathos, the rawest misery of the human condition, no heroic exit may seem as poignant as one we hear of from a photographer out in the Arctic with his camera. In an icy igloo he found and photographed a helpless old woman, left abandoned by the harsh but inevitable custom of her people. She sat motionless and silent, in threadbare clothing. 'I put some tobacco into her soapstone pipe, but she was too weak to suck on it. By next morning she had died of cold and hunger' (Harrington, p 128).

10

Men of Action

The greater part of Men make their way with ... the same animal eagerness as the Hawk. The Hawk wants a Mate, so does the Man ... They both want a nest ... they get their food in the same manner – The noble animal Man for his amusement smokes his pipe – the Hawk balances about the clouds ...

Keats, Spring 1819 (Letters, p 236)

Peter the Great was one of the first great men of action to be also a great smoker; Pushkin depicts him, at a convivial gathering, playing chess with an English skipper, each saluting the other with salvoes of tobacco fumes (p 441). Frederick the Great showed his greatness by having waistcoat pockets to hold a quantity of snuff worthy of a great man. He was also one of the early collectors of snuff-boxes. But it is Napoleon who stands out as the first grand snuff-taker. We see him, in his minister Count Molé's account of him, presiding over his Council of State – hunched in his chair, talking in his jerky energetic fashion, careless of logic, often absent-minded, with

> that long, small gold snuff box which he was always mechanically opening to help himself to a pinch of snuff, which he took quite noiselessly, and most of which fell on the white lapel of his uniform until it was quite dusted with it, and last but not least the mechanical movement of his arm in handing back the snuff box to the chamberlain, who soon filled it up and returned it. (p 84)

He carried a snuff-box with him to the battlefield. At Waterloo in a pause of exhaustion he betrayed his uneasiness 'by taking copious pinches of snuff. He mounted his horse and rode to the front, receiving there the cheers of his blood-stained lancers and battered infantry.' Meanwhile many of the Dutch or Flemish troops in Wellington's army had – much more sensibly, one must say – removed to the shelter of some trees behind the front, where an English officer saw whole companies lounging, '"fires blazing under cooking kettles, while men lay about smoking!"' (Rose, chap 40).

In the year of peace between Napoleon's first abdication and his return from Elba, Samuel Rogers the literary banker seized, as many other Britons did, the first chance for a dozen years of a visit to France. He was conducted through the palace of St Cloud by an old body-servant of its former occupant. 'He never changed his servants', according to this informant.

> A new face was death to him . . . A mouse stirring would wake him . . . Walked fast with eyes on the ground and his hands joined behind . . . Ate little at dinner, some bouillon, some poulard, that was all, his snuff-box by his side. Beaucoup de tabac, beaucoup de café. (Clayden, vol 1, p 169)

Napoleon III, his nephew, smoked cigarettes; an unroyal thing to do in those days, but he had grown up in exile, knocking about the world, a conspirator in Italy, a special constable in London, a State prisoner in France – he had even been in the USA – so it was no wonder he had picked up plebeian habits. He was Britain's ally in the Crimean War, however, and on 5 September 1854, Prince Albert, who was visiting him at Boulogne, wrote to Queen Victoria:

> The Emperor thaws more and more. This evening after dinner I withdrew with him to his sitting-room for half an hour before rejoining his guests, in order that he might smoke his cigarette, in which occupation, to his amazement, I could not keep him company. (Martin, T., vol 3, p 103)

Bismarck, the man destined to overthrow him, was a Prussian squire, contemptuous of cigarettes, though he lived to see them entering court life when his old master's grandson, the Kaiser Bill of 1914, sat on the throne. It was a dictum of Bismarck's (a person who in youth thought nothing of swimming across the Rhine after dinner and a bottle of port) that a man should not dream of dying before he had drunk five thousand bottles of champagne and smoked a hundred thousand cigars.

Mazzini's birthplace, and now museum or burial place, in the Via Lomellini at Genoa, holds among its relics two clay pipes, one quite elaborate, with what looks like an amber mouthpiece and three small classical figures perched on the stem, one playing a harp. But it was as a cigarette smoker that his acquaintances knew him. Among them were the Carlyles. 'He lived almost in squalor', Carlyle said after his death. 'His health was poor from the first; he took no care of it. He used to smoke a great deal, and drink coffee with bread crumbled in it' (Wilson and MacArthur, pp 248-9). Life, health, revolutionary plots, patriotic hopes, all went up in smoke.

Another of the fellow smokers whom Carlyle took an interest in – an extraordinary contrast with Mazzini – was the Paraguayan dictator Francia, about whom he wrote a long essay. Of the two, he could feel with Francia, a strong man instead of a dreamer, an enlightened despot such as Carlyle would have liked to be, living among a nation of blockheads as Carlyle felt himself to be living. 'Only persons of no understanding being near him for the most part, he had to content himself with silence, a meditative cigar and cup of _maté_. O Francia, though thou hadst to execute forty persons, I am not without some pity for thee!' (Carlyle, 'Francia', p 297). Carlyle quotes from two Europeans who had ventured into Paraguay the dictator's private routine. He is up before dawn; a Negro brings the tea apparatus, and he prepares for himself, with studious care, his maté tea. Then he walks in the portico, 'and smokes a cigar, which he first takes care to unroll, in order to ascertain there is nothing dangerous in it, though it is his own sister who makes-up his cigars for him.' After dinner a siesta, followed by tea and cigar, 'with the same precautions as in the morning' (pp 294-5). An explosive cigar would have been no Christmas cracker joke in Francia's country.

Another remote, isolated ruler was Gordon, as governor-general at Khartoum, toiling at business in the equatorial heat. 'He chain-smoked fat cigarettes, rolled by a *cavasse* standing behind his chair with one ready to slip between his fingers when he silently held up a hand for it.' As the Sudan fell, gradually and then more and more quickly, into the hands of the Mahdi, and the rebel hosts closed in on Khartoum, Gordon sat there, smoking; the day before his death he sat all day in his palace, and then on till midnight, smoking (Trench, pp 142, 255, 289).

Of the colossi bestriding our own century, which has seen far too many, Stalin had his pipe; Churchill, a duke's grandson, was never seen without a cigar; Mao, from a middle-peasant family, was content with a cigarette, and wanted it so badly that at Yenan after the Long March he grew tobacco himself – the only Great Man known to have done so – near his cave, and so fulfilled the obligation laid on all Party office-holders to perform some manual labour. Only Hitler smoked nothing; in his last and most virulently wicked years he kept himself going by being injected daily with chemicals. Kemal Pasha or Atatürk, founder of modern Turkey, shared Mao's love. One day in 1936 he dropped in at a ministry of education tea party, taking a group of foreign scholars by surprise, and grilled them for two-and-a-half hours on the subject of etymology. (Language reform was part of the modernising programme.) He addressed most of his questions to Sir Denison Ross, who answered in Turkish, or when words failed him in French, and who was fascinated by his 'marvellous eyes'. All the time Atatürk smoked cigarettes, and drank cold water and finally a cup of coffee. 'We in the front circle had as many cigarettes as we wanted, but nothing else' (pp 235-6)

To common thinking a man of action is first and foremost a man at arms, and Marshal Ney is said to have led cavalry charges with a cigar in his mouth or hand. Fighting men can safely be said to belong to a calling with a professional debt to tobacco, ever since this came in sight. Their life is an unnatural one, with as a rule little mental activity to sustain it. An old colonel of Balzac's, for example, reduced to poverty in the years after 1815, has to try to prove his identity in order to claim an inheritance. He interviews a lawyer, who ends by giving him a letter, with two 20-franc pieces slipped into it. Outside he stops to look at it under a street lamp. It is the first gold he has touched for nine years; his first thought – 'Je vais donc pouvoir fumer des cigares!' (Balzac, *Chabert*, p 40).

A Frenchman who was with General Lamoricière on a tour during the conquest of Algeria describes him sitting after breakfast in a vast marble hall, and, 'smoking cigars without end', conversing with his senior officers (Castellane, vol 2, p 112). A British officer was with General de Jourville in a later phase of French operations. In the cool night air the camp came to life. 'Bright specks here and there might be seen, marking the lucky possessors of cigars'; Jourville, he felt certain, 'would try to smoke a last cigar, if he knew he were sure to be shot before he could quite finish it'. On one occasion there was a sudden interruption, the cries of captured women as 'the far-famed prophetess Lalla Fathma', who had been inspiring the resistance, was brought in (Walmsley, p 365). A more attractive picture is cited by Cunninghame-Graham from an Englishman who served as a volunteer in the Venezuelan struggle for freedom from Spain. He disliked Venezuela, but admired the leader, General Páez. After the day's marching or fighting 'Páez would be seen dancing with his people in the ring formed for that purpose, smoking with them, drinking from the same cup, and lighting the fresh segar from the one in the mouth of his fellow soldier' (*Páez*, pp 103-4).

It is astonishing to remember that the first Portuguese sailed to India, the first Spaniards to America, with no tobacco smoke to speed them over the waves. In spite of this it is hard to resist a conviction that the expansion of Europe could not have been kept going without its aid. Seamen were ill fed, and doomed on those interminable voyages – as long today as the journey from earth to Venus – to celibacy, with harsh maritime discipline to worsen it. By contrast, Herman Melville's shipmate in the US navy, the foretopman 'Landless', was always cheerfully carefree, though always in trouble, his back covered with the scars of many floggings. He shed no tears, but spat out instead 'the golden juice of a weed, wherewith he solaced and comforted his ignominious days. "Rum and tobacco!" said Landless, "what more does a sailor want?"' (*White Jacket*, chap 90).

'Smoke all day and take no exercise', was Joseph Chamberlain's prescription for success in political life, and tobacco has undoubtedly meant much to modern politicians as a class. They lead lives of busy, mostly empty, activity; smoke helps to pump up the flaccid balloon. Gladstone was an outstanding exception. Still a boy at Eton, he persuaded a friend to give up smoking. His secretary Algernon West records an incident that occurred when the two of them were staying at Walmer Castle with Lord Granville, a pillar of the Liberal party and at the time Warden of the Cinque Ports. 'As we were walking on the ramparts one evening after dinner we persuaded Mr. Gladstone to smoke a cigarette, but it was a terrible failure. Tobacco to him was an abomination.' He is only known to have made one other attempt, when he took a cigarette out of politeness to the Prince of Wales who was dining with him (p 261).

One of Gladstone's plagues in his last years was Lord Randolph Churchill, who stood at the opposite pole from him in this field as well as politically. In 1885 he became Secretary for India, the youngest member of a Tory cabinet. One day the Queen enquired 'why the India Office box had reached Balmoral full of grey substance and this was discovered to be ash from the innumerable cigarettes which the highly-strung Lord Randolph had smoked in London'; she 'laughed heartily' (Leslie, p 103). Since those days a number of British politicians, like Baldwin and Wilson, have made a parade of their pipes, as more democratical than the cigar, more solidly John Bullish than the cigarette.

However, more flamboyant airs have been cultivated, privately at least, by some foreigners. Lassalle, the German socialist, strewed his Berlin flat in the early 1860s with Turkish hookahs and small tables laden with all kinds of smoking materials (Schiroauer, p 222). Karl Radek, a shining light of the communist movement until extinguished by the Stalin whom he had eulogised, was described in 1918 as a small spectacled man with a big head, a huge pipe or cigar always in his mouth.

> As he jaunts from the Dom Sovietov to his office, an English cap on his head, his pipe puffing fiercely, a revolver strapped to his side and a bundle of books under his arm, he looks like a cross between a bandit and a professor. (Radek, p xiv)

A successful politician must have a good deal of the diplomat in him. A diplomat 'lies abroad for the good of his country'; a politician lies at home for the good of his party, and few men have been so completely immersed in the business of diplomacy, or in tobacco smoke, as G.W.F. Villiers, fourth Earl of Clarendon. 'Throughout his life', says his biographer, he kept the love of cigarettes he acquired at Madrid in the 1830s, a taste then almost unknown in England; and he 'turned night into day, and day, or the best part of it, into night', working till 4 or 5 am. 'The tradition still lingers in Downing Street how, when Foreign Minister, he used to sit down to a batch of papers with a bundle of cigarettes beside him, which was usually finished before the papers' (Maxwell, H., vol 1, p 109).

A foreign minister of our more limelight-loving era, and later premier until removed and hanged by the army, was Mr Bhutto of Pakistan. As befitted a wealthy landowner he went in for expensive European clothes and refreshments; he liked good cigars, and was fond of dipping them in choice brandy while smoking. In 1965 as Foreign Minister he was prominently identified with the brief war with India over Kashmir. When Pakistan was compelled to accept Soviet mediation and agree to terms at the Tashkent conference which left Kashmir in Indian hands, Bhutto submitted reluctantly. At the ceremonial signing of the Tashkent Declaration of peaceful intentions, he was reported by Indian journalists to have shown his ill-humour in an undignified way, by blowing contemptuous smoke rings, until called to order by his leader, President Ayub (Taseer, pp 68, 197).

Diplomats try to ferret out one another's official secrets; detectives ferret out those of the criminal classes, which are apt to be about equally disreputable. Nearly all the detectives of fiction and screen, from Sherlock Holmes onward, seem to have been incessant smokers. Whether or not detectives of flesh and blood consume so much nicotine, the fictional image shows how ready the man in the street is to feel that systematic thinking must be impossible without some artificial stimulus. We regard mental activity, by detective or philosopher or anyone else, as unnatural. By emitting volumes of smoke our mystery-solvers advertise the extreme complexity of their task and the intensity of their exertions. Concentrated thinking requires a concentrated atmosphere, as Holmes once said to Watson in some of the silliest words he was ever guilty of.

Conan Doyle was a doctor as well as writer, and Watson a doctor as well as Holmes's partner. Medical men have been notorious smokers, and few – till lately – have grudged them the indulgence. Many might be critical of the army surgeon who, after the storming of a Maori stockade in a war of 1863, skinned 'an old tattooed chief who was found on a nearby spur just after dying of wounds ... to make a tobacco pouch from the "beautiful *rapa*, or spiral pattern over his buttocks"' (Scott, D., p 19). (Some nurses too must have felt the soothing call of tobacco, like Charlotte Brontë's Mrs Horsfall, a 'dragon' from whom others fled, and who 'took her dram three times a day, and her pipe of tobacco four times' (*Shirley*, chap 32).)

Actors and entertainers, too, have very often been drawn to tobacco; they also lead strenuous and stressful lives. Their audiences may slip through their fingers as unexpectedly as a doctor's patients. Like statesmen they live by conjuring up a world of illusion, and the free-floating eddies of smoke round them may help them to feel that their spells are dissolving all resistant disbelief. On the first night of *Lady Windermere's Fan* Oscar Wilde appeared in front of the curtain, opera hat in one hand, a lighted cigarette in the other, to congratulate the audience on its intelligent appreciation of his play (Le Gallienne, p 263). On the last night of *A Woman of No Importance* he was at the Haymarket with a pair of friends, all three with clusters of vine-leaf in their hair. But Max Beerbohm said in a letter that he had never seen Oscar look so fatuous, as he 'waved his cigarette round and round his head' (Jullian, p 250).

And that twentieth-century phenomenon, the cinema, has combined many of the effects and resources of fiction and visual art. No one was more inventive in his use of them, and of smoking tricks among many others, than Charlie Chaplin, from his earliest films to some of the latest. There is a brilliant stroke in *City Lights* (1931), for example, when Chaplin the tramp, ejected from his patron's house, is driving off in the Rolls-Royce given him in a drunken freak. Seeing a half-smoked cigar on the ground, he stops and jumps out to snatch it, jostling aside another vagrant who was about to pick it up, and drives away with it between his lips, while the other man stares after the car in bewilderment.

Chaplin was librettist, composer, director, as well as actor. Some unpublished memoirs of one of his leading ladies, the charming Georgia of his finest farce, *The Gold Rush*, recall that 'While working he smoked incessantly.' He noticed that she seemed to feel no need of it, and added,

> 'I don't like to see a girl smoke.' I answered, 'Really, I don't care about seeing a man smoke either.' He said, with a finality, 'I'm stopping here and now.' Then he proceeded to throw all his packages of cigarettes into the waste-paper basket. This scene and dialogue were repeated many times during our companionship.

They were on a boat trip to Catalina Island, near Hollywood, when Chaplin lost his temper with a man who came and sat in front of them, puffing cigarette smoke that blew into their faces. He began talking, louder and louder, about this man's rudeness, and the evils of smoking, as virtuously as if he himself had never smoked. 'His voice filled the deck . . . everyone's eyes were on the man. He arose and silently stole away.' But Chaplin did turn into a confirmed non-smoker, and would expatiate on the risks of cancer long before they became accepted doctrine. 'Later, when he lived in Switzerland, he'd sometimes make his guests freeze by opening the windows to let the fumes escape' (Epstein, p 52).

Thought and Fancy

He snuffed and smoked cigars and drank liquors, and talked in the most indescribable style . . . Now and then he sank in to a brown study, and seemed dead in the eye of law. About two o'clock he was sitting in this state smoking languidly, his nose begrimed with snuff, his face hazy and inert, – till he suddenly asked his young host: 'I hope, Mr. Gordon, you don't believe in universal damnation?'

> Carlyle on John Wilson ('Christopher North'), Professor of Moral
> Philosophy, at a party (Froude, *Carlyle*, vol 2, pp 412-13)

If men of action have needed tobacco, the activities of the mind seem to have called for it at least as insistently. There may be evidence here that these two spheres of human effort have more in common than appears on the surface, just as men and women have, or Eskimos and Brahmins – or even, despite a wider gap than either, rich and poor.

Among earlier modern philosophers Hobbes is reported to have been a devoted smoker, whose pipe partnered his thinking and writing; he survived, none the less, to the age of 92. Tom Paine, as much a preacher of liberty as Hobbes of authority, may be said to have had the closest tie with tobacco of any philosopher, since during his years at Lewes he married a shopkeeper's daughter and took over the business, largely in tobacco; the awkward thought can hardly have escaped him that some of the wares he had sold were the product of slave labour.

But it was the rise of German metaphysics that established the link in people's minds between pipe smoking and a shaggy, absent-minded type of professor, usually German, sinking into profundities of cloudy thought amid rolling billows of pipe smoke. And indeed it may not be fanciful to suppose a psychological influence of this smoke on the mysteries of Germanic philosophy. Marx and Engels, it is true, heirs to Hegel's dialectic yet combining in themselves the impulses of thought and action, theory and practice, were also voracious smokers. In a great deal of his work Marx's companions were tobacco and midnight oil, as his son-in-law Paul Lafargue observed.

> 'Capital', he said to me once, 'will not even pay for the cigars I smoked writing it.' But he was still heavier on matches. He so often forgot his pipe or cigar that he emptied an incredible number of boxes of matches in a short time to relight them. (Anon., *Reminiscences*, p 7)

Tobacco could find a place in Marx's economics, or in a love letter. 'A volume of Propertius and eight ounces of snuff may have the same exchange value . . .' (Prawer, p 304). His eyes, he wrote to his wife in 1856, 'however spoiled by lamplight and tobacco', still showed her to him lovingly, in dreams or awake (Siegel, p 288). His youngest daughter Eleanor was given a packet of cigarettes by a friend in 1875, just before her 21st birthday, perhaps in its honour (Kapp, p 173).

All but volume 1 of *Capital* was left to Engels to sort out and edit, with much strain on his eyesight; Marx's handwriting was as incomprehensible as the academic philosopher's thinking. Indeed at one point Engels thought he had found the cause of his sore eyes in excessive use of fertiliser on the tobacco fields his cigars came from, and changed to other brands. But two years later he was feeling that he must take a summer rest by the seaside; he would try, he said, 'to put myself in condition again to be able to smoke a cigar which I have not done for more than two months, about a gramme of tobacco every other day being as much as I can stand' (Engels, *Lafargue*, vol 2, pp 43-4, 275-6). Another who worked his way from German – and Greek – philosophy to a version of his own of socialism, and with the same vital assistance, was Lassalle. He was labouring at his book on Heraclitus, he wrote to his father, and in the last three days had got through 7 pens and 39 cigars, and was feeling fagged (Schiroauer, p 96).

Marx and Engels proclaimed their theories of socialism to be 'scientific'; a good many scientists have shared their addiction to nicotine. Newton is said to have been one of these. Freud paid the penalty for his love of smoking with the cancer of the mouth that killed him. How much tobacco meant to Darwin is clear from the details recorded of his daily life. He learned to take snuff while a student at Edinburgh, and in a youthful letter, after giving it up for a month, he confessed to feeling 'most lethargic, stupid, and melancholy'. Smoking he picked up while riding over the pampas with the gauchos, 'and I have heard him speak', says his chronicler, 'of the great comfort of a cup of *maté* and a cigarette when he halted after a long ride, and was unable to get food for some time.' In later life 'He only smoked when resting, whereas snuff was a stimulant, and taken during working hours.' To check overindulgence he sometimes kept the snuff-jar outside his study, so that to take a pinch he had to get up and go for it (Darwin, *Autobiography*, Appendix 1).

German students, of what may be called their great age, between the 'War of Liberation' from Napoleon in 1813-14 and the revolutions of 1848, must have spent a good part of their money on tobacco, and may be supposed to have been sometimes aping their learned seniors, and borrowing the motto 'I smoke, therefore I think'. 'A common amusement at the German Universities', Coleridge found, was 'for a number of young men to smoke out a Candle – i.e. to fill a room with Tobacco-smoke till the Candle goes out' (*Collected Letters*, pp 462-3). (Professorial philosophy might be called by analogy a game of filling the world with ink so as to drown the candle of common sense.) Scott thought of the academic tribe of his day as good at Greek, 'connoisseurs in tobacco, and not wholly ignorant of the mystery of punch-making', but deficient in the higher faculties (letter to J. Villiers, 6 April 1821). Their pupils emulated them in some if not all of these pursuits. Trollope's young man at Oxford tells his aunt, Lady de Courcy, that he is determined not to get plucked in the examination, like his friend Baker.

> 'He got among a set of men who did nothing but smoke and drink beer. Malthusians, we call them.'
> 'Malthusians!'
> '"Malt", you know, aunt, and "use", meaning that they drink beer.'
> (*Doctor Thorne*, chap 5)

At Cambridge I remember the mathematician Littlewood, always companionable, telling me that he used formerly to start his morning's work after breakfast by filling five pipes, to be smoked one after the other. Mathematicians have often had an expert knowledge of music, and composers have often shared the fondness of many of them for tobacco. Young Ernest Pontifex in *The Way of All Flesh*, for example, was thrilled to hear from an aged rector that he had known Dr Burney, the musicologist – 'for he knew that Dr Burney, when a boy at school at Chester, used to break bounds that he might watch Handel smoking his pipe in the Exchange coffee-house' (Butler, *All Flesh*, chap 37). Bach would invite a visitor, after dazzling him with a display on the harpsichord, to join him in a soothing pipe. A poem by him on smoking has survived.

Mozart carried a snuff-box, but thick tobacco smoke poisoned him. A letter to his father from Augsburg in October 1777 tells of a clavichord maker who, after hearing him play, embraced him and carried him off to a coffee-house. 'When I entered I thought that I should drop down, overcome by the stink and fumes of tobacco. But with God's help I had to stand it for an hour; and I pretended to enjoy it all, though it seemed to me as if we were in Turkey' (p 316). Mozart could relish a quiet pipe on his own, at any rate in his later years; in one of his last letters he told his wife how he had played a game of billiards with himself – 'then I told Joseph to get Primus to fetch me some black coffee, with which I smoked a splendid pipe of tobacco; and then I orchestrated nearly the whole of' the rondo of the clarinet concerto (7 October 1791, p 967).

Beethoven, for his part, enjoyed an occasional small pipe while working. And there is a story of Schubert welcoming a youngster, taken to see him one morning, by playfully puffing smoke at him from a long pipe. When Brahms visited him in his sanatorium, after his mental collapse, Schumann complained of cigars sent him being purloined, or failing to reach him. We hear of Wagner singing at the piano for friends until his snuff was all used up, and then exclaiming petulantly: 'No more snuff – no more music.' And there was an anxious period in Sibelius's life when he was being treated for a suspected cancer, and had to give up cigars, which he found a wrench. A musical comedy of 1904 by Herbert Haines, *The Catch of the Season*, had a song, 'Cigarette', that for a while was on all lips. Stravinsky's spacious studio at Hollywood was furnished with what has been called 'obsessional ritualisation'; one of the tables was devoted to boxes of cigarettes, lighters, holders, flints, pipe cleaners (Storr, p 131).

Artists at work, by comparison with composers, may have found snuff more convenient than smoking. Sir Joshua Reynolds, for example, when provoked, only shifted his ear-trumpet, and took snuff. A contemporary of Sir Joshua's was the eccentric sculptor Nollekens, of whom we read that 'He took snuff, but seldom used his handkerchief.' He chewed tobacco, of any kind, usually taken from his workmen's iron box; he got snuff mostly from visitors, apologising for having left his own box in a coat pocket (Smith, J.T., chap 20). A friend of Turner's says that in his later years the great painter suffered from sore gums, and his teeth deserted him. '"He was very fond of smoking and yet had a great objection to any one knowing of it. His diet was principally at that time rum and milk"' (Lindsay, p 197). Daumier, on the contrary, did not mind being seen with an elegant little pipe, and some of his brilliant caricatures were of smokers or snuffers.

Artists, whether themselves addicts or not, were often in fact fond of such subjects. Frans Hals painted a nameless smoker holding his pipe and smiling broadly; Teniers liked to do genre pictures of Dutch boors puffing away in their beer-houses. In fact there was for long a tendency, as in literature, to give such scenes a moralising turn. Jan Steen's tavern scene (in Norwich Castle) has a fat woman dozing off, an empty glass in her hand, while a man behind puffs smoke at her indignantly from his clay pipe. In the same painter's 'Evils of Intemperance' (in the National Gallery) a youngish woman, a stall-keeper, is slumped on the ground in tipsy oblivion, a long pipe dangling from her hand; children stand round, jeering.

One 18th-century fashion was the pastoral, which might be romantic or humorous. Gainsborough's 'Peasant Smoking at a Cottage Door' (1788) shows him with pipe and family, at peace with a world suggested by an attractive background of hill and trees, while, in 'The Catastrophe', by Morland (1791), a horse has fallen at a ford, and its bald middle-aged rider is sprawling on the ground, while a yokel, pipe in mouth, and his stout wife stare in consternation. But portrait-painting was to leave the pastoral behind, and to grow increasingly sophisticated; even so, it too found room for tobacco. Typical of one phase is a man of Byronic aspect, painted by Monvel; he is standing, with long dark hair, open neck, left hand in pocket, the other holding a half-smoked cigar. In the Toulouse-Lautrec collection at Albi is an 1893 portrait of Louis Pascal, a middle-aged gentleman standing erect, a top hat adding to his altitude, cane under arm, cigar in moustached mouth, the embodiment of bourgeois self-satisfaction. Renoir painted a well-dressed trio at the end of an opulent restaurant meal, one woman sitting, another standing, a handsome bearded man lighting a cigarette, his profile and its glowing tip turned towards us.

Cézanne's pipe smoker, seen sideways at the café table, on the other hand, is a return to a simpler, less prosperous world. It has been remarked that the *Naïf* group of French painters, in search of an artless naturalistic style, had a liking for similar subjects (Jakovsky, p 15). Someone in England produced a picture called 'A Pinch of Snuff', an attempt to show a snuff-taker in the very act of sneezing; 'the result', says someone who saw it, 'was not very satisfactory' (Nevill, p 177). At the opposite end from such realism was a growing taste for the exotic, as Europeans moved out across a world which oftener than not they saw through a glass, darkly. It afforded new footholds for tobacco, and the hookah caught the spirit of Orientalism perfectly. John Lewis (1805-76) spent a decade at Cairo, in search of local colour; his 'Pipe-Bearer' is a black attendant holding an ornate hookah as he stands beside his tall Arab master. (Easterners had meanwhile been learning to paint themselves and their pipe dreams. Under the Mughuls, Muslim India had shaken off the Islamic taboo against the human form in art, and their successors, many petty hill-rulers among them, survive in the charming miniatures of the 18th century. Each sits with his ornate hookah beside him, its coiling pipe in his hand; it has become almost a part of the insignia of royalty, like the sceptre in Europe. Their consorts are painted with the same accompaniment, as in the elegant 'Princess and Her Ladies by the Lake', painted about 1753 at the northern court of Guler, and now in the Victoria and Albert Museum.)

Exotic in a very different mode was the art hobby of Bodle of Kilmarkeckle, a comic invention of the Scottish novelist John Galt. A laird of old family, his whole life was snuff, and he devoted 20 years to decorating his parlour walls with drawings of birds and beasts, made with a variety of snuffs: his aim was to express the nature of each of them through his choice of tobaccos. 'Linty' snuff, he declared, induced a feeling as of being seated on a green hillock in hay-time, with birds singing in the sunlight. Sadly, when he was helping to lower his daughter into her grave a gust of wind blew away his pinch of canary snuff (Galt, chaps 24, 51).

Pipes and snuff-boxes inspired a true folk art, a lingering into modern times of the creative work of nameless medieval crafts-men; it may be compared with their gargoyles and carvings on misericords in old churches. An example from some Catholic region is a papier mâché snuff-box whose lid exhibits a monk smuggling a girl into the monastery, hidden in a sheaf of corn on his back (Libert, p 22). In early 19th-century England there was a vogue – a reflection, it may be, of prevailing moods in the shadow of steam-mills and wars – of pipes adorned with portraits of the Devil, or of Death driving a winged chariot, with a skeleton posti-lion. And in Mayhew's time street-sellers were still carrying stocks of pipes with death's-heads and grinning demons (p 176). A caricature much in demand was one of a huge-nosed Wellington, after his order banning smoking in barracks.

Clay pipes with spectacles of current events could be mass-produced. Frenchmen had a besetting taste for military topics and Napoleons; also for episodes of the revolutions of 1789 and 1830. Every prominent public man of the 19th century was caricatured on the bowl of some pipe or other, often with much ingenuity (Fairholt, pp 180ff; Libert, p 57). In each country patriotic spirit could be fomented by this art, and its reminders of national glories: faces of rulers and heroes, battle scenes, triumphs like William III's descent on Ireland, the Seven Years War victories of Frederick the Great, the Duke of Brunswick driving the French back over the Rhine in 1758 (Phillips, P., pp 63-8).

The English clay pipe, sold by the gross, belonged to an uprooted, urbanised population, a peasantry proletarianised; the elaborately hand-carved Bavarian pipe was the work of peasants or village craftsmen whiling away their winter leisure, for themselves and then for a widening market of connoisseurs. In those carvings a thousand fantasies, wishes, alarms, may be seen coming to life amid the curling smoke. A bamboo stem a yard long terminates in a hand holding a metal-crowned skull three inches high. A fight between lion and crocodile; a horse and rider perched on a stem, the animal's nose just above the bowl, as if savouring the smell; many Red Indian and Turk heads, feathered or turbaned; on a short clay stem a man seated cross-legged at a round table with a tankard on it; a seaman stepping over an anchor. There is no end to the wealth of motifs in this art akin to the toymaker's.

On other continents other pre-industrial artists were turning out miniature works of art as remarkable as any of Europe's. Earthenware pipes of the Iroquois and Algonquian tribes of eastern Canada sometimes had bowls modelled into bird or human heads, facing towards the smoker. Out on the plains, human figures and bears were common, or an owl might perch on the rim. On the Pacific coast pipes of carved argillite, made for sale to white men, shone in artistic style as much as in technical resource.

Often they depicted the newcomers' dress, dwellings, machines, steamboats, as well as figures from mythology; a pipe might have its stem ornamented with a wonderfully exact imitation of a ship's rigging. A very striking one, from before 1913, has men and bears along the stem: one bear, on its back, grips a man with all its four paws, with his head in its mouth, while another squats with its front paws resting on the bowl (Wyatt, pp 9,42, 60-62). In western Africa a kindred art was flowering: some massive pipe-bowls had stylised figures on them, or faces with a touch of the demonic, resembling those made famous by African masks. Others had long stems decorated with metal rings or small pierced coins.

Tobacco has endowed writers with wings; it seems also to inspire readers with faith in them, to judge by the frequency with which a modern author's photograph appears, on the jacket of his book, together with his pipe and an assurance that he is married and has three children. All this apparently is to be taken as a guarantee of his reliability; another mark of the popular association between mental activity and tobacco smoke. From authors to their paymasters tobacco may be supposed to have spread by natural contagion. In the early 1860s the publisher Macmillan held a weekly 'tobacco parliament' – an echo of King Frederick William's – for his quill-drivers (Murray, K.M.E., p 141). In the 1890s we hear from Richard Le Gallienne, a 'prentice writer then, of another such gathering, always animated and 'with the usual humanizing accompaniments of tobacco and whisky-and-soda' (p 165).

Dekker was one of the first English writers to appreciate the importance of the newcomer from across the Atlantic, though his opinion of it sounds ambiguous when, instead of invoking the Muse, he calls on the god of tobacco – 'thou beggarly Monarche of _Indians_, and setter-up of rotten-lungd chimneysweepers' – to help him to give 'the phantastick _Englishmen_' a greater knowledge of leaf and flavour than 'the whitest toothd Blackamoore in all Asia' (_Hornbook_, pp 12-13). And Milton is said to have smoked a pipe and drunk a glass of water before his early bed; at his widow's death his Bible and tobacco box were found among her possessions (Hansford, p 199). Molière could sound as enthusiastic about snuff as Falstaff about sack. His *Don Juan* opens with a speech by Sganarelle, the part he took himself, holding a snuff-box: 'Whatever Aristotle and all the philosophers may say, there's nothing to equal tobacco; it's the passion of all decent folk, and a man who lives without it doesn't deserve to live.'

It is surprising, on the other hand, that Burns's letters reveal so little interest in tobacco, which ought to have been invaluable to a man of his restless temperament. (It was the Third or 'Tobacco' Division of the Customs that he was posted to at Dumfries.) Boswell tried smoking, briefly; Johnson never did, though he could praise it as a sedative. Of one of the poets included in his *Lives*, John Philips, he says: 'I have been told that he was in company silent and barren, and employed only upon the pleasures of his pipe'; this devotion failed to raise him above a very humble literary rank.

Scott's changing feelings, the drying up of an old fountain of comfort, can be tracked through his letters and diaries. He sounds a resolute smoker when in 1819 he writes to his army son, at Cork –

> As you Hussars smoke, I will give you one of my pipes, but you must let me know how I can send it safely. It is a very handsome one, though not my best. I will keep my *Meer-schaum* until I make my continental tour, and then you shall have that also. (4 September 1819; Lockhart, *Scott*, chap 45)

On 24 February 1829, he is not pleased at having to drive 8 miles to dinner with someone, and getting no work done. 'Smoked a cigar on my return, being very cold' (*Journal*). A month later, on 17 March, after his solitary meal he gets through the last two hours of his solitary work by smoking, 'which I find a sedative without being a stimulant'. Next year, on 26 May, 'I have laid aside smoking much; and now, unless tempted by company, rarely take a cigar. I was frightened by a species of fit which I had in February.' He adds to this entry: 'Well, be it what it will, I can stand it.' Without any bombast Scott can sound at times as much a hero as any of his characters. By 1831 all is over. He is on an invalid diet; 'after dinner I am allowed half a glass of whisky or gin made into weak grog. I never wish for more, nor do I in my secret soul long for cigars, though once so fond of them' (16 March 1831, *Journal*).

A Romantic ought to be romantic about his pipe; but the only one of the English Romantics who was truly a disciple was Charles Lamb. (It seems to have been the actor Macready who heard his celebrated saying that he would like to draw in his last breath through a pipe and exhale it in a pun.) He had the unluckiest life of them all, and needed the comforter most. Only an occasional versifier, he was never more a poet than in his 'Farewell to Tobacco'. He was always making good resolutions about giving it up, not for the last time on 28 September 1805, when he sent this poem to Wordsworth and talked hopefully about his writing plans – hitherto only

> an idle brag or two of an evening, vapouring out of a pipe, and going off in the morning; but now I have bid farewell to my 'sweet enemy', Tobacco, I shall perhaps set nobly to work ... Tobacco has been my evening comfort and my morning curse for these five years. (vol 1, p 240)

Coleridge wrote to his wife from Ratzeburg on 14 January 1799 that he was learning from German example what 'a great addition to the comforts of Life' a pipe after breakfast was: he meant to smoke at no other time when back home, though at present he was taking a whiff four times daily (*Collected Letters*, p 462). But how odd an effect smoking could have on him stands out in the story, which Hazlitt quoted as characteristic,

> of his being asked to a party at Birmingham, of his smoking tobacco after dinner and going to sleep on a sofa, where the company found him, to their no small surprise, which was increased to wonder when he started up of a sudden, and rubbing his eyes, looked about him, and launched into a three hours' description of the third heaven, of which he had had a dream. ('My First Acquaintance with the Poets')

Coleridge's pipe did not always propel him to celestial heights, however. 'I smoked yesterday afternoon', he wrote in a letter of 1795, 'and then imprudently went into the Sea – the Consequence was that on my return I was taken sick – and my triumphant Tripes cataracted most Niagara-ishly' (*Collected Letters*, p 163). Possibly as a result of miscarriages like this, he had transferred his allegiance to snuff, by the time De Quincey came to know him, in 1807. Coleridge was then living at Nether Stowey, in Somerset, where his neighbour Lord Egremont one day brought him 'a canister of peculiarly fine snuff which Coleridge now took profusely'. He seems to have meant it as a spur to composition, for he lamented to a friend that Coleridge was now writing nothing, only talking, and proposed the history of Christianity as a suitable subject (De Quincey, p 10). This work remained unwritten; but to some friends who were denouncing snuff he once indignantly retorted that the human nose might very likely have been created for its reception (*Table Talk*, 4 January 1823).

But if ever a man really smoked with all his might, it was Thomas Carlyle. Whether there was any subterranean, or sub-nasal, connection in his mind between his love of good, cheap tobacco, and his endorsement of Negro slavery, is a question his biographers have not asked. He must have smoked away, beginning at the age of 11, a whole plantation. He suffered chronically from dyspepsia, and once made a journey to Edinburgh to consult a doctor about it. '"It is all *tobacco*, Sir"', was the response;

> 'give up tobacco;' gave it instantly and strictly up; – found, after long months, that I might as well have ridden sixty miles in the opposite direction, and 'poured my sorrows into the long hairy ear of the first jackass I came upon', as into this select medical man's. (*Reminiscences*, p 242)

Carlyle was one of a great many who took refuge in the thought of nicotine when some stern ordeal awaited him. Writing to his Jane about the journey they were to make after their wedding at Haddington to their first home, on Comely Bank in Edinburgh – only 20 miles away – he asked her to let him, 'by the road, as occasion serves, *smoke three cigars* without criticism or reluctance, as things essential to my perfect contentment'. To his credit he added (with a painful effort, we may guess) that if she objected he would submit (Froude, vol 1, p 376).

When they moved to London they had at first no garden, and being forbidden to smoke indoors he had to perch on a cistern in the rear, long pipe in mouth, 'for all the world like the emblem over a tobacconist's door' (Hanson, p 163). In time he got leave to smoke up the chimney. When they went to Chelsea he had a garden seat to smoke on, but it was just below the window of his neighbour, a retired civil servant who abhorred the smell. An angry correspondence broke out, until a tactful acquaintance – a budding diplomat – managed to patch up a compromise: he was to move his seat further away, and the four daughters next door were to remove their piano – a fearful affliction, no doubt – from the party-wall between the houses (Hornby, pp 45-6).

This relief did not keep Carlyle from being always deeply sorry for himself; he had some reason, during his long years of self-imposed and barren toil on his *Frederick the Great*. Relics preserved in his birthplace at Ecclefechan include a small oblong tobacco box, from the 18th century, whose metal lid has a crude effigy of the hero – 'Fredericus Magnus Rex Borussorum'. There is a bigger metal box with a tobacco-chopping apparatus, a cigar-case, and a round embroidered smoking cap, an article that must have been intended to ward off the smell of smoke from the hair, as a smoking jacket did from the clothes.

Carlyle despised poetry, though much of his own prose was highly poetical; yet his companion of many a smoking bout was Alfred Tennyson, a poet as hopelessly dependent on tobacco as himself. Alfred, too, was a pipe smoker from very early days, and of the most abandoned kind, already as a student at Cambridge smoking a 'dreadful shag' whose pungent reek bore down all other pipes at meetings of the Apostles Society (Martin, R.B., p 89). When Tennyson called in her husband's absence one day Jane Carlyle was flattered to find that she could keep him talking to her, as an equal, for three hours, with the aid of brandy and pipes as well as tea (Hanson, p 312). A much less idyllic story, however, is of Lord Lansdowne meeting him in the Cosmopolitan Club, and Tennyson, learning that he was not a smoker, insisting on his trying a whiff from his own dirty clay pipe, dripping with nicotine juice at the mouthpiece. Lansdowne lacked courage to refuse, but shuddered whenever he thought of it. Yet exquisite poetry came into Tennyson's mind, often taking shape from cloudlets of smoke, as he sat composing on a hard wooden chair in a little room at the top of the house. 'His "sacred pipes", as he called them, were half an hour after breakfast, and half an hour after dinner, when no one was allowed to be with him, for then his best thoughts came to him.' 'Hundreds of lines were, as he expressed it, "blown up the chimney" with his pipe-smoke, or were written down and thrown into the fire, as not being then perfect enough' (Tennyson, H., vol 1, pp 377-8, vol 2, p 124).

'No woman should marry a teetotaller or a man who does not smoke'; R.L. Stevenson must have been at least half serious, and have felt that a man with neither of the two grand creature comforts to humanise him *must* be a bad-tempered brute. Smoke hung over his memories of 'Skelt's Juvenile Drama' and its illustrations, prophetic of *Treasure Island* – 'Captain Luff and Bold Bob Bowsprit', an inn parlour with 'red curtains, pipes, spittoons, and eight-day clock . . .' ('Penny Plain'). At San Francisco in 1879 it was noticed that he loved to 'talk and smoke by the hour', despite his weak chest (Nickerson, p 69). But like so many brain-workers he found that his blessing could turn into a curse. Near the end of his life, in 1893, he wrote to a friend about a story he was struggling to finish, and said literature was 'the basest sport in creation': he was feeling 'nearly dead with dyspepsia, over-smoking, and unremunerative overwork' (*Vailima*, p 209).

Nineteenth-century England has a gallery of other smoking writers to exhibit. Thomas Hood, the great punster, wrote touching verses entitled 'My Cigar and I'; Macready the Shakespearian actor had occasion one day to call on Edward Bulwer-Lytton, fashionable novelist and politician and would-be dramatist.

> He was in very handsome chambers in the Albany, dressed, or rather
> _déshabillé_, in the most lamentable style of foppery – a hookah in his
> mouth, his hair, whiskers, tuft, etc., all grievously cared for. (23
> February 1836, vol 1, p 278)

And Thackeray was a 'tobacconist' to the backbone, declaring his
faith in his essay 'Memorials of Gormandizing', when he talked of
two gentlemen he had watched sipping punch in the Café Foy in
Paris. 'Both were silent; both happy; both were smoking cigars, –
for both knew that the soothing plant of Cuba is sweeter to the
philosopher than the prattle of all the women in the world' (_Cathe-
rine_, p 521). Samuel Butler, the novelist, only allowed himself to
smoke in the evening in his staid later years. He would come home
about 9.30, he says, 'have some bread and milk, play two games of
patience, smoke a cigarette and go to bed about 11' (Henderson,
p 202). But George Gissing spoke, through his 'Henry Ryecroft',
of how contentedly in his years of strength he could live in Grub
Street poverty. 'A door that locked, a fire in winter, a pipe of
tobacco – these were things essential; and granted these, I have
been often richly content in the squalidest garret' (Part 1 sec 10).

Hack writers of adventure stories for boys might have as much
need as their betters of the friendly fumes. G.A. Henty worked
with his secretary or assistant Griffith in a study crammed with the
rifles and spears and so on he had collected when a war correspondent.

> Henty, with a well-coloured clay pipe in hand, would recline his mas-
> sive frame on a sofa and begin to dictate: settings, character sketches,
> plot outlines – under a cloud of tobacco smoke a book would take
> shape.

Six thousand words, morning and evening, were reckoned a good
day's work. In 1880 two of the smaller fry fled from London to a
hotel in Margate, where they pawned their clothes for the sake of
costly cigars, iced claret and stout. A friend soon had to be summoned by telegraph to bring a loan. 'I went upstairs', he says, 'and
when I entered their combined room, which reeked of stale
tobacco smoke and beer, they were both sitting at a small table,

writing . . . ' (Dunae, pp 20, 30).

James Russell Lowell's poem in praise of tobacco speaks of how it can stir even 'Arctic regions of the brain' to life and warmth (Sims, p 35); one of the finest touches to be found in the literature of nicotine. Not surprisingly, sundry American writers were roused to eloquence by the theme, but also, like others, learned that smoking has its penalties. For Melville, for example, it was ruined, in his life afloat, by the rule restricting it to the vicinity of the cook's galley on the gun-deck, after meals. It was good to watch the crew gathering there, chatting and joking in the recesses between the cannon, all transformed, 'so long as the vapoury bond united them', into a band of brothers. But he found it disgusting to have the enjoyment cut short at the end of a half-hour, 'when those sedative fumes have steeped you in the grandest of reveries . . . as if from one of Mozart's grandest marches a temple were rising, like Venus from the sea . . .' Rather than this, he gave it up altogether (*White Jacket*, chap 91). A smoker must have liberty to smoke when the mood seizes him.

Among Europeans, Balzac was a cigar enthusiast. Two great poets, Goethe and Heine, detested smoke. But Manet painted Mallarmé holding a cigar; and Baudelaire had the happy idea of making his pipe talk about him, instead of the other way about. I am an author's pipe, its ode begins, and my visage, dark as an Abyssinian or Kaffir woman's, shows what a mighty smoker he is. When he is sorrowful I pour out smoke like the chimney where a labourer's food is being got ready for his return; I cradle his spirit on the blue fumes curling from my mouth . . . (Baudelaire, LXXI). Petőfi the Hungarian poet – a revolutionary of 1848, killed in battle in 1849 – reproaching a friend for not writing, assured him that he was not asking for a long, heavy letter:

> I swear this by whatever I hold dearest in the world,
> By tobacco, by pâtes of white cheese. (no 115, 1847)

In 1882 the critic N.K. Mihaylovski got to know Tolstoy, and found him an agreeable companion. If they got into a too warm argument he would say '"Let us each smoke a cigarette and rest a bit." We smoked cigarettes, and that of course did not end our dispute, but the very fact of interrupting it for a few moments really calmed it' (Maude, vol 2, p 117). But in his ascetic old age Tolstoy turned against tobacco, as firmly as if he saw in it the head and front of all a wicked world's vices. 'I abstain from writing', he wrote once to a friend, 'and feel a kind of purity, such as one feels from not smoking.' To someone else he is said to have declared – with some degree of clairvoyance – 'The man who does not smoke, saves ten years of his life, and the man who does not drink, saves twenty.' Always a missionary, eager to convert others as well as himself, he called a village meeting and got the peasants to promise to abandon both tobacco and vodka. 'They even sacrificed their pipes, tobacco and tobacco-pouches, but there was much subsequent backsliding' (Maude, vol 2, pp 243, 179, 240).

In this century, too, writers have pondered over the secret of nicotine, as well as the meaning of life. 'This transformation of a dry herb', Pavese, the Italian novelist, wrote in his diary, 'into a cloud of fragrant, lively fertilizing smoke is not without significance. In other days it would quickly have become a symbol (like the pipe of Gitche Manito in Longfellow)' (3 September 1944, p 156). It did indeed become a kind of symbol for Brecht, particularly in his play *The Good Person of Szechwan* (1959), where Chen Teh used a gift of money from the gods to start a small tobacco shop in order to make money for charity. The play's editors point out how frequently smoking played a part in Brecht's plays, boldly experimental in form as well as in spirit, and in this one 'had an almost ritual quality' (pp xi-xii). He advocated a 'smoking-theatre', on the theory that an audience could be got to *think* if allowed to smoke at the same time (Willett, pp 145-6).

And near the end of the War of 1914-18, when tobacco had become one of the great shortages, Katherine Mansfield wrote to a friend that she was not in want, because Virginia Woolf had sent her six packets of Belgian cigarettes. They were not doing much to cheer her up, it seems, for she went on: 'I feel ever so much better – Hate life more than ever – see MORE CORRUPTION every day –

and everybody seems to be evil and vile. Nearly everybody' (Baker, pp 116-17). Her friend Virginia Woolf was another sufferer from life, to whom the magic herb, if it failed in the end to save her, brought much relief.

> Her cigarettes were made from a special tobacco called My Mixture. Mr Woolf bought it for her in London and, in the evenings, they used to sit by the fire and make these cigarettes themselves. It was a mild sweet-smelling tobacco, and she would not have any other cigarettes, though sometimes she smoked a long cheroot which she enjoyed very much. (Noble, p 190)

Another English writer of the troubled inter-war years had a singular sensation in 1933 when he was living on a Greek island and trying, under difficult conditions, to write a novel. One day, upset by the yelling of people round him, he inadvertently inhaled smoke from the cigarette in his mouth – for the first time, though he had been a smoker for ten years. He felt as if intoxicated, as if levitating, and from that moment was a regular inhaler, 'a nicotine addict for the next thirty years' (Isherwood, p 139).

A comrade of George Orwell's in the International Brigade in Spain

> remembered how they suffered in his dug-out through Orwell's incessant smoking of cigarettes while he wrote, rolled from the strongest, coarsest black shag pipe tobacco. He kept a rope cigarette lighter hanging from his belt all the time. (Crick, p 217)

Writing to his wife Ellen after a three-day visit from her, behind the front, Orwell assured her: 'Dearest, you really are a wonderful wife. When I saw the cigars my heart melted away' (p 218); did his wife wonder whether it was she or her offering that had inspired so warm a tribute?

But a more unequivocal one was paid by Sir Compton Mackenzie, when he wrote near the end of a long life that he was just finishing his 81st book, had probably smoked nearly a quarter-million pipefuls, was still in excellent shape, and was 'seriously handicapped' when obliged to write without aid from tobacco (pp 335, 343). With abstainers multiplying, we may soon have to ask whether literature is going to become impossible – or has already begun to be impossible.

For a modern reader the Dickensian haze of tobacco smoke is as intrinsic a part of Victorian London and its purlieus as its fogs and smogs. At the naval dockyard at Chatham are 'great chimneys smoking with a quiet – almost a lazy – air, like giants smoking tobacco' (Dickens, *Traveller*, chap XXVI). At the 'Three Cripples', in search of Bill Sikes, Fagin went upstairs into a room redolent of vice and squalor, despite its piano and singer; it was lit by two gas jets, but 'the place was so full of dense tobacco smoke, that at first it was scarcely possible to discern anything more' (*Oliver*, chap 26). Flaubert was himself an inveterate smoker, and it has been noticed that in *Madame Bovary* the smell of tobacco is everywhere, and helps the plot to unfold. Emma reads romances about sultans with long pipes, admires her gentleman-lover with his cigars, despises her husband, the struggling country doctor, all the more because he cannot smoke one without coughing and choking (Jakovsky, pp 26-30).

Writers have thus had quick eyes for the mannerisms or modes of tobacco takers, and what they can tell us. Thoreau observed how people losing ground in an argument would gain a breathing space by resorting to a pinch of snuff, and then go on as obstinately as before (p 81). George Eliot's Bartle, having eaten his supper and got to his pipe and ale, began by saying that he had news to impart, but broke off and

> gave a series of fierce and rapid puffs, looking earnestly the while at Adam. Your impatient loquacious man has never any notion of keeping his pipe alight by gentle measured puffs; he is always letting it go nearly out, and then punishing it for that negligence. (*Adam Bede*, chap 21)

Tobacco could blend equally with the most heartfelt sentiment. When Susan Ferrier's heroine was taking leave of her Highland friends, assembled to see her off, even old Donald the family retainer had his farewell gift, 'and, as he stood tottering at the chaise-door, he contrived to get a "bit snishin mull" laid on Mary's lap, with a "Bless her bonny face, an' may she ne'er want a good sneesh!"' (chap 31). And another poem by Petöfi is about his going into the kitchen, lighting his pipe as he did so, to see a pretty girl: as soon as she looked at him his torpid heart was set ablaze, while his pipe went out (p 16).

Tobacco smoke could have a kinship with daydreams and regrets, as well as with philosophical thought. Edward Thompson quotes in his biography of William Morris a poem of his about a refugee of 1848, and his old ardent hopes 'that melted in air like the smoke of his evening pipe' (*Morris*, p 277) – as Morris's own hopes of socialism may have done before his death. Another old hopeful was the Chartist bookseller in *Alton Lock*, Sandy Mac-Kaye, who rejected all London food and water as noxious, and would eat only Scots oatmeal, mixed with whisky and made into 'Athol brose'. 'But it was little he either ate or drank – he seemed to live upon tobacco. From four in the morning till twelve at night, the pipe never left his lips, except when he went into the outer shop. "It promoted meditation, and drove awa' the lusts o' the flesh,"' he averred (Kingsley, chap 6).

Comic characters with pipes have also abounded. Scott's Dominie Sampson seldom opened his mouth to speak, but was always ready to emit from it 'huge volumes of tobacco smoke', and appeared to a stranger an 'eating, drinking, moving, and smoking automaton' (*Guy Mannering*, chap 3). And a Dickens oddity as sparing of words as the Dominie is sitting one stormy night in the comfortable parlour of his 'Maypole' tavern, 'giving no other signs of life than breathing with a loud and constant snore (though he was wide awake), and from time to time putting his glass to his lips, or knocking the ashes out of his pipe, and filling it anew'. Mr Willet and his two old cronies have not uttered a word for over two hours, but all feel they are having a convivial evening. About 10.30 pm Mr Willet is beginning to nod, but he has 'perfectly acquired, by dint of long habit, the art of smoking in his sleep' (*Barnaby Rudge*, chap 33).

Thackeray has a Byronical painter who walks the town wrapped in a ponderous Spanish cloak, with 'a large pipe full of the fragrant Orinoco . . . Andrea did not like smoking, but he used a pipe as part of his profession as an artist, and as one of the picturesque parts of his costume; in like manner, though he did not fence, he always travelled about with a pair of foils' (*Shabby Genteel*, chap 4). Thackeray's too is the rich old miser Sir Pitt Crawley whom we first see sitting at his fireside with the 'pipe and a paper of tobacco' he has sent his Mrs Tinker out for, and insisting on a farthing change from the penny-ha'penny entrusted to her (*Vanity Fair*, chap 7).

Sherlock Holmes wrote a peerless monograph on the 140 varieties of tobacco ash that a detective should be able to identify (Doyle, 'Boscombe Valley'). One splendid moment in the saga is when Watson throws down his cigarette before nerving himself to enter the prehistoric hut on Dartmoor and face the dangerous criminal supposedly lurking there – and another when Holmes, returning to his hiding place, recognises the cigarette as his friend's and knows Watson must be inside (*Hound*, chap. oo). But Doyle could be philistine enough to let an American actor make up a play where Holmes, lured to a gas chamber in Stepney, fixed his glowing cigar to the window-frame to make the gang think him still here, while he escaped through the door (Pearsall, p 97). The Challenger epic makes amends, at any rate as regards the dignity of the cigar. 'Real San Juan Colorado', says the professor, handing one to the young journalist Malone after their fight on the doorstep. 'Heavens! don't bite it! Cut – and cut with reverence!' (*Lost World*, chap 4). And there is the climactic scene when the friends, last survivors as they believe of the human race, agree to devote what they expect to be their final minutes to a last farewell smoke (*Poison Belt*).

When a ship was wrecked off Crusoe's island, and a drowned boy washed ashore, 'He had nothing in his pocket but two pieces of eight and a tobacco-pipe. The last was to me of ten times more value than the first' (Defoe, p 113). (But do we ever hear of Crusoe having any tobacco to put in it?) When Long John Silver came to negotiate with Captain Smollett, on Treasure Island, the latter coldly filled his pipe; the pirate leader, in token of the equality he claimed, followed suit, and 'the two men sat silently smoking for quite a while, now looking each other in the face, now stopping their tobacco, now leaning forward to spit. It was as good as the play to see them' (Stevenson, *Treasure Island*, chap 20).

One of Kipling's less convincing puppets is the fascinating courtesan Lalun, an intriguer whose power in Lahore rivals that of the British governor – an enticing amorist who also 'knew how to make up tobacco for the *huqa* so that it smelt like the Gates of Paradise' (Wurgaft, p 102). Lower still on the literary ladder we meet 'Sapper's' hero Bulldog Drummond with his cigarette case – 'Turkish this side, Virginia the other' – and his antagonist Carl Peterson with his 'eternal cigar' and its imperturbable glow.

Tobacco has also found its way into tales for young people quite different from the blood-and-thunder sort. After a picnic lunch the 'Little Women' and their friends played the game of taking turns at improvising bits of a kaleidoscopic story. Meg called up a Gothic setting, a knight plucked back by a spectre which 'waved, threateningly, before him a – '

> 'Snuff-box,' said Jo, in a sepulchral voice, which convulsed the audience. 'Thankee', said the knight politely, as he took a pinch, and sneezed seven times so violently that his head fell off. (Alcott, chap 12)

When Alice in Wonderland stood on tiptoe to peep over the edge of a mushroom,

> her eyes immediately met those of a large blue caterpillar, that was sitting on the top, with its arms folded, quietly smoking a long hookah, and taking not the smallest notice of her or of anything else. ('Carroll', chap 4)

(Esoteric interpretations have been put forward; it may be simplest, if one is needed, to take it as a skit on clerical drones.)

In our own time the tobacco cloud has drifted far out into space. In one science-fiction story men on a remote planet are addressed by a mysterious voice, and brought a tray of refreshments by a robot waiter. 'The whisky was smooth, tasted far more like real

Scotch than do the imitations distilled on a score of planets. The cigarettes were not at all bad', and self-igniting (Chandler, A.B., chap 6). The newest series of television space episodes has a bland Alien officer on board the starship who sports a curved pipe in imitation of Sherlock Holmes, and has made a study of all the master's problems.

12

To Smoke or Not to Smoke

In principle, I'm entirely against smoking – it is unchristian and unnecessary – it makes me sick to see a gang of little punks puffing at coffin nails – I know for a fact that all labour agitators smoke cigarettes. But my doctor, a Christian man, advises me to take an occasional cigar for the sake of my throat . . .

Mr Knife, in Sinclair Lewis, *Gideon Planish*, chap 21

As late as about 1660 a medical work on tobacco, by Dr Everard and others, could still be entitled *'Panacea' or the Universall Medicine*. But medical opinion, always divided, was shedding most of its early enthusiasm, and tobacco being pushed, so far as health was concerned, on to the defensive. There might be a lingering faith in its efficacy as a prophylactic, even in the 19th century when cholera epidemics swept across Europe: in 1832 when his Somerset parish was attacked, the Rev. J. Skinner arranged for a house where some patients had died to be fumigated with tobacco, as well as with burning tar ropes (p 453). But medical uses of tobacco were coming to be more marginal, even freakish. There was, for a time, much reliance on rectal inflation, with tobacco smoke blown into the anus, as a means of resuscitating the drowned. And a booklet of advice to soldiers in World War One recommended them to abandon smoking, but to make use of tobacco ash for padding sensitive corns (Cairncross, pp 17, 19).

Some pawky verses quoted in *The Scots Magazine* for 1803 (p 30) viewed the question with Caledonian caution, from both sides –

Tobacco reek, Tobacco reek,
When I am well, it makes me sick:

Tobacco reek, Tobacco reek,
It makes me well when I am sick.

Defenders mostly fell back on other arguments than straight-forward ones of health. An old one already mentioned, and frequently refurbished, was the value of tobacco for warding off worse odours. After all, the first home of the pipe was the Red Indian lodge, or collective long-house, which missionaries venturing into found indescribably malodorous. Whether or not its occupants felt tobacco's virtue as a protective screen, some Europeans at home were quick to do so. They were exposed to all kinds of effluvia, rural or urban; and these have been very slow to take their departure, even in countries priding themselves on their attention to hygiene, while many new ones have joined their ranks.

Thackeray was one modern who appreciated these facts. On a festival day in Paris in 1841 he witnessed an open-air play about a Spaniard captured by the Turks, with a Moorish castle and other fine sights. 'All persons who frequent these public spectacles should take the writer's advice, and have a cigar to smoke. It is much more efficacious than scent-bottles of any sort' ('A St Philip's Day'). A Dutch colonel in Java in 1911 maintained that 'it was necessary for him to light a cigar first before talking to a group of Javanese, in the hope that the cigar odour would drown the stench from their clothes' (Alatas, p 120). Some European prejudice is evident in such dicta; and the native nose may have found the colonel equally distasteful.

It was chiefly those well-off enough to be fastidious who wanted protection from smells. Those poor enough to be hungry might look to tobacco for a different kind of relief. There was firm evidence, Chute held in 1595, that the inhabitants of Florida could subsist for four or five days on tobacco smoke, without food or drink (p 45). Either by stimulating and mobilising in some fashion the bodily energies, or by acting as a narcotic and dulling the craving for food, tobacco really could be a temporary substitute for it. (This was of course convenient for those who ought to have been providing food for the needy.) A French savant declared in 1688, in the midst of Louis XIV's wars, that soldiers with tobacco could do without other nourishment for days on end (Fairholt, p 243); Braudel quotes another who in 1703 classified tobacco among the *aliments* that sustain mankind (Braudel, pp 188-9). And during the agitation against Walpole's Excise Bill in 1733 it was urged that cheap tobacco was a necessity of the workers, who often tasted no food until midday or later (Mackenzie, p 180). As Marie Antoinette might have said: If the poor have no bread, let them chew tobacco.

Later in the 18th century an English medical writer, discussing narcotics, pointed out that

> various substances of this class are used by the inhabitants of different countries, as opium and bang by the Turks and East Indians, and tobacco by all others . . . as stimulants and cordials, that give vigour to the system, raise the spirits, call forth agreeable feelings, and render the body, for a time, capable to bear fatigue and privation of food. (Trotter, T., p 34)

We do not hear of the well-to-do going over to this economical diet. More surprising, they do not seem to have made serious efforts to feed their horses or dogs on smoke. There were other ways, however, in which it could be supposed to benefit their animals. Pepys and his wife were on their way to Islington in their carriage one day, when a horse suddenly fell ill with staggers. The coachman cut its tongue and tail, to bleed it, but instead of responding it seemed ready to drop down. He then blew some tobacco into its nostrils, on which it sneezed, recovered, and went on as well as ever. 'One of the strangest things of a horse I ever observed,' Pepys comments, 'but he says it is usual' (18 August 1667).

Whether or not tobacco could be of use to animals useful to men, it could certainly help to get rid of some other kinds. A young British nobleman making a stay on a ranch in Argentina saw it in action against the *escuerzo*, a venomous toad with fangs. A young fellow wearing high boots for protection would tease one with a stick, while it kept jumping up in an attempt to reach his hands. When it had been worked into a fury, the stick was dipped into the oily residue from a pipe, and held out to the toad, 'who would fasten on to it like a mad creature, only to die in a few seconds of the nicotine' (Hamilton, *Here, There*, p 237). From Argentina also we hear of how rats on a plantation were kept down by 'the "smoking machine", which pumped the fumes of sulphur, bad tobacco, and other deadly substances into their holes and suffocated them' (Hudson, p 44). In Britain garden pests were tackled for long in the same way: 'In 1851 there appears to have been a mobile machine in use for fumigating with tobacco smoke' (Hadfield, p 350). At a somewhat earlier date there had been dark suspicions of nicotine being employed in Spain, and by Jesuits, as a poison.

In 1951 when the French were trying, with the help of German mercenaries, to regain control of Vietnam, a detachment was moving through the mountainous country of the Meo tribe, close to the Chinese border. They saw hardy hill-women carrying heavy burdens up steep ascents, mouths stained red with betel-nut and usually smoking clay pipes. They learned that leeches dropped out of trees on to the unwary, and that to pull them off left a festering sore, but that a lighted cigarette would usually banish them (Scholl-Latour, pp 67-8). Tobacco smoke has been a cherished auxiliary in man's long struggle against flying insects, above all the mosquito; Europeans finding their way into Canada were unpleasantly struck by the clouds of mosquitoes on the wing every summer. But man and his ally have not always been the winners. An artist on holiday with a party of Britons in another northern region, Lapland, sat down when they came on a picturesque deserted hamlet and tried to sketch it, but was at once enveloped in mosquitoes.

> He battled with them bravely for a long time; he smoked like a chimney; he slapped himself with frantic industry; and at last he gave it up in despair. He had covered three pages of his sketch-book with blood – his own blood – and pencil scratches, and dishevelled insect corpses. (Hyne, p 102)

There used to be a shop in Cambridge that sold bags of assorted cigarettes, of all colours, dimensions, flavours – Egyptian, Russian, Balkan Sobranie, and the rest – on whose wings the buyer could float luxuriously from continent to continent, as if on a magic carpet. Personal preferences, on the other hand, have often been narrow and tenacious. James Joyce's Mr Daedalus had to get Uncle Charles to take his morning whiff of black twist in the outhouse.

> Damn me, said Mr Daedalus frankly, if I know how you can smoke such villainous awful tobacco. It's like gunpowder, by God.
> – It's very nice, Simon, replied the old man. Very cool and mollifying.
> (*Portrait*, p 67)

National or regional choices have also established themselves. A city – Paris, for instance – will come to be recognisable by its tobacco smell. Wilfred Owen summed up French cigarettes as 'a species of poisonous straw' (p 267), and many born outside France would concur; but more recently a French writer has complained of regional preferences in Europe being too much overborne by Anglo-American tastes (Jakovsky, p 35).

With this diversity of choice, it is not surprising that tobacco has often been mixed with other ingredients, to create novel sensations. A seeker of information in the Sahara some years ago stayed awhile with a friendly household at El Golea. Its head forbade the women to ask for cigarettes, but when his back was turned his old mother 'would make violent signs in dumb show' for him to slip one or two under the mat. She took the tobacco out and mixed it with herbs, and perhaps opium (Ross, M., p 94). It is a far cry from that old lady to Oscar Wilde, lunching in a Paris restaurant, but someone who knew him says that 'While eating – very little – he ceaselessly half-smokes Egyptian cigarettes mixed with opium, and is a terrible drinker of absinthe' (Jullian, p 204).

But there has also, sadly often, been a search for substitutes, when the true leaf has been missing; war has been the chief stimulus to the search. An old Russian soldiers' song about a long siege recounts how men had to eat their horses, use gunpowder for salt, smoke hay in their pipes, make clothes out of sacks (Baddeley, p 371). And in the siege of Lucknow during the Indian Mutiny men were reduced to stealing from one another. Food too ran short, but

> what most of the soldiers and volunteers missed far more than good food was tobacco . . . They tried to smoke green leaves and became ill in consequence. They filled their pipes with tea leaves and dried guavas. (Hibbert, p 317)

In the later stages of World War One things were getting bad for smokers on the Allied side, still worse for their retreating foes. On 15 September 1918, Wilfred Owen wrote home that 'Cigs are scarcer and scarcer. *Verb. Sap.* The poor boys were smoking grass in envelopes in the line last week' (p 577). On the Long March, Mao and his comrades tried all sorts of wayside plants. And in beleaguered Malta during World War Two smokers took to 'a mixture of dried fig, lemon and strawberry leaves which that "mother of invention" discovered to be the best herbal substitute for tobacco' (Shankland and Hunter, p 44). I myself have been told by a Yugoslav friend, the virologist Dr Vesenjak, who as a young woman was a medical volunteer in the Resistance, that dried horse-dung was one of the materials tried by the partisans. (In one of my own fits of economy I remember trying used tea leaves; they proved nauseating.)

Many other experiments have been tried by seekers not in want of something to smoke themselves, but desirous of increasing profits on tobacco by adulterating it. Their doings are a tribute to human ingenuity in a commercial era: capitalism and tobacco have run their course side by side. Complaints began almost as soon as smoking. Dr Barclay of Edinburgh was criticising malpractices in 1614, and we can suspect them when the grocer's wife in the Beaumont and Fletcher play *The Knight of the Burning Pestle* says she has been called a 'damned bitch' by customers, a hundred times, 'about a scurvy pipe of tobacco' (Act 1 Scene 3). And in his book on working-class conditions in England in the 1840s Engels cited an article in the *Liverpool Mercury* on the way tobacco was being

> 'mixed with disgusting substances of all sorts . . .' I can add that several
> of the most respected tobacco dealers in Manchester announced
> publicly last summer, that, by reason of the universal adulteration of
> tobacco, no firm could carry on business without adulteration, and that
> no cigar costing less than threepence is made wholly from tobacco.
> (*Working Class*, pp 105-6)

The few prosecutions that took place bore no relation, as *The Times* wrote, to the frequency of cheating, which included use of 'sugar, alum, lime, flour of meal, rhubarb leaves, saltpetre, fullers' earth, starch, malt consumings, chromate of lead', and a dozen other things (14 August 1855, p 10). Milk, bread, and other foods were being doctored similarly; it was always the poor who were cheated most.

Capitalism was only refining on what the untutored instinct of the dealer had always pointed out to him as the way to prosper. Hajji Baba, for example, laid in tobacco from different regions of Persia and Syria, and greatly enlarged his stock 'with the assistance of different sorts of dungs'. He knew real connoisseurs when he saw them, and sold them almost pure leaf; what other customers got was less and less genuine, in gradations down to the dullest, who received hardly any tobacco at all (Morier, chap 10).

Surely, one must think, the nose of childhood and innocence cannot relish the smell of tobacco smoke, still less its depressing residue of staleness, enough by itself to warn any of us that nicotine joys carry a taint of mortality. A 1990 enquiry confirms that most children between 10 and 15 dislike a smoky atmosphere; but as they grow, and come under insidious influences – the worst being parental example – this healthy reaction wears off. From the unwholesome curiosity that too many develop, a few have been rescued as if by a special providence. At the age of 8, for example, the American novelist Upton Sinclair was given a cigarette, in a Baltimore street, by a bigger boy. He began to smoke it, but, he says, 'another boy told me a policeman would arrest me, so I threw the cigarette away, and ran and hid in an alley, and have never yet recovered from this fear. It has saved me a great deal of money' (p 12).

Too many others have been born into environments where smoking was as natural as breathing. On a country walk Jane Carlyle met a boy of 7 driving cattle, 'and – smoking a pipe! I asked him when he learned to smoke, and he answered that *he did not remember!*' (Hanson, p 324). In a play of 1863 a garrulous Mrs Willoughby deplores her grandson's precocious yielding to temptation:

> Many's the time when he've come in, I've said, 'Sam,' I've said, 'I smell tobacco,' I've said. 'Grandmother,' he'd say to me, quite grave and innocent, 'p'raps it's the chimbley' – and him a child of fifteen, and a short pipe in his right-hand pocket! (Taylor, Act 2)

Most boys – and now girls – have had to learn to smoke, as an accomplishment qualifying them for adult life, and an exciting pointer to a world full of mysterious promise. By way of prelude they may have learned to blow soap bubbles through pipes, or 'smoke' edible cigarettes. Dylan Thomas remembered these as part of the Christmas sports of boyhood in a small Welsh town – 'you put one in your mouth and you stood at the corner of the street and you waited for hours, in vain, for an old lady to scold you for smoking a cigarette, and then with a smirk you ate it' ('A Child's Christmas'). Stevenson had memories of a small place in Scotland, a sunless ingle called the Lady's Walk, a cheap cigar called the 'Pickwick'. 'To fit themselves for life, and with a special eye to acquire the art of smoking', boys gathered there and shared 'a single penny pickwick', cut into lengths with a blunt knife ('The Lantern-Bearers'). At Lerwick in the Shetlands in those days, boys when let out of school would roam the streets begging for bits of tobacco, mostly from the Hollanders always to be met with. These shreds they smoked in black clay pipes purloined from their homes. 'After a few "rooks" a deathly pallor as a rule o'erspread the countenance of the youthful devotee', and very likely a beating followed when he got home. 'But all this notwithstanding, with a bravery and perseverance worthy of a better cause, most of the boys learned to smoke' (Manson, p 417). Multitudes of such youngsters, when only a few years older, in the same daredevil spirit have gone off to the wars, and been seen no more.

Dickens's schoolboy Toots had the misfortune of possessing more money and less brains than these little Scots or Vikings. He had sometimes to be helped into the open air 'in a state of faintness', after trying to smoke 'a very blunt cigar' bought on the beach from 'a most desperate smuggler', who boasted a price of £200 on his head. Toots had also been sold an expensive jar of snuff warranted to have been 'the genuine property of the Prince Regent' (*Dombey*, chap 14). In another Dickens novel a man of the world, with his eye on an unhappily married young woman, gets her young cub of a brother on his side by means of flattery, drink, and tobacco – Tom reclining on a sofa, half-tipsy, and 'smoking with an infinite assumption of negligence' (*Hard Times*, chap 3). Far more pardonable is Samuel Butler's hero Ernest, who as a schoolboy at 'Roughborough', or Rugby, soon stopped making himself sick with beer, but could not give up a habit acquired at 13 or 14 of smoking. Later on he was always reproaching himself for this vice; but, harassed by a bullying father and a nagging mother anxious about his 'purity', he often slunk away into a grove behind the rectory,

> and consoled himself with a pipe of tobacco. Here in the wood with the summer sun streaming through the trees and a book and his pipe the boy forgot his cares and had an interval of that rest without which I verily believe his life would have been insupportable. (*All Flesh*, chap 40)

And it seemed to Jerome K. Jerome, writing in the 1920s, as if smoking had come to be a hereditary human accomplishment, so quickly was it picked up.

> Your veriest flapper, nowadays, will enjoy her first cigarette. It was less in our blood when I was a boy . . . But with pluck and perseverance one attains to all things – even to the silly and injurious habit of pumping smoke into one's heart and liver. (*Life*, p 38)

Various ways of putting a stop to juvenile smoking have been canvassed. Corporal punishment was authority's inbred instinct. About 1900 an Essex boy doing odd jobs on a farm before school was caught smoking in the woodshed. The farmer hit him, he ran home crying, his father on learning the cause hit him again, he got to school late and was caned (Thompson, P., pp 72-3). (It would be interesting to know whether this cured him.) James Joyce's Stephen is told by his father of the more civilised way *his* father had treated the matter. Catching sight of him smoking a pipe in the street with other boys, his father said nothing, but next day he remarked in a casual tone: 'If you want a good smoke, try one of these cigars. An American captain made me a present of them last night in Queenstown' (*Portrait*, p 104).

Nearer to today, a Department of Education pamphlet on 'Smoking and Health in Schools', discussing the fascination of cigarettes for youngsters, remarks: 'Girls need to understand that some boys believe that girls prefer boys who smoke.' And in Britain in 1983 it was estimated that £60 million-worth of cigarettes had been bought by children under 16 (British Medical Association, p 1). An obvious remedy, which few parents will be firm enough to adopt, lies in economic sanctions: children should cease to be given far more pocket money than they have any rational need of.

While boyhood has panted for its baptism of nicotine, manhood has lost innumerable hours in regrets, vows of reform, efforts too often vain to escape from thraldom to Circe. Two medical experts describe their 'withdrawal symptoms': irritability, insomnia, weakened memory, and so on, penalties that only a quarter of those making the effort manage to endure for a year. Others may be predestined to failure. Smokers seem to be 'more impulsive' by nature, and more prone to 'antisocial behaviour' (Kaplan and Sadock, pp 538-43).

But of all unfortunates torn between the need to make a fresh start and the clinging embrace of an old consort, Charles Lamb is the most eloquent. His 'Confessions of a Drunkard' are a lament over his fall into the company of smokers while striving to break away from that of drinkers. 'The Devil could not have devised a more subtle trap to re-take a backsliding penitent.' Soon he was drinking and smoking at once. 'This is Sunday,' he wrote to Wordsworth in 1815, when he was 40, 'and the head-ache I have is part late hours at work the two preceding nights, and part later hours over a consoling pipe afterwards' (*Letters*, vol 1, pp 329-30). His poem 'Farewell to Tobacco' had been written ten years before – an elegy over what he was losing, and the thought that from then on he would only be able to catch stray whiffs from other pipes,

> Sidelong odours, that give life
> Like glances from a neighbour's wife.

Love and hate had wrestled as he thought of tobacco,

> Filth of the mouth and fog of the mind . . .
> Hemlock, aconite –
>> Nay, rather
> Plant divine, of rarest virtue . . .

Lamb was a clerk at India House, the East India Company office, where he felt like a lost soul; by the time he was able to retire on a pension, it was too late for a new life. He was the only one of the English Romantics to be subjected to the dismal slavery of a regular paid job.

Longfellow was a poet free of financial worries, but a prey to similar painful wrestlings. 'I have smoked myself into an ill humour', he could write, 'and am peevish and discontented' (Wagenknecht, p 171). Many times he gave up smoking, but never for long. Karl Marx was more firm-minded. He stopped writing poetry after his adolescence, and stopped smoking, on his doctors' order, in his late fifties. 'This was a terrible sacrifice', an acquaintance wrote.

> On my first visit to him after the doctors' order he was quite pleased and proud to be able to tell me that he had not smoked for so and so many days . . . On every subsequent visit he would tell me how long it was since he had given up smoking . . . His pleasure was all the greater

when some time later the doctor allowed him a cigar a day. (Lessner, pp 165-6)

And his disciple Gramsci calculated in December 1932, four years before his death, that his living expenses came to 122 lire a month, 15 of them for tobacco. He was only smoking one-fifteenth as much as before his imprisonment: still too much, but 'it is very hard to give up altogether a habit so old and fixed' (*Lettres de la prison*, p 280).

Tolstoy was briefly a soldier, and always an ardent sportsman until 1885, when he killed his last hare and put away his gun. He was then 57. Next, a governess in the family wrote, came the turn of tobacco.

> He suffered unendurable torment, positively not knowing what to do with himself. He would pick up a cigarette-end here and there like a schoolboy, to have but a single whiff, or dilating his nostrils he would eagerly inhale the smoke when others smoked in his presence ... (Maude, vol 2, p 172)

At last he triumphed over himself. We may wonder whether for Tolstoy, at his age, and perhaps for Marx, the cost to his creative powers was too heavy.

Bad health forced Pavese, like Marx though not Tolstoy, to call a very unwilling halt. 'A feverish cold', says his diary on 10 February 1948. 'Two days ago I started smoking again, and felt the same terrible, unbearable irritation. Stop it! Stop it! The same game as when I was twenty...' (10 February 1948, p 188). And an English essayist wrote of his struggles to emancipate himself from the 'Giant Nicotine', ever since 'that far-off day when I burned a hole in my jacket pocket with a lighted cigar that I hid at the approach of danger'. He cheered himself with an argument by some wit that tobacco prolonged life. ' "Look at the ancient Egyptians", he said. "None of them smoked, *and they are all dead*" ' ('Alpha', pp 43ff).

Mark Twain must have been touching up a real experience, on the other side of the Atlantic, with his tale of being lost in the snow one night with two companions. Death seemed close; it was time for repentance; Twain threw away his beloved pipe, another man his whisky bottle, the third his greasy pack of cards: all felt true relief on being freed at last from a burdensome vice. Dawn came, and revealed that they were only a few yards away from the nearest house of a settlement. Twain was soon hunting for his pipe, though deeply ashamed of this speedy fall from grace; lighting it and going behind a barn to hide, he found his companions there with their bottle and cards (*Roughing It*, pp 219-23). Babbitt turned over his new leaf at least once a month.

> He went through with it like the solid citizen he was: admitted the evils of Tobacco, courageously made resolves, laid out plans to check the vice, tapered off his allowance of cigars, and expounded the pleasures of virtuousness to everyone he met. He did everything, in fact, except stop smoking. (Lewis, *Babbitt*, chap 4)

To the young, of course, it must seem easy for the old to stop, since they have to learn to give up so much else. The truth seems at odds with this, whether old people still wanting to be active are in question, or those who have no more business in the world, like Old Jolyon of *The Forsyte Saga*. He prized his independence, would not see his doctor, smoked three, sometimes four cigars daily instead of his former two; often feeling that he ought to give them up, but unable to make up his mind (Galsworthy, *Indian Summer*, sec 5). The feat being so difficult, then, credit for success in renouncing tobacco has often been given to the supernatural. William James cites several cases in his study of religious experiences. A woman wrestled in vain with her pipe for years, until at last, when she was 53, as she sat smoking by the fire a voice sounded. 'I did not hear it with my ears', she testified, 'but more as a dream or sort of double think. It said, "Louisa, lay down smoking."' This kept being repeated until she got up and laid her pipe aside; she 'never smoked again or had any desire to' (p 266). And an Oxford graduate, son of a clergyman, underwent religious conversion at 3 pm on 13 July 1886, at his father's rectory: he was soon delivered both from periodic bouts of drinking and, after 12 years of the pipe, from smoking (pp 222ff, cf pp 286-7).

As the 19th century wore on, smoking came to be felt as part of the normal condition of masculine life, like wearing trousers. 'You're a smoker, of course, Dr. Grimstone?' says Mr Bultitude to the redoubtable headmaster on their railway journey together ('Anstey', _Vice Versa_, chap 4), one of the funniest pieces of comedy ever written. All the same, warning voices were being lifted here and there, and clearly those who tried to give up smoking felt it was doing them no good. More specific attacks on it came in waves, one of which had its high point in the 1850s. George Borrow, that champion of English beer, launched a diatribe against the cant of teetotalism, above all in America – 'the land, indeed, par excellence, of humbug and humbug cries ... Tobacco-smoke is more deleterious than ale, teetotaller' (_Romany_, Appendix to chap 8). Thackeray might be a wholehearted smoker, but he was not blind to the risks. His silly young Ensign Famish, home on sick leave from his regiment in India, 'recruits his health by being intoxicated every night, and fortifies his lungs, which are weak, by smoking cigars all day' (_Snobs_, chap 10).

By about 1880 an _Anti-Tobacco Journal_ was coming out, and the connection between clay pipes and cancer of mouth or nose was being recognised. While practising at Plymouth, Conan Doyle

> went up country once, and operated upon an old fellow's nose which had contracted cancer through his holding the bowl of a short clay pipe immediately beneath it. I left him with an aristocratic, not to say supercilious organ, which was the wonder of the village (_Memories_, p 61)

In the next century conviction of the dangers quickened. In the 1930s an 'Anti-Cigarette League' was active. By mid-century tobacco was entering its penumbral stage, when uneasiness was darkening into fear, even though doctors did not take the lead in surrendering their pipes or cigarettes. In October 1978 the always slow-moving Labour Party decided to allow no more smoking at its annual conference. And under pressure of enlightened opinion some government action began to be taken, mostly halting and grudging. Counter-pressure from the tobacco lobby was powerful, especially with Downing Street oftener than not in Tory occupation, and Profit the sacredest of words. On 14 October 1990, the *Observer* published a survey of MPs, on both sides, having professional links with the tobacco industry, or tobacco interests in their constituencies; how politicians and such interests are likely to interact was wittily brought out in an episode in the television series *Yes, Prime Minister* (Lynn and Jay, no 7).

Lobbyists could be eloquent about tobacco revenue. In 1968-9 it paid for nearly half the cost of Britain's armed forces, so the common sense remedy might be for Britain to give up smoking, and what politicians and profiteers call 'Defence', together. Officially preferred policy has been to raise taxation on tobacco, which keeps revenue buoyant while having some deterrent effect on smokers. In October 1984 the British Medical Association launched its strongest campaign against tobacco advertising; the vendors muttered threats of libel suits, but did not venture to start them. (In the USA advertising on radio or television had been banned by Congress in 1971.) No-smoking notices in British railway carriages, ignored at first, have become effective. More and more people object to being poisoned by other people's smoke, which may lead to smoking at work coming to an end. At the same time, some smokers or lobbyists are falling back on the contention that the right to smoke is part of individual liberty, and anyone who questions it must be a Marxist in sheep's clothing.

In the USA between 1964 and 1978 the percentage of adults who smoked fell from 42 to 34, though that of women and adolescents rose (Kaplan and Sadock, pp 538-43). It seems that there and in Britain and western Europe the dividing-line has come to be one of class: the better-off give up smoking, the less well-off go on – whether because they are less well educated, or because life gives them more need of tobacco. We are seeing something like a return to the 18th-century position, when ordinary men and women smoked, gentlemen and ladies did not. Or as a priggish American put it a long time ago, tobacco should be eschewed by 'all persons of well regulated minds and correct moral principles' (Wallis, p 225). Once a class difference makes itself felt in any matter of social habit, snobbery will come in too and widen it. Not to smoke is one easy way of being a gentleman, or – in modern rig-marole – belonging to the Top People, or upper echelons.

Tobacco is thus ceasing to be a leveller, as to some extent it has been – when gentlemen did not smoke, they could take snuff. But there have always, of course, been class differentials in the mode of taking nicotine. Mr Chucks the bosun in _Peter Simple_, for example, smitten by a Spanish girl's charms, won her father's heart, if not hers, by pressing on him a handful of cigars – 'having very fortunately a couple of dozen of real Havannahs in my pocket (for I never smoke anything else, Mr. Simple, it being my opinion that no gentleman can)' (Marryat, chap 16). And until about the time of World War One, British officers were only allowed to smoke Turkish cigarettes, as somehow more distinguished, ie less liked than Virginian by most Britons.

Within the English working class, decent status came to depend partly on ability to buy and exchange cigarettes. In the hard times before World War Two a family man, to keep his self-respect, even when unemployed, needed enough pocket money for cigarettes and beer: 15 cigarettes a day might be customary. This may sound like an excessive demand on the family income. But such small luxuries were felt to be 'part of life; without them, life would not be life' (Hoggart, pp 39-40). King Lear thought the same. A derelict old man picking up cigarette-ends in the street has made a good symbolic figure of poverty's lower depths.

In 1978 seven multinationals controlled 80 per cent of world production (Norton-Taylor, R., _Guardian_, 2 October 1978), and by 1984 world sales reached £31 billion a year (British Medical Association, p 139), yielding profits of an order that no sellers want to relinquish. To make up for shrinking markets at home, produc-ers are energetically pushing sales in the Third World; among other things they are getting cultivators to grow tobacco, with technical aid from them, on soil that ought to be used for growing food. In India the fading of the old Trichinopoly cigar is blamed on multinational competition: it was traditionally produced by small firms and cottage industry, and so could be defended as being in line with Gandhi's economic ideals (Winchester, S.,

Guardian, 29 July 1978). Educated Indians are turning away from smoking, but Third World population is growing terribly rapidly, and most of it is terribly poor and ignorant. It is given few health warnings, and there are – in Pakistan, for example – few checks on advertising. With all this, the Third World is a ready-made market for narcotics.

13

Man's Best and Worst Friend

On a Philippine island; people bringing for sale sea-shells, birds, a snake. I threw a cigar butt on the ground; they eagerly snatched it and shared smoking it. I gave them a cigar each: with what happiness and what deep bows did they thank me for this gift! I then wanted to lie down on a board in the tent; they hastened to be helpful, cleaned the board, and put little stones under it.

Ivan Goncharov, The Frigate Pallada, p 517

Cant terms for tobacco and its appendages have abounded, testimonies to the wit of the man in the street. In English a cigarette has been christened a 'cig', a 'fag' (fag-end), 'weed', 'gasper'. By analogy with 'picturesque', a smoker well supplied with cigars, or sporting an expensive one, might in the 1840s be dubbed 'cigaresque'. Tobacco likewise supplied nicknames for other things, seemingly remote. De Quincey derided the 'Gothic' style of architecture fashionable in his time, with its 'little gingerbread ornaments, and "tobacco pipes", and make-believe parapets' (p 246). Ringlets worn by London costers and gypsies came to be known as 'tobacco-pipe curls'. French soldiers called the new rifle issued in 1867 a *fusil à tabatière*, or snuff-box gun. A crimson tropical flower got the name, probably from the size of its bell, of 'Dutchman's pipe'.

Colloquial phrases twined round the fragrant leaf. Men have indulged in 'pipe dreams' of fame and fortune. To smoke a pipe, about 1700, was to 'raise a cloud', later on to 'blow a cloud'. When cigar smokers were gathered together they were said to be sitting 'under a canopy of Havannah'. In the 19th century a man might 'cock' a pipe, and particularly 'cock a broseley', the Shropshire district of Broseley being renowned for its churchwardens. To 'put someone's pipe out' was to upset him. 'Put *that* in your pipe and smoke it' went with a clinching point in a dispute. Not long after World War Two a phrase came into circulation about politics being made in 'smoke-filled back rooms', originally an allusion to the choosing of election candidates in America by professional operators behind the scenes.

Snuff, like smoke, has stimulated verbal fancy. There used to be a saying about a sneeze being 'cheap snuff', a pleasure not paid for. Anything of value is 'not to be sneezed at' – not to be blown or thrown away as worthless. To be 'up to snuff' meant to be as smart as the next man. Another turn of speech came from the throwing of snuff into a person's face, for insult or injury. When the British ambassador at Vienna in 1908 got into an altercation with the foreign minister, the latter talked disparagingly of British treatment of prisoners in the recent Boer War – 'for which', Goschen wrote in his diary, 'I gave him snuff' (4 November 1908, p 177). In French, *passer à tabac* has come to mean thrashing someone, an idiom presumably suggested by the grinding of tobacco into snuff.

For very long tobacco has furnished individuals, not writers only, with imagery or other means of expressing their feelings. The poet Samuel Butler, censuring 'The Licentiousness of the Age', compared men who by shunning one extravagance run into another to pipes which, 'at one end hit', break at the other end (*Poems*, vol 3, p 76). And Kingsley's old Scots Chartist, son of a strict old Covenanter, in his deathbed ramblings wonders whether he will get to heaven . . . 'Katie, here, hauds wi' purgatory, ye ken; where souls are burnt clean again – like baccy-pipes' (chap 33). It was a natural thought to an author who, on a visit to Tennyson, 'walked hard up and down the study for hours smoking furiously, and affirming that tobacco was the only thing that kept his nerves quiet' (Tennyson, H., vol 1, p 443). There is an old story in the Shetlands, recalled by one T. Henderson in *Shetland Life* (June 1982), about two old fellows dumbfounded by their first sight of a steamship entering their harbour, and one saying to the other (in broad dialect): 'Have a pinch of snuff with me, Lowrie, for you and I will snuff no more till we snuff together in Glory!'

Tobacco found its way into folk culture as well as literature. _J'ai de bon tabac dans ma tabatière_ . . . a collector might come on a great many such songs up and down the world. Old King Cole, one of the legendary rulers of ancient Britain, called for his pipe as well as his glass and his fiddlers. We may guess that after a few generations of smoking, ordinary folk supposed that the world had always been smoking, as well as fighting, kissing, and praying. Larry Hogan, in an Irish novel, compares a pipe and the spark of life in it to a human being and its breath of life, which must also go out; and he trolls snatches of an old song –

> A pipe it larns us all this thing, –
> 'Tis fair without and foul within,
> Just like the soul begrim'd with sin.
> Think o' this when you're smoking tiba-akky!

Though the pipe was never prime favourite in Spain, in the folklore of Catalonia and the Balearic Islands there are festival days when children smoke one, and girls present a lighted pipe to the young men of their choice (Jakovsky, pp 25-6). Among Muslims in southern India, one of them wrote early in the 19th century, 'the right to use the caste or tribal pipe is carefully restricted, and exclusion from its use is a common form of social boycott' (Sharif, p 328). In the old Punjab, too, refusal of a share of hookah or water was a customary mode of excommunication, akin to interdiction from fire and water in medieval Europe.

And competitions connected with tobacco have been widespread. At the annual Egremont Crab Fair in Cumbria contestants would stand with their heads through a horse collar, trying who could pull the ugliest face or smoke the fastest pipe, while a north of Ireland contest to keep a pipe alight longest was won in November 1982 by a woman. In both Britain and Germany there have been snuff tournaments, won by entrants able to take the most pinches of snuff within a given number of seconds.

Men have liked to imagine animals, as well as gods, in their own image. David Teniers the younger, for example, painted a group of sociable monkeys smoking their pipes together. Uncle Remus, the fabled Negro story-teller, always scraping through his pockets for grains of tobacco to put in his pipe, had one tale about how Brer Rabbit tricked Brer Fox into letting him ride on his back, with bridle and spurs, to a party – where he 'sa'nter inter de house, he did, en shake han's wid de gals, en set dar, smokin' his seegyar same ez a town man', and boasting of Brer Fox having been for many years his family riding-animal (Harris, chap 6).

In more practical fashion, smoking could serve, in days before everyone carried a watch, as a time-measurer, a kind of hour-glass. 'If you ask how far off a place is', a traveller home from southern Spain informed his readers, 'you may be told *dos cigaritos*, i.e. as far as you can go while smoking two cigars.' On the other hand boiling an egg, which required more precision, would be regulated by the number of *credos* that could be repeated in the time specified (Meyrick, p 65). In a German novella a pedestrian enquiring the distance to a lake was told that it was quite near, he would be there 'in scarcely half a pipe of tobacco' (Storm). In Canada the *voyageurs*, or French-Indians conveying goods or pas-sengers by canoe, would halt now and then to smoke a pipe, and a journey could be referred to as a three-pipe one, or a five-pipe one. And when the Russian radical Alexander Herzen was arrested a police inspector told him admiringly about how his pre-decessor had induced some men to make a false confession of theft by threatening to have them flogged 'for two pipes'. Asked what this meant, the inspector explained:

> One gets bored, you know, while a flogging is going on; so one lights a pipe; and, as a rule, when the pipe is done, the flogging is over too. But in special cases we order that the flogging shall go on till two pipes are smoked out. The men who flog are accustomed to it and know exactly how many strokes that means. (pp 223-4)

From the rude wigwam has sprouted a world-wide industry; mankind has squandered on tobacco incalculable millions, for which there is nothing tangible to show, not so much as a pyramid or a statue of a lord mayor. Turgenev speaks of watching from a train window the smoke eddying from the locomotive, changing shape, dissolving, like everything human, especially everything Russian (*Smoke*, p 53). Pipe smoke has evoked the same reveries, drawn on the air patterns as evanescent as most human thoughts or doings. Many have seen 'pictures in the fire' while dozing over it; tobacco smoke has been a still more persuasive wooer of fantasy.

Tobacco has been, especially when smoked, the most universal new pleasure mankind has acquired. It has appealed to, and been able at times to transfigure, the most unexpected human beings. Even a military mandarin of the old Chinese school might unbend from his rigid dignity under the amiable fumes. For example, the mission led by Lord Amherst in 1816 was Britain's second effort to push open the locked doors of China, a failure like the first, but Basil Hall, captain of the ship conveying Amherst and his assistants, recounts an incident that Sir Toby Belch might well have dismissed as an 'improbable fiction'. Some Chinese officials had come on board for a diplomatic ceremony, and Hall noticed one of them, an army man, returning to his junk close by. There he threw off his cumbrous robes and 'great unwieldy velvet boots, with soles an inch thick', and reappeared in slippers, a pipe hanging from one corner of his mouth – to begin a playful series of 'monkey tricks', throwing peaches to midshipmen in the rigging (Hall, vol 1, p 35).

Tobacco's universal appeal should have been an eloquent reminder to Adam's children of their common descent. Modern men have enjoyed their social smoking, and offered each other cigarettes before smoking themselves; a vestigial sharing can outlive by ages the collective ownership of bygone times. But modern civilities are faint echoes of older customs. Poncins living and travelling with his Eskimos felt the joy of being part of a community, however small, performing its tasks together in 'harmony and serenity', and after they were over rolling cigarettes out of a common tin (p 262). On Melville's Pacific island of Typee tobacco was a scarce luxury, obtained in small amounts from foreigners. This compelled sparing use, and made sharing all the more brotherly.

> The islanders, who only smoke a whiff or two at a time, and at long intervals, and who keep their pipes going from hand to hand continually, regarded my systematic smoking of four or five pipefuls in succession, as something quite wonderful. (chaps 20, 23)

And in the Spanish- and Portuguese-speaking lands, more than in others, rich and poor could be brought together by their common love of tobacco in simple acts of helpfulness. At Pará, deep in the interior of Brazil, Bates the naturalist observed 'a gentle courtesy' among people of all conditions. 'I have seen a splendidly-dressed colonel, from the President's palace, walk up to a mulatto, and politely ask his permission to take a light from his cigar' (p 45).

Tobacco helped to see Britain through the twin ordeals of industrial revolution and Napoleonic Wars without either collapse or explosion. (An explosion may, no doubt, be what would have done it most good.) More generally, it has smoothed humanity's passage through its most tumultuous epoch of upheaval and change. Exploration and discovery have been a vital part of this: the film of the Soviet scientists settling down at the North Pole for a long season on floating ice showed them all puffing at cigarettes as they began the task of sorting out their equipment and setting up house in a strange new environment. For an individual who has lived long with the same pipe, it may grow into a trusted helpmate, somewhat like an African fetish; its familiar proximity is an assurance of life being on an even keel. Moreover the smoker, unlike the more materialistic chewer or snuffer, as a kindler of fire has some touch of the Promethean spirit. In times of stress the glowing pipe-bowl or cigarette-tip can resemble Portia's little candle, or 'a good deed in a naughty world'.

The benison has fallen in countless ways on different mortals. Fretted by a talk with a young son unable to pass his Latin test but wanting a car of his own, Babbitt 'lighted the gloriously satisfying first cigar of the day and tasted the exhilarating drug of the *Advocate-Times* headlines' (Lewis, *Babbitt*, chap 2). A woman in a Pavese novel, revelling in a hot bath in her hotel in Turin, recalled her last stay, during the War when all the pipes were broken and a bath was not to be had.

> I thought with pleasure: as long as you can have a bath, living is worth the effort.
> A bath and a cigarette. While I smoked, my hand dangling above the surface of the water, I contrasted the protracted bathing which now lulled me with the exciting days I had seen . . . (*Women*, p 6)

Tobacco as a dear companion has earned thanks as warm as Horace lavished on wine as a loosener of frozen tongues, a seal of friendship, an emboldener of the oppressed poor; an anthology like the one put together by A.E. Sims is evidence of how many and eloquent have been the tributes paid to it. English-speakers have surely stood first among the givers of praise. When someone told Carlyle that he was doing articles for the trade journal *Tobacco Plant*, it was enough to set the great smoker off into a paean to tobacco as

> one of the divinest benefits that had ever come to the human race, arriving as compensation and consolation at a time when social, political, religious anarchy and every imaginable plague made the earth unspeakably miserable . . . [in short a] miraculous blessing from the Gods. (Wilson and MacArthur, p 256)

Gissing made a more temperate but no less heartfelt acknowledgement of the twin virtues of tea and tobacco: an elevating theme in itself, for it is remarkable that nicotine has been able to blend so well with each of earth's three sovereign beverages, tea and coffee and wine. He comes home from a walk in chilly rain, and luxuriates in the restoring first cup, while he looks round at his books and pictures. 'I cast an eye on my pipe . . . And never, surely, is tobacco more soothing, more suggestive of humane thoughts, than when it comes just after tea – itself a bland inspirer' (*Ryecroft*, Part 4 sec 6). And Sir James Barrie divided English history into two halves, before and after tobacco. 'I know, I feel, that with the introduction of tobacco England woke up from a long sleep. Suddenly a new zest had been given to life. The glory of existence became a thing to speak of' (pp 106-7).

Hispanics, another race of devotees, have not been far behind in the chorus. One who stands out is Sarmiento, the Argentine writer who became president in 1868 and bequeathed his name to a city. He extolled smoking, in his narrative of travels in Europe in 1846-7, as 'the sole habit that makes brothers of all earth's peoples; for tobacco, in the three hundred years between its glorious discovery and our enlightened age has won more prose-lites [sic] than Christianity in two thousand, and without spilling a drop of blood' (p 153). Sarmiento inveighed against state mono-polies of tobacco as a villainous impost on 'man's prime need'. And in India by the late 19th century tobacco could be included by economists calculating 'the lowest absolute scale of necessaries' for the poorest. For an agricultural labourer in the Bombay Pre-sidency it would cost 5 rupees a year, as compared with 43½ rupees for food (Naoroji, p 27, cf p 171).

In the light of such testimonials, it may well seem that tyrants of the past who tried to prevent their subjects from smoking were betraying an inhuman mentality. But now a sterner veto than any of theirs is being imposed by Science, or the goddess Hygeia. Lauded so often as a good angel, tobacco has turned out at last a malignant witch, as Red Riding Hood's grandmother turned out to be a wolf. Only a sturdy optimist can fail to see here one more facet of a universal phenomenon of disenchantment. Everything that man delights in is bad for him, it appears, as is so often stated. Nicotine, sugar, alcohol and the rest are all 'pleasant vices' sent to plague him. The nursemaid's instruction – 'See what the children are doing, and tell them they mustn't' – might be just as well addressed to grown-ups. It may be more exact to say that the com-forts men have designed for what they call civilised life, passed in noisy crowded masses, may be psychologically helpful but phys-ically bad, because designed for a radically bad mode of living. Alone of the animals, they exist on two planes that are only loosely linked, and as a result, it may be surmised, of an accidentally speeded-up evolution of one part of themselves, their brain.

As for men's relations with one another, privately tobacco may well have improved them, but publicly its reign has coincided with an epoch of ferocious greed and crime, as well as of virtue and progress. Tobacco has been an innocent accomplice in colonial wars, slave trading, exploitation of labour. It has been, and is now when known to be a poison, sold by selfish men for profit, as others sell guns and bombs. There may have been something prophetic of how nicotine would turn to man's harm in the report by the Spanish invaders of America that some Indians had a method of fighting by squirting tobacco juice into their enemies' eyes (Fairholt, p 14).

Van Gogh in hospital complained pathetically of being forbidden to smoke; with nothing to distract him he lay all day and all night thinking about all the people he knew (p 473). If tobacco is abandoned, men may live longer, but not more happily. Today neuroses of all kinds seem (doubtless not for this reason alone) to afflict the literate classes which are giving it up, and to find disordered reflections in their arts and mode of living. Twenty years ago a hopeful believer writing to the press argued that everything made by God must contain good, and tobacco companies should devote their researches to finding what the good thing in the nicotine plant is; they would then be able to set themselves right with the world 'by producing something . . . of lasting benefit to the race, and of greater profit to themselves' (Bateman, p 124). But either the attempt has not been made, or it has not yet borne fruit.

Reasons for not smoking are various and unanswerable. It does physical harm to smokers and those near them, and financial harm to the public by straining medical resources. It is not an adequate reply to point out, as some have been doing, that smokers often die before being able to collect pensions, and thus cancel out the social cost they are responsible for. It is another black mark against them that while they choke their lungs with toxins, they help to choke every corner of the country with litter; their empty cigarette packets mingle with empty cans along every road and lane, and surround every rural bench. In Britain penalties for this behaviour are purely nominal, and its inhabitants must be the worst litter-louts in Europe. And official measures to dissuade smokers, not only here, have a make-believe look. In 1989 the European Community spent the equivalent of $8 million on anti-smoking publicity, and $1,190 million on subsidies to tobacco growers (*European*, 3-5 August 1990).

It is the poorer classes and countries that go on smoking. Clearly the best remedy would be to abolish poverty and ignorance. Most of the ills that nicotine has been needed to soothe have been man-made: war, hunger, overwork, lack of work. If these are allowed to continue, removal of tobacco will open the door further to other and worse drugs. Aldous Huxley had an acute sense of the human need for tranquillisers or pick-me-ups. He condemned alcohol and tobacco as 'very unsatisfactory euphorics, pseudo-stimulants and sedatives', on which people were ready to spend much more than on their children's education; he seemed to rest his hopes on new and better artificial substitutes. Looking back in 1959 on his Brave New World of 1932 he pointed out that improvements on its chemical pill 'Soma' had become possible – though he also saw the danger of their being utilised by dictators to manage public opinion (pp 99, 104-5). Mankind should throw physic of this kind to the dogs, and cure itself instead by radical reform of the worm-eaten social fabric, the moral slum we all inhabit today.

Kilvert, the Victorian curate on the Welsh Marches, heard of a 'Tom Tobacco' buried somewhere on the moors, but few claimed to know where his grave was, or its 'mysterious story' (pp 197, 201). In 1988 a two-minute film called *The Last Smoker* was heard of from Germany: 'When everybody thinks smokers are extinct, the last Smoker is sighted, in an isolated retreat.' So the Age of Tobacco is passing away (unless the reckless human race is dooming itself to pass away first), bequeathing to posterity a rich store of relics. Museums hold an immense array of pipes, snuff-boxes, and so on, to feed our curiosity and let our minds stray to departed owners who little knew that their treasures would one day repose in glass cases, under our gaze. Even fragments of old clay pipes turned up by the spade or washed up in Thames mud can make us think of the wisps of smoke that once stole through them, and guess at the wisps of thought that passed through their smokers' minds.

Tobacco faces banishment, but this ought not to mean oblivion. It has meant very much to legions of human beings, brought untold comfort to sufferers, performed innumerable small acts of kindness. It has allayed fears, consoled misfortune, lulled anger, called spirits from the vasty deep. A devotee who has abandoned its aid may well say with Macduff.

> I cannot but remember such things were,
> That were most precious to me.

It is time for us to take leave of tobacco, but it should not be an ungrateful farewell.

Books and Other Sources Quoted

Adolphus, J.L., *Letters from Spain in 1856-1857*, London, 1858.
Ahmed, Leila, *Edward W. Lane*, London, 1978.
Alatas, S.H., *The Myth of the Lazy Native*, London, 1877.
Alcott, Louisa M., *Little Women*, 1869.
'Alpha of the Plough', *Leaves in the Wind*, London, 1920.
Andros, A.C., *Sketches of a Holiday Scamper in Spain*, London, 1860.
Anon., 'An English Liberal', *Italy, its Condition; Great Britain, its Policy*, London, 1859.
Anon., 'Ghost Town', *Calico Ghost Town*, Calico: Cal., 1959.
Anon., Hist. Mss. Commission, *Newark on Trent: The Civil War Siegeworks*, London, 1964.
Anon., *Inside Sebastopol and Experiences in Camp*, London, 1856.
Anon., *Reminiscences of Marx and Engels*, Instit. of Marxism-Leninism, Moscow, nd.
Anon., 'Notes of a Tour through the Border States during the Civil War', *Macmillan's magazine*, VI, May–October 1862.
Anon., 'A Resident Officer', *Madrid in 1835*, London, 1836.
Anon., 'Reverend Doctor Syntax', *A Tour in Search of the Picturesque*
Anon., 'A Subaltern', *The Campaign in the Punjaub*, Edinburgh, 1849.
Anon., 'A Travelling Artist', *A Tour in Spain*, London, 1833.
Anon., *The Two Commissars* (an unpublished satire, Bombay, 1944).
Anon., 'A Young American' (H. Slidell-Mackenzie)
Anon.,
'Anstey, F.' (T.A. Guthrie), *Vice Versa*, London, 1882.
  Voces Populi, 1st Series, London, 1912.
Atteridge, A.H., *Famous Modern Battles*, London, 1913.
Aubrey, John, *Scandals and Credulities*, ed. J. Collier, New York, 1931.
Aulnoy, Mme d', *Travels into Spain*, 1691, 1930.
Austen, Jane, *Mansfield Park*, 1814.
Avrich, Paul, *Russian Rebels 1600-1800*, London, 1973.
Aytoun, W.E., *Stories and Verse*, ed W.L. Renwick, Edinburgh, 1964.
Baddeley, J.F., *The Russian Conquest of the Caucasus*, London, 1908.
Baker, Ida, *Katherine Mansfield*, 1971, 1985.
Balzac, H. de, *Les Chouans*, 1829.

Le Colonel Chabert, 1832.
La Maison Nucingen, 1838.
Barrie, J.M., *My Lady Nicotine*, London, 1890.
Bateman, M., ed, *This England. Selections from the New Statesman Column, 1934-1968*, Harmondsworth, 1969.
Bates, H.W., *The Naturalist on the River Amazon*, London, 1915.
Bateson, F.W. and Joukovsky, N.A., eds, *Alexander Pope*, Harmondsworth, 1971.
Baudelaire, C.P., *Les Fleurs du mal,* 1857.
Bayer, P., *Art Deco Source Book*, Oxford, 1988.
Beames, John, *Memoirs of a Bengal Civilian*, 1896; London edn, 1984.
Bell, G.H., ed, *The Hamwood Papers of the Ladies of Llangollen*, London, 1930.
Bell, J.H., *British Folks and British India Fifty Years Ago*, Manchester, nd.
Benham, W.G., *Cassell's Classified Quotations*, London, 1920.
Best, G., *Humanity in Warfare*, London, 1980.
Bierhorst, J., trans, *Four Masterworks of American Indian Literature*, New York, 1974.
Bird, Isabella, *The Yangtze Valley and Beyond*, 1899, 1985.
Blelhynden, K., *Calcutta Past and Present*, London, 1905.
Boas, F.S., *Marlowe and His Circle*, Oxford, 1929.
Boelcke, W.A., ed, *The Secret Conferences of Dr Goebbels October 1939 – March 1943*, London, 1967.
Bohannan, P., ed, *Law and Warfare. Studies in the Anthropology of Conflict*, New York, 1967.
Borrow, George, *Lavengro*, 1851.
The Romany Rye, 1857.
Boswell, James, *The Journal of a Tour to the Hebrides with Samuel Johnson*, 1775.
Boswell in Holland 1763-1764, ed. F.A. Pottle, London, 1952.
Bownas, G., ed, *The Penguin Book of Japanese Verse*, Harmondsworth, 1964.
Boxer, C.R., *The Dutch Seaborne Empire 1600-1800*, 1965, 1973.
The Portuguese Seaborne Empire 1415-1825, London, 1969.
Brand, John, *Popular Antiquities of Great Britain*, ed. Sir H. Ellis, London, 1854, 3 vols.
Braudel, Fernand, *Capitalism and Material Life 1400-1800*, London, 1973.
Brecht, Bertolt, *The Good Person of Szechwan*, 1943, 1987.
Brewer, J., *The Sinews of Power. War, Money and the English State 1688-1783*, London, 1989.
Briggs, Asa, *A Social History of England*, London 1983.
British Medical Association, *Smoking Out the Barons: The Campaign against the Tobacco Industry*, Chichester, 1986.
Brontë, Charlotte, *Jane Eyre*, 1847.
Shirley, 1849.
Browne, E.G. *A Year among the Persians* (1887-8), Cambridge, 1893.
Bryant, Arthur, *Triumph in the West 1943-1946*, London, 1959.

Bryant, W.C., *Letters from Spain and Other Countries in 1857 and 1858*, London, 1859.
Burke, Peter, *Popular Culture in Early Modern Europe*, London, 1978.
Burton, Richard R., *Pilgrimage to Al-Medinah and Meccah*, 1855-56.
   First Footsteps in East Africa, 1856, 1910.
   A Mission to Gelele King of Dahome, ed. C.W. Newbury, London, 1966.
Burton, Robert, *The Anatomy of Melancholy*, 1621; London, 1923.
Butler, Samuel (1612-80), *Poems*, ed. R. Bell, London, nd.
Butler, Samuel (1835-1902), *The Way of All Flesh*, London, 1903.
Calder, Angus, *Revolutionary Empire. The Rise of the English-Speaking Empires*, London, 1981.
Caldwell, Erskine, *Tobacco Road*, London, 1934.
Campbell, Thomas, *Letters from the South*, London, 1837.
Cardus, Neville, *Autobiography*, London, 1949.
Carlyle, Thomas,
   'Dr Francia' (1843), in *Scottish and Other Critical Miscellanies*, 1915.
   Latter-Day Pamphlets, no 2, 1850.
   Reminiscences, 1881, 1932.
Carroll, Lewis (C.L. Dodgson), *Alice's Adventures in Wonderland*, 1865.
Cartwright, F.W., *Disease and History*, New York, 1972.
Castellane, Count P. de, *Military Life in Algeria*, London, 1853.
Cather, Thomas, *Journal of a Voyage to America in 1836*, London, 1955.
Cayley, G.J., *Las Alforjas*, London, 1853.
Cederroth, S., 'Javanese and Sasak Folk Beliefs', in M. Lundahl and T. Svensson, eds, *Agrarian Society in History*, London, 1990.
Chakrabarty, D., *Rethinking Working-Class History. Bengal 1890-1940*, Princeton, NJ, 1989.
Chambers, R., *History of the Rebellion of 1745-6*, 1827.
Chandler, A.B., *Rendezvous on a Lost World*, London, nd.
Chelebi, Katib, *The Balance of Truth*, 1656, trans G.I. Lewis, London, 1957.
Chen, Jack, *The Sinkiang Story*, New York, 1977.
Chesneaux, J. et al, *China from the 1911 Revolution to Liberation*, Hassocks, 1977.
Christiansen, E., *The Origins of Military Power in Spain 1800-1854*, London, 1967.
Chute, Anthony, *Tabacco*, 1595, 1961.
Clark, G.N., *The Wealth of England from 1496 to 1760*, London, 1946.
Clark, Peter, *The English Alehouse: A Social History 1200-1830*, London, 1983.
Clayden, P.W., *Rogers and his Contemporaries*, London, 1889.
Cobbett, William, *Rural Rides*, 1912.
Cockburn, Lord, *Circuit Journeys*, 1888, 1983.
Coe, M.D., *The Maya*, Harmondsworth, 1971.
Coleridge, Hartley, *Letters*, ed. G.E. and E.L. Griggs, London, 1937.
Coleridge, S.T., *Collected Letters*, ed. E.L. Griggs, Oxford, 1966.
Coleridge, S.Y., *Table-Talk*, ed. H.N. Coleridge, 1840.
Collins, Mary, *Women at Prayer*, New York, 1987.

Colvin, Sir A., *The Making of Modern Egypt*, London, 1906.

Connolly, T.W.J., *The Romance of the Ranks; or, Anecdotes, Episodes and Social Incidents of Military Life*,

Conrad, Joseph, *Nostromo*, New York, 1904.
Chance, 1913, 1927.
The Rescue,
Last Essays, New York, 1926.

Coon, C.S., *The Hunting Peoples*, Harmondsworth, 1976.

Cooper, Fenimore, *The Pioneers*, 1823.

Cowper, William, *Letters*, ed. E.V. Lucas, London, nd.

Craig, David, *On the Crofters' Trail. In Search of the Clearance Highlanders*, London, 1990.

Cranmer-Byng, J.L., *An Embassy to China. The Journal Kept by Lord Macartney. 1793-1794*, London, 1962.

Crick, Bernard, *George Orwell*, London, 1980.

Cross, J.W., *George Eliot's Life*, New York, 1885.

Crow, Carl, *Harris of Japan*, London, 1939.

Cunninghame-Graham, R.B., *José Antonio Páez*, London, 1929.
Portrait of a Dictator: Francisco Solano Lopez, Paraguay, 1865-1870, London, 1933.

Curzon, Robert, *Visits to Monasteries in the Levant*, London, 1865.

Dalhousie, Marquess of, *Private Letters*, ed. J.G.A. Baird, Edinburgh, 1910.

Darby, H.C., *The Draining of the Fens*, Cambridge, 1940.

Darwin, Charles, *Autobiography*, added to by his son, London, 1929.

Dauchez, F., *Mon premier voyage en Espagne*, Paris, 1908.

Day, Robin, *Time for Lovers. A Personal Anthology*, London, 1977.

Deedy, J., *Literary Places. New York and New England*, Kansas City, 1978.

Defoe, Daniel, *Robinson Crusoe*, 1719; Everyman ed, 1906.

Dekker, Thomas, *Old Fortunatus*, 1600.
The Wonderful Year, 1603.
The Gul's Hornbook, 1609.

De Quincey, Thomas, *Reminiscences of the Lake Poets*, 1834-51, 1907.

Dermigny, L., *La Chine et l'occident. 1719-1833*, Paris, 1964.

Devine, T.M., *The Tobacco Lords. A Study of the Tobacco Merchants of Glasgow. c. 1740-90*, Edinburgh, 1975.

Dickens, Charles, *Oliver Twist*, 1837-39.
Barnaby Rudge, 1841.
Dombey and Son, 1848.
Hard Times, 1854.
The Uncommercial Traveller, 1861.

Dimbledy, D. and Reynolds, D., *An Ocean Apart. The Relationship between Britain and America in the Twentieth Century*, London, 1988.

Diösy, Arthur, *The New Far East*, 6th edition, London, 1904.

Disraeli, B., *Sybil; or, The Two Nations*, 1845.

Dixon, J.H., *Ballads and Songs of the Peasantry of England*, ed. R. Bell, London, nd.

Donaldson, Gordon, *Scotland. The Making of the Kingdom: James V – James VII*, Edinburgh, 1965.
Donkin, J.G., *Trooper in the Far North-West*, 1889; Saskatoon, 1987.
Doveton, F.P., *Reminiscences of the Burmese War in 1824-5-6*, London, 1852.
Doyle, A. Conan, *The Hound of the Baskervilles*, London, 1901.
The Lost World, London, 1912.
The Poison Belt,
Memories and Adventures, 1924; Oxford, 1989.
Dunae, P.A., in J. Richards, ed., *Imperialism and Juvenile Literature*, Manchester, 1989.
Dunn, R.S., *Sugar and Slaves. The English West Indies, 1624-1713*, London, 1973.
Durand, Col. A., *The Making of a Frontier*, London, 1900.
Durrell, G., *The Bafut Beagles*, London, 1954.
Eastman, L.E., in J.K. Fairbank and A. Feuerwerker, eds, *Cambridge History of China*, vol 13, 1986.
Eden, Emily, *Up the Country. Letters . . . from the Upper Provinces of India*, 1866; Oxford, 1937.
Edgeworth, Maria, *Ormond*, 1817.
Eeman, H., *Prelude to Diplomacy. My Early Years 1893-1919*, London, 1983.
Eisenstein, S.M., *Selected Works, Vol I, 1922-34*, London, 1988.
'Eliot, George' (Mary A. Evans), 'Amos Barton', in *Scenes of Clerical Life*, 1857.
Adam Bede, 1859.
Felix Holt, 1866.
Elliott, J.G., Maj-Gen, *Field Sports in India 1800-1947*, London, 1973.
Ellis, Havelock, *The Soul of Spain*, London, 1908.
Elwin, Verrier, *Leaves from the Jungle. Life in a Gond Village*, London, 1936.
Emery, F., *The Red Soldier. Letters from the Zulu War, 1879*, London, 1977.
Engels, Friedrich, *The Condition of the Working Class in England*, 1849; Harmondsworth, 1987.
Socialism: Utopian and Scientific, 1892.
Correspondence with Paul and Laura Lafargue, Moscow, 1960.
Epstein, Jerry, *Remembering Charlie*, London, 1988.
Erickson, John, *The Road to Stalingrad*, vol. 1, 1975; London edn, 1985.
Fairholt, F.W., *Tobacco: Its History and Associations*, London, 1859.
Farquhar, George, *The Beaux' Stratagem*, 1707.
Featherstone, D., *Colonial Small Wars 1837-1901*, Newton Abbot, 1973.
Fergusson, James, *John Fergusson 1727-1750*, London, 1948.
Ferrier, J.P., *Caravan Journeys and Wanderings*, 1857; Karachi, 1976.
Ferrier, Susan, *Marriage*, 1818.
Firth, C.H., *Cromwell's Army*, London, 1902.
Fletcher, J., Chap 2 of J.K. Fairbank, ed, *Cambridge History of China* Vol 10, 1978.
Forbes, Archibald, *Memories and Studies of War and Peace*, London, 1898.
Ford, Richard, *Gatherings from Spain*, London, 1846.

Forster, E.M., *The Hill of Devi*, 1953; Harmondsworth, 1965.

Fountaine, Margaret, *Love among the Butterflies: Diaries, 1878-1913*, ed. W.F. Cater, Harmondsworth, 1982.

Franchère, Gabriel, *Journal of a Voyage on the North-West Coast of North America*, 1820; Toronto, 1969.

Franklin, Sir John, *The Journey to the Polar Sea*, 1910.

Fraser, Ronald, *Blood of Spain. The Experience of Civil War, 1936-1939*, London, 1979.

Froude, J.A., *Thomas Carlyle. A History of the First Forty Years of His Life 1795-1835*, London, 1896.

Gade, J.A., *Christian IV King of Denmark and Norway*, London, 1927.

Galbraith, J.K., *The Scotch*, Toronto, 1964.

Galsworthy, John, *In Chancery*, London, 1920.

'The Indian Summer of a Forsyte', in *The Forsyte Saga*, London, 1922.

Galt, John, *The Entail*, 1822.

Gaskell, Elizabeth, *Mary Barton*, 1848.

Cranford, 1853.

Gaskell, P., *The Manufacturing Population of England*, London, 1833.

Gautier, Théophile, *Wanderings in Spain*, London, 1853.

Gay, John, *The Beggar's Opera*, 1727.

Gell, Sir W., *Narrative of a Journey in the Morea*, London, 1823.

Ginger, R., *Eugene V. Debs. The Making of an American Radical*, 1949; New York, 1962.

Gissing, George, *The Private Papers of Henry Ryecroft*, London, 1903.

Gledhill, C., ed, *Home is Where the Heart Is. Studies in Melodrama and the Woman's Film*, London, 1987.

Goldsmith, Oliver, *The Good-Natur'd Man*, 1768.

Goncharov, I.A., *The Same Old Story*, 1847; English edition, Moscow, nd.

The Frigate Pallada, 1856; trans K. Goetze, New York, 1987.

Gordon, P.L., *Belgium and Holland*, London, 1834.

Gramsci, Antonio, *Lettres de la prison*, trans J. Noaro, Parish, 1953.

Grant, Elizabeth, *Memoirs of a Highland Lady*, ed. A. Tod, 1898; Edinburgh, 1988.

Grant, I.F., *Highland Folk Ways*, London, 1961.

Grant, James, *The Romance of War*, London, 1889.

Graves, Charles, *A Pipe Smoker's Guide*, London, 1969.

Graves, R. and Hodge, A., *The Long Week-End. A Social History of Great Britain 1918-1939*, London, 1940.

Gray, Thomas, *Poems . . . Letters and Essays*, 1912.

Gregorovius, F., *Siciliana. Sketches of Naples and Sicily in the Nineteenth Century*, London, 1914.

Gregory, J.S., *Great Britain and the Taipings*, London, 1969.

Grimble, Sir A., *A Pattern of Islands*, London, 1952.

Grogan, E.S. and Sharp A., *From the Cape to Cairo*, London, 1899.

Gross, John, *The Rise and Fall of the Man of Letters*, Harmondsworth, 1973.

Grunberger, R., *A Social History of the Third Reich*, Harmondsworth, 1974.

Guevara, Che, *Guerrilla Warfare*, 1961; Harmondsworth, 1969.
Guillet, E.C., *Early Life in Upper Canada*, Toronto, 1933.
Gurr, A., *Playgoing in Shakespeare's London*, Cambridge, 1987.
Habib, Irfan, *The Agrarian System of Mughul India (1556-1707)*, Bombay, 1863.
Hadfield, M., *A History of British Gardening*, Harmondsworth, 1965.
Hafen, L.R., *The Life of Thomas Fitzpatrick: Mountain Man, Guide and Indian Agent*, 1931; 1973.
Hale, Georgia, *Memoirs*, unpublished.
Haliburton, Thomas C., *The Clockmaker . . . Samuel Slick of Slickville*, 1st series, 1836; Toronto, 1958.
Hall, Capt. Basil, *Voyages*, Edinburgh, 1826.
Halliwell, L., *Halliwell's Filmgoer's Companion*, 9th edn, London, 1988.
Halter, T., in R.R. Bezzola, ed, *Anthology of Swiss-Romansch Literature*, London, 1971.
Hamilton, Lord Frederick, *The Days Before Yesterday*, London, 1920.
Here, There and Everywhere, London, 1921.
Hanford, J.H., *John Milton, Englishman*, London, 1950.
Hanson, L. and E., *Necessary Evil. The Life of Jane Welsh Carlyle*, London, 1952.
Hardman, F., *The Spanish Campaign in Morocco*, Edinburgh, 1860.
Hardy, J.B., *Papers*, in National Army Museum, London.
Harrer, H., *Seven Years in Tibet*, London, 1953.
Harrington, R., *The Inuit. Life As It Was*, Edmonton, 1981.
Harris, Joel C., *Uncle Remus*, 1880.
Harrison, J.F.C., *The Common People*, London, 1984.
Hazlitt, William, *Winterslow*, 1839.
Heide, R. and Gilman, J., *Starstruck. The Wonderful World of Movie Memorabilia*, New York, 1986.
Heine, Heinrich, *Italian Travel Sketches, etc.*, trans E.A. Sharp, London, nd.
Henderson, P., *Samuel Butler. The Incarnate Bachelor*, London, 1953.
Henry, R.S., *The Story of the Mexican War*, New York, 1961.
Herbert of Cherbury, Lord, *Autobiography*, ed. S. Lee, 1886.
Herbert, F.W. von, *The Defence of Plevna, 1877*, revised edition, London, 1911.
Herr, R., *Modern Spain*, Berkeley, Cal., 1971.
Hervey, M.H., *Dark Days in Chile. An Account of the Revolution of 1891*, London, 1892.
Herzen, Alexander, *Childhood, Youth and Exile*, 1852-3; Oxford, 1980.
Hewison, J.K., *The Covenanters*, Vol 2, Glasgow, 1908.
Hibbert, C., *The Great Mutiny. India 1857*, Harmondsworth, 1980.
Higginson, T.W., *Army Life in a Black Regiment*, New York edn, 1962.
Hill, Christopher, *The World Turned Upside Down. Radical Ideas during the English Revolution*, Harmondsworth, 1975.
A Turbulent, Seditious, and Factious People. John Bunyan and His Church 1628-1688, Oxford, 1988.
Hobbs, Maj. H., *John Barleycorn Bahadur. Old Time Taverns in India*, Calcutta, 1944.

Hobhouse, L.T., *Morals in Evolution*, 1906; London, 1951.

Hodgkin, Thomas, *Vietnam. The Revolutionary Path*, London, 1981.

Hoggart, R., *The Uses of Literacy*, Harmondsworth, 1958.

Hornby, Sir Edmund, *An Autobiography*, London, 1929.

Horne, A., *The Price of Glory. Verdun 1916*, 1962; Harmondsworth edn, 1964.

Hudson, W.H., *Far Away and Long Ago*, London, 1918.

Hughes, Geoffrey, *Words in Time. A Social History of the English Vocabulary*, Oxford, 1988.

Hughes, G.B. et al, *The Country Life Antiques Handbook*, Twickenham, 1986.

Hughes, Robert, *The Fatal Shore. A History of the Transportation of Convicts to Australia, 1787-1868*, London, 1987.

Hughes, Thomas, *Tom Brown's Schooldays*, 1857.

Hughes, T.M., *An Overland Journey to Lisbon*, London, 1847.

Hutchinson, Lester, *Conspiracy at Meerut*, London, 1935.

Huxley, Aldous, *Brave New World Revisited*, London, 1959.

Huxley, Francis, *The Way of the Sacred*, London, 1980.

Hyne, C.J. Cutliffe, *Through Arctic Lapland*, London, nd.

Irving, Gordon, *The Solway Smugglers*, Dumfries, 1972.

Isherwood, Christopher, *Christopher and his Kind*, New York, 1976.

Israel, J.I., *Dutch Primacy in World Trade 1585-1740*, Oxford, 1989.

Izumo, Takeda, etc., *Chushingura*, 1748; trans D. Keene, New York, 1971.

Jakovsky, A., *Tabac-magie*, Paris, 1961.

James, Henry, *The Princess Casamassima*, 1886.

James, Henry, *Washington Square*, 1881.

James, William, *The Varieties of Religious Experience*, 1901-2; Glasgow, 1979.

Jefferies, R., *Hodge and his Masters*, 1880; London, 1979.

Jefferys, J.B., ed, *Labour's Formative Years (1848-1879)*, London, 1948.

Jerome, Jerome K., *Three Men in a Boat*, 1888; annotated edition by C. Matthew and B. Green, London, 1982.
Three Men on the Bummel, 4th edition, 1926.
My Life and Times, 1926; London, 1984.

Joffe, Maria, *One Long Night*, trans V. Dixon, London, 1978.

Jonson, Samuel, *Lives of the English Poets*, 1777.

Johnson, Ben, *The Complete Plays*, 1910.

Joyce, James, *A Portrait of the Artist as a Young Man*, 1916.

Jullian, Philippe, *Oscar Wilde*, London, 1971.

Kaplan, Fred, *Thomas Carlyle. A Biography*, Cambridge, 1983.

Kaplan, H.I. and Sadock, B.J., *Comprehensive Textbook of Psychiatry III*, 3rd edition, Baltimore, 1981.

Kapp, Yvonne, *Eleanor Marx*, Vol 1, *Family Life 1855-1882*, London, 1972, 1979.

Keats, John, *Letters*, ed. Sidney Colvin, 1891; London, 1935.

Keddie, N.R., ed., *Scholars, Saints, and Sufis*, Berkeley, Cal., 1978.

Kelly, Rev. Charles,

Kilvert, Rev. Francis, *Diary 1870-1879*, ed. W. Plomer, Harmondsworth, 1977.

Kincaid, D., *British Social Life in India, 1608-1937,* 1938; London, 1973.

Kinglake, A.W., *Eothen,* 1844; London, 1948.

Kingsley, Charles, *Alton Locke,* 1850.

Knox, Bernard, in ed. P. Sloan, *John Cornford. A Memoir,* London, 1938.

Kunene, Mazisi, trans, *Emperor Shaka the Great. A Zulu Epic,* London, 1979.

Lafargue, Paul, *The Right to be Lazy,* 1883; Chicago, 1975.
    Textes choisis, ed. J. Girault, Paris, 1970.

Lamb, Charles, *Letters,* London, 1909.

Landes, D.S., *Revolution in Time. Clocks and the Making of the Modern World,*
    Cambridge, Mass., 1983.

Lane, E.W., *Manners and Customs of the Modern Egyptians,* 1860, 1908.

Lee, Sir Sidney, et al, eds, *Shakespeare's England,* Oxford, 1916.

Lefebure, Molly, *Samuel Taylor Coleridge. A Bondage of Opium,* London,
    1974.

Le Gallienne, R., *The Romantic '90s,* New York, 1926.

Legge, J.G., *Rhyme and Revolution in Germany . . . 1813-1850,* London, 1918.

Lehmann, J.H., *All Sir Garnet. A Life of Field-Marshal Lord Wolseley,*
    London, 1964.

Leslie, Anita, *Jennie. The Life of Lady Randolph Churchill,* London, 1969.

Lessner, F. *see* Anon., *Reminiscences of Marx and Engels.*

Lever, Charles, *A Rent in a Cloud,* London, 1969.

Levi, P., *The Life and Times of William Shakespeare,* London, 1988.

Lewis, Maj. Gen. H.V., Papers, Imperial War Museum, London.

Lewis, Sinclair, *Babbitt,* 1922.
    Gideon Planish, 1943; London, 1966.

Leyda, Jay, *A History of the Russian and Soviet Film,* 3rd edn, London, 1983.

Libert, Lutz, *Tobacco, Snuff-Boxes and Pipes,* London, 1986.

Lindsay, Jack, *J.M.W. Turner,* London, 1966.

Livingstone, David, *Missionary Correspondence 1841-1856,* London, 1961.

Lockhart, J.G., *Peter's Letters to his Kinsfolk,* 1819; London, 1952.
    The Life of Sir Walter Scott, 1838.

Lockwood, D., *I, the Aboriginal* (London, 1963).

'Long Lance', *Autobiography of a Blackfoot Indian Chief,* London, 1976.

Longford, Elizabeth, *Wellington. The Years of the Sword,* London, 1969.

'Loti, Pierre' (L.M.J. Viaud), *Le Roman d'un Spahi,* 1881.
    Vers Isfahan 1904.

Lover, Samuel, *Handy Andy,* 1842.

Luke, Sir Harry, *Malta,* 1949; London, 1968.

Lynn, J. and Jay, A., 'The Smokescreen', *Yes, Prime Minister,* no 7, London,
    1989.

McClellan, G.B., *Venice and Bonaparte,* Princeton, NJ, 1931.

Macartney, Lord, *An Embassy to China,* journal, ed. J.L. Cranmer-Byng,
    London, 1962.

MacDermott, Mercia, *A History of Bulgaria 1393-1885,* London, 1962.

Mackenzie, Sir Compton, *Sublime Tobacco,* London, 1957.

Macpherson, G., *Life of Lal Behari Day,* Edinburgh, 1900.

Macready, William Charles, The Diaries of, 1833-1851, London, 1912.
Malmesbury, Earl of, *Memoirs of an Ex-Minister,* Leipzig, 1885.
Manson, Thomas, *Lerwick During the Last Half Century,* Lerwick, 1923.
Markham, C.R., *The War between Peru and Chile 1879-1882,* London, 1882.
Marryat, Capt. F., *Peter Simple,* 1834.
Mr Midshipman Easy, 1836.
Martin, R.B., *Tennyson, the Unquiet Heart,* Oxford, 1983.
Martin, R.G., *Lady Randolph Churchill,* London, 1972.
Martin, Theodore, *The Life of His Royal Highness the Prince Consort,* London, 1877.
Marvin, C., *The Russians at Merv and Herat,* London, 1883.
Marx, Karl. *The Eighteenth Brumaire of Louis Bonaparte,* 1852.
Mason, J.A., *The Ancient Civilizations of Peru,* Harmondsworth, 1957.
Mason, Philip, *A Matter of Honour. An Account of the Indian Army,* 1974; Harmondsworth edn, 1976.
Massingham, H.J., ed, *A Treasury of Seventeenth-Century English Verse,* London, 1919.
Maude, Aylmer, *The Life of Tolstoy,* 1908-10; London, 1930.
Maxwell, Constantia, *Country and Town in Ireland under the Georges,* London, 1940.
Maxwell, Sir Herbert, *The Life and Letters of George William Frederick Fourth Earl of Clarendon,* London, 1913.
Mayhew, Henry, *London Labour and the London Poor.* (Selections by P. Quennell: *Mayhew's London,* London, nd.
Melville, Herman, *Typee,* 1846.
White Jacket, 1850.
Meyrick, Rev. F., *The Practical Working of the Church of Spain,* Oxford, 1851.
Michell, Lynn, *Growing up in Smoke,* London, 1990.
Miller, D.H., *Custer's Fall. The Indian Side of the Story,* 1957; London, 1965.
Milne, James, *The Epistles of Atkins,* London, n d.
Molé, Count (1781-1855), The Life and Memoirs of, London, 1974.
'Molière' (J.-B. Poquelin), *Don Juan,* 1665.
Moore, D.L., *Lord Byron. Accounts Rendered,* London, 1974.
Moore, William, *See How They Ran,* London, 1970.
Morier, James, *The Adventures of Hajji Baba of Ispahan,* 1824.
Morton, A.L., *The World of the Ranters,* London, 1970.
Mozart, W.A., *The Letters of Mozart and his Family,* ed. E. Anderson, 3rd edition, London, 1985.
Murray, K.M.E., *Caught in the Web of Words. James A.H. Murray and the Oxford English Dictionary,* Oxford, 1979.
Naoroji, Dadabhai, *Poverty and Un-British Rule in India,* London, 1901.
Nef, J.U., *War and Human Progress,* London, 1950.
Nevill, Lady Dorothy, Leaves from the Note-Books of, ed. R. Nevill, London, 1910.
Nickerson, R., *Robert Louis Stevenson in California,* San Francisco, 1982.
Noble, J.R., ed., *Recollections of Virginia Woolf,* Harmondsworth, 1975.

O'Brien, G., *The Economic History of Ireland in the Seventeenth Century*, Dublin, 1919.
O'Casey, Sean, *Drums under the Window*, London, 1945.
O'Donnell, P., *The Irish Faction Fighters of the 19th Century*, Dublin, 1975.
O'Donovan, E., *Merv*, London, 1883.
Orwell, George (Eric Blair), *Down and Out in Paris and London*, 1933; Harmondsworth, 1974.
Oudendyk, W.J., *Ways and By-Ways in Diplomacy*, London, 1939.
Owen, Wilfred, *Collected Letters*, London, 1967.
Palmerston, Lord, *Letters to L. and E. Sulivan 1804-1863*, London, 1979.
Park, Mungo, *Travels in Africa*, 1799, 1805, 1907.
Parkman, Francis, The Journals of, ed. M. Wade, London, 1946.
Parry, J.H., *The Spanish Seaborne Empire*, London, 1966.
Pavese, Cesare, *Among Women Only*, London, 1953.
  A Diary: 1935-1950. This Business of Living, London, 1961.
Payne, S.G., *Politics and the Military in Modern Spain*, Stanford, 1967.
Pearman, *Sergeant Pearman's Memoirs*, ed. Marquess of Anglesey, London, 1968.
Pearsall, R., *Conan Doyle*, Glasgow, 1989.
Pemble, J., *The Raj, the Indian Mutiny and the Kingdom of Oudh 1801-1859*, Cranbury, N.J., 1977.
Pennycuick, Lt.Col. J., *Papers*, in National Army Museum.
Penzer, N.M., *The Harem*, London, 1936.
Pepys, Samuel, *Diary*, ed. H.B. Wheatley, London, 1949.
Petöfi, Sándor, anthology: French trans by J. Rousselot, Budapest, 1971.
Phillips. A., *My Uncle George*, London, 1986.
Phillips, Phoebe, ed, *The Collectors' Encyclopaedia of Antiques*, London, 1973.
Pinero, Arthur, *The Magistrate*, 1885.
  The Gay Lord Quex, 1899.
Plaatje, Sol T., The Boer War Diary of, ed. J.L. Comaroff, London, 1973.
Poncins, G. de, *Kabloona*, London, 1942.
Post, Laurens van der, *The Lost World of the Kalahari*, London, 1958.
Pottle, F.A., *James Boswell, The Earlier Years 1740-1769*, London, 1966.
Prawer, S.S., *Karl Marx and World Literature*, Oxford, 1976.
Prebble, John, *Glencoe*, Harmondsworth, 1968.
Prendergast, John, *Prender's Progress. A Soldier in India, 1931-47*, London, 1979.
Prichard, Iltudus, *The Chronicles of Budgepore*, 1870; Delhi, 1972.
Priestley, Philip, *Victorian Prison Lives*, London, 1985.
  Jail Journeys. The English Prison Experience Since 1918, London, 1989.
Proust, Marcel, *Cities of the Plain, Part 2* (1922), trans C.K. Scott-Moncrieff, London, 1941.
Pushkin (Poushkin), Alexander, Prose Tales, trans. T. Keane, London, 1914.
Radek, Karl, *Portraits and Pamphlets*, London, 1935.
Rahim, Muhammad Abdur, *Social and Cultural History of Bengal*, Karachi, 1963.

Ramsay, Allan, *The Gentle Shepherd*, 1725.
Ramsay, Dean, *Reminiscences of Scottish Life and Character*, 1857-61; 26th edition reprint, Edinburgh 1947.
Raychaudhuri, T., 'Mughal India', in *Cambridge Economic History of India*, vol. 1, 1982.
Reed, John, *Ten Days that Shook the World*, 1919; Harmondsworth, 1977.
Renoir, Jean, *Renoir, My Father*, London, 1988.
Richard, et Quétin, *Guide du voyageur en Espagne et en Portugal*, Paris, 1853.
Ridley, J., *The Tudor Age*, London, 1988.
Rijnhart, S.C., *With the Tibetans in Tent and Temple*, Edinburgh, 1901.
Robert, J.C., *The Story of Tobacco in America*, New York, 1952.
Rose, J.H., *The Life of Napoleon I*, London, 1913.
Ross, Sir E. Denison, *Both Ends of the Candle*, London, 1943.
Ross, Michael, *People of the Mirage*, London, 1952.
Rowse, A.L., *The Elizabethan Renaissance*, London, 1974.
Royle, E., *Modern Britain. A Social History 1750-1985*, Baltimore, 1987.
Rudman, H.W., *Italian Nationalism and English Men of Letters*, London, 1940.
Rumbold, Sir H., *Further Recollections of a Diplomatist*, London, 1903.
Russell, Ralph, *Ghalib, The Poet and His Age*, London, 1972.
Sabri-Tabrizi, G.R., *Iran: A Child's Story, a Man's Experience*, Edinburgh, 1989.
Sachse, W.L., *The Colonial American in Britain*, Madison, 1956.
Saikaku, Ihara, *The Life of an Amorous Woman*, 1686; London, 1964.
Saint-Amand, I. de, *Napoleon III and his Court*, London, 1900.
Saltykov-Shchedrin, N.E., *The Golovlyov Family*, 1934.
Sanderson, E., *Africa in the Nineteenth Century*, London, 1898.
Sarmiento, D.F., *Viajes por Europa, Africa i América 1845-1847*, 1849; Collected Works, vol. 5.
Sassoon, Siegfried, *Memoirs of an Infantry Officer*, 1930; new edition, London, 1944.
Schama, S., *The Embarrassment of Riches. An Interpretation of Dutch Culture in the Golden Age*, London, 1987.
Schiroauer, A., *Lassalle*, London, 1931.
Scholl-Latour, P., *Death in the Ricefields*, London, 1981.
Scott, Dick, *Ask That Mountain. The Story of Parihaka*, Auckland, 1975.
Scott, Michael, *Tom Cringle's Log*, 1836, 1915.
Scott, Walter, *Guy Mannering*, 1815.
    The Bride of Lammermoor, 1819.
    The Fortunes of Nigel, 1822.
    St Ronan's Well, 1823.
    The Surgeon's Daughter, 1827.
    Journal, 1825-32, 1890; London, nd.
Seidensticker, E., *Kafu the Scribbler. The Life and Writings of Nagai Kafu, 1879-1959*, Stanford, 1965.
Seigel, J., *Marx's Fate. The Shape of a Life*, Princeton, NJ, 1978.
Selden, John, *Table Talk*, 1689; London, 1887.

Shankland, P. and Hunter, A., *Malta Convoy*, 1963.

Sharar, Abdul Halim, *Lucknow: The Last Phase of an Oriental Culture*, London, 1975.

Sharif, Ja'far, *Islam in India*, ed. G.A. Herklots, 1832; London, 1972.

Shepperson, G.A., 'Cecil Rhodes', Seminar paper, Edinburgh University, 9 February 1981.

Shooter, Rev. Joseph, *The Kaffirs of Natal and the Zulu Country*, London, 1857.

Silva, C.R. de, *Ceylon under the British Occupation 1795-1833*, Colombo, 1962.

Simpson, R.B., *Robert Louis Stevenson's Edinburgh Days*, London, 1898.

Sims, A.E., ed, *The Witching Weed. A Smoker's Anthology*, London reprint, 1927.

Sinclair, Upton, *Autobiography*, London, 1963.

Singh, Bawa Satinder, *The Jammu Fox. A Biography of Maharaja Gulab Singh of Kashmir 1792-1857*, 1974.

Singh, N. Iqbal, *The Andaman Story*, Delhi, 1978.

Sita Ram, *From Sepoy to Subedar*, 1873; London, 1970.

Skinner, Rev. John, *Journal*, ed. H. and P. Combs, Oxford, 1971.

Smailes, Helen, *Scottish Empire*, Edinburgh, 1981.

Small, Maj. A.R., *The Road to Richmond*, 1957.

Smith, Adam, *The Wealth of Nations*, 1776; London, 1904.

Smith, Albert, *A Month at Constantinople*, London, 1850.
The Pottleton Legacy, London, 1856.

Smith, J.T., *Nollekens and his Times*, London, 1828.

Smollett, Tobias, *The Expedition of Humphrey Clinker*, 1771, 1943.

Snowden, Philip, *An Autobiography*, London, 1934.

Sobel, R. and Francis, D., *Chaplin: Genesis of a Clown*, London, 1977.

Solzhenitsyn, Alexander, *One Day in the Life of Ivan Denisovich*, Harmondsworth, 1963.

Spalding, H., trans, *Khiva and Turkestan*, London, 1874.

Speke, J.H., *Journal of the Discovery of the Source of the Nile*, 1863, 1906.

Spence, J.D., *The Gate of Heavenly Peace. The Chinese and their Revolution, 1895-1980*, London, 1982.

Spenser, Edmund, *The Faerie Queene. Books I-III*, 1589.

Stanhope, Philip Earl, *Conversations with the Duke of Wellington 1831-1851*, 1888; London, 1938.

Stark, Freya, *The Valleys of the Assassins*, London, 1934.

Steedman, Carolyn, *The Radical Soldier's Tale. John Pearman, 1819-1908*, London, 1988.

Steinbeck, John, *The Log from the 'Sea of Cortez'*, 1941; New York, 1977.

Steinmetz, A., *The Romance of Duelling*, London, 1868.

Stenton, J., in *The Beaver*, Winnipeg, April-May 1987.

Stern, J.P., *Hitler. The Führer and the People*, Glasgow, 1975.

Sterne, Laurence, *A Sentimental Journey*, 1768.

Stevenson, Robert Louis, 'The Lantern Bearers', *Across the Plains*, 1883.
Treasure Island, 1883.

Prince Otto, 1885.
Kidnapped, 1886.
Vailima Letters, ed. Sir C. Colvin, Edinburgh, 1895.
In the South Seas, London, 1896.
'"A Penny Plain and Twopence Coloured'", in *Memories and Portraits*, London, 1912.
Storm, Theodore, *Immensee*, 1852.
Storr, Anthony, *The Dynamics of Creation*, Harmondsworth, 1976.
Strickland, Gen. Sir Peter, Diaries, Imperial War Museum, London.
Stuart, Col. W.K., *Reminiscences of a Soldier*, London, 1874.
Sudermann, H., *Frau Sorge*, New York, 1891.
Surtees, W., *Twenty-Five Years in the Rifle Brigade*, Edinburgh, 1833.
Tanner, J.R., ed, *Tudor Constitutional Documents 1485-1603*, Cambridge, 1930.
Taseer, Salman, *Bhutto: A Political Biography*, London, 1979.
Taylor, Tom, *The Ticket-of-Leave Man*, 1863.
Teng, S.Y., *The Taiping Rebellion and the Western Powers*, Oxford, 1971.
Tennant, C., *The Radical Laird. A Biography of George Kinloch 1775-1833*, Kineton, 1970.
Tennyson, Hallam, *Alfred Lord Tennyson*, London, 1897.
Tetens, Alfred, *Among the Savages of the South Seas. Memoirs of Micronesia, 1862-1868*, Stanford, 1958.
Thackeray, W.M., *A Shabby Genteel Story*, 1840.
Catherine, 1838.
Vanity Fair, 1847-48.
'A St Philip's Day at Paris', in *Sketches by M.A. Titmarsh*, 1841.
Notes of a Journey from Cornhill to Grand Cairo, 1846.
The Book of Snobs, 1848.
The English Humourists, 1851.
The Four Georges, 1855.
Thayer, W.T., *From Log Cabin to White House. The Life of James A. Garfield*, 1882.
Theobald, A.B., *The Mahdiya*, London, 1951.
Thesiger, W., *Arabian Sands*, London, 1960.
Thieblin, N.L., ('Azamat-Batuk'), *Spain and the Spaniards*, London, 1874.
Thomas, Dylan, *A Child's Christmas in Wales*, 1954.
Thompson, David, *Narrative of Explorations of Western America 1784-1812*, ed. J. B. Tyrrell, Toronto, 1916.
Thompson, E.P., *The Making of the English Working Class*, London, 1963.
William Morris, 2nd edition, London, 1977.
Thompson, Flora, *Lark Rise*, Oxford, 1939.
Thompson, Paul, *The Edwardians. The Remaking of British Society*, St Albans, 1977.
Thomson, W.H., *History of Manchester to 1852*, Altrincham, 1966.
Thoreau, Henry, *Journals*, ed. O. Shepard, New York, 1961.
Thorburn, S.S., *Bannu; or our Afghan Frontier*, London, 1876.
Thornbury, W., *Life in Spain, Past and Present*, London, 1859.

Thurston, E., *The Madras Presidency*, Cambridge, 1913.
Tolstoy, L.N., *'The Cossacks' and Other Stories*, Harmondsworth, 1960.
Tomlinson, H.M., *Tidemarks*, London, 1924.
Tracy, Honor, *The Straight and Narrow Path*, Harmondsworth, 1960.
Trench, C. Chevenix, *Charley Gordon*, London, 1978.
Tressell, R., *The Ragged Trousered Philanthropists*, 1914; London, 1955.
Trevor-Roper, H.R., *The Last Days of Hitler*, new edition, London, 1962.
Trollope, Anthony, *The Warden*, 1855.
    Doctor Thorne, 1858.
    The American Senator, 1877.
    Is He Popenjoy?, 1878.
    Thackeray, 1879.
    The Duke's Children, 1880.
    An Autobiography, 1883; World's Classics edn, 1923.
Trollope, Frances, *Domestic Manners of the Americans*, 1832; London, 1927.
Trotter, Thomas, *An Essay Medical, Philosophical, and Chemical on Drunkenness*, 1804; ed. Roy Porter, London, 1988.
Tung, Wu, *The Flight of an Empress*, ed. I. Pruitt, New Haven, Conn., 1931.
Turgenev, I.S., *Smoke*, 1867; English edn, London, 1949.
    On the Eve, Harmondsworth, 1950.
Turner, Thomas, *The Diary of, 1754-1765*, ed. D. Vaisey, Oxford, 1985.
'Twain, Mark' (S.L. Clemens), *Roughing It*, 1871; ed. F.R. Rogers, 1972.
    Life on the Mississippi, 1883.
    Tom Sawyer Abroad, 1894.
Tylor, Charles, *The Camisards*, London, 1893.
Tyndall, John, *Glaciers of the Alps*, 1860, 1906.
Valensi, L., *Fellahs tunisiens*, Paris, 1977.
Van Gogh, Vincent, *Lettres à son frère Théo*, trans L. Roëdlandt, Paris, 1988.
Vassiltchikov, Marie, *The Berlin Diaries 1940-1945*, London, 1990.
Victoria, The Letters of Queen, ed. A.C. Benson and Lord Esher, London, 1908.
Vigny, Alfred de, *Servitude et grandeur militaires*, 1935; Paris, nd.
Vitzthum von Eckstaedt, Count C.F., *St. Petersburg and London in the Years 1852-1864. Reminiscences*, London, 1887.
Wagenknecht, E., *Longfellow*, New York, 1955.
Wale, H.J., *Sword and Surplice*, London, 1880.
Walker, A., *The Shattered Silence. How the Talkies Came to Stay*, London, 1986.
Wallis, S.T., *Glimpses of Spain*, New York, 1849.
Walmsley, H.N., *Sketches of Algeria during the Kabyle War*, London, 1958.
Washington, Booker, T., *Up From Slavery*, 1901; Oxford, 1945.
Waterfield, The Memoirs of Private, ed. A. Swinson and D. Scott, London, 1968.
Waterton, Charles, *Wanderings in South America*, 1825.
Watt, Sir George, *The Commercial Products of India*, London, 1908.
Webb, Beatrice, *My Apprenticeship*, London, 1926.

Wedgwood, J.C. (Lord Barlaston), *Papers*, in Imperial War Museum.
West, Sir Algernon, *Recollections 1832 to 1886*, London, 1899.
Wheatley, *The Diary*, ed. C. Hibbert, London, 1964.
Whitman, Sidney, *German Memories*, London, 1912.
Whymper, E., *Travels among the Great Andes of the Equator*, London, 1892.
Wilde, Oscar, *The Picture of Dorian Gray*, 1891.
Willett, John, *The Theatre of Bertolt Brecht*, revised edition, London, 1977.
Williams, Gwyn, *The Land Remembers. A View of Wales*, London, 1978.
Wilson, D.A., *Carlyle to Threescore and Ten (1853-1865)*, London, 1929.
Wilson, D.A., and MacArthur, D.W., *Carlyle in Old Age (1865-1881)*, London, 1934.
Wilson, John, ('Christopher North'), *Noctes Ambrosianae*, Edinburgh, 1822-34, 1892.
Winnington, Alan, *The Slaves of the Cool Mountains*, 1959; Berlin edn, 1962.
Witte, Sergei, *Memoirs*
Woodham-Smith, C., *The Reason Why*, Harmondsworth, 1958.
Woolf, Virginia, *To the Lighthouse*, London, 1927.
Wordsworth, Dorothy, *Journals*, ed E. de Selincourt, Vol 2, London, 1952.
Wright, L.B., *Middle Class Culture in Elizabethan England*, London, 1935.
Wurgaft, L.D., *The Imperial Imagination*, Middletown, Conn., 1983.
Wyatt, Victoria, *Shapes of Their Thoughts. Reflections of Culture Contact in Northwest Coast Indian Art*, 1984.
Yeats, Jack B., *Ah Well. A Romance in Perpetuity*, 1942; London, 1974.